Ruling the Margins

I0125760

Administrative rule is a type of rule centred on devising and implementing regulations governing how we live and how we conduct ourselves economically and politically, and sometimes culturally. The principle feature of this type of rule is that the important question about how things should be arranged and for what purpose becomes a bureaucratic matter.

Histories of the global south are rarely used to explain contemporary political structures or phenomena. This book uses histories of colonial power and colonial state-making to shed light on administrative government as a form of rule. Prem Kumar Rajaram eloquently presents how administrative power is a social process and the authority and terms of rule derived are tenuous, dependent on producing unitary meaning and direction to diverse political, social and economic relationships and practices.

Prem Kumar Rajaram is Associate Professor of Sociology and Social Anthropology at the Central European University, Hungary. In his research, Prem Kumar Rajaram is particularly interested in questions of marginality and depoliticisation. His research has focused on the government of asylum seekers, particularly those in detention in Europe and Australia, and on colonial histories of state-making. He is particularly interested in the limits of politics, looking at individuals and groups excluded from political participation and seeing what their exclusion says about the nature of the political.

Interventions

Edited by: Jenny Edkins, Aberystwyth University and
Nick Vaughan-Williams, University of Warwick

For a full list of titles in this series, please visit www.routledge.com

'As Michel Foucault has famously stated, "knowledge is not made for under-standing; it is made for cutting." In this spirit the Edkins–Vaughan-Williams Interventions series solicits cutting-edge, critical works that challenge main-stream understandings in international relations. It is the best place to contribute postdisciplinary works that think rather than merely recognize and affirm the world recycled in IR's traditional geopolitical imaginary'

Michael J. Shapiro, University of Hawai'i at Mānoa, USA

The series aims to advance understanding of the key areas in which schol-ars working within broad critical poststructural and postcolonial traditions have chosen to make their interventions, and to present innovative analyses of important topics.

Titles in the series engage with critical thinkers in philosophy, sociology, politics and other disciplines and provide situated historical, empirical and textual studies in international politics.

Production of Postcolonial India and Pakistan
Meanings of partition
Ted Svensson

War, Identity and the Liberal State
Everyday experiences of the geopolitical in the armed forces
Victoria M. Basham,

Writing Global Trade Governance
Discourse and the WTO
Michael Strange

Politics of Violence
Militancy, international politics, killing in the name
Charlotte Heath-Kelly

Ontology and World Politics
Void universalism I
Sergei Prozorov

Theory of the Political Subject
Void universalism II
Sergei Prozorov

Visual Politics and North Korea
Seeing is believing
David Shim

Globalization, Difference and Human Security
Edited by Mustapha Kamal Pasha

International Politics and Performance
Critical aesthetics and creative practice
Edited by Jenny Edkins and Adrian Kear

Memory and Trauma in International Relations
Theories, cases, and debates
Edited by Erica Resende and Dovile Budryte

Critical Environmental Politics
Edited by Carl Death

Democracy Promotion
A critical introduction
Jeff Bridoux and Milja Kurki

International Intervention in a Secular Age
Re-enchanting humanity?
Audra Mitchell

The Politics of Haunting and Memory in International Relations
Jessica Auchter

European-East Asian Borders in Translation
Edited by Joyce C.H. Liu and Nick Vaughan-Williams

Genre and the (Post)Communist Woman
Analyzing transformations of the Central and Eastern European female ideal
Edited by Florentina C. Andreescu and Michael Shapiro

Studying the Agency of being Governed
Edited by Stina Hansson, Sofie Hellberg Maria Stern

Politics of Emotion
The Song of Telangana
Himadeep Muppidi

Ruling the Margins
Colonial power and administrative rule in the past and present
Prem Kumar Rajaram

Ruling the Margins

Colonial Power and Administrative Rule
in the Past and Present

Prem Kumar Rajaram

Routledge
Taylor & Francis Group

NEW YORK AND LONDON

First published 2015
by Routledge
711 Third Avenue, New York, NY 10017, USA

and by Routledge
2 Park Square, Milton Park, Abingdon, Oxfordshire OX14 4RN

First issued in paperback 2016

*Routledge is an imprint of the Taylor & Francis Group,
an informa business*

© 2015 Taylor & Francis

The right of Prem Kumar Rajaram to be identified as author of this work
has been asserted by him in accordance with sections 77 and 78 of the
Copyright, Designs and Patents Act 1988.

All rights reserved. No part of this book may be reprinted or reproduced or
utilized in any form or by any electronic, mechanical, or other means, now
known or hereafter invented, including photocopying and recording, or in
any information storage or retrieval system, without permission in writing
from the publishers.

Trademark Notice: Product or corporate names may be trademarks or
registered trademarks, and are used only for identification and explanation
without intent to infringe.

Library of Congress Cataloging-in-Publication Data

Rajaram, Prem Kumar.
Ruling the margins : colonial power and administrative rule in the past and
    present / by Prem Kumar Rajaram.
    pages cm. — (Interventions)
    Includes bibliographical references and index.
    1. Colonies—Administration—History. 2. Bureaucracy—History.
    3. Power (Social sciences)—History. 4. Citizenship—History.
    5. Southern Hemisphere—Social conditions. 6. Southern Hemisphere—
    Politics and government. I. Title.
    JV412.R35 2015
    325'.3—dc23
    2014017865

Typeset in Sabon
by Apex CoVantage, LLC

ISBN 13: 978-1-138-28622-1 (pbk)
ISBN 13: 978-1-138-80387-9 (hbk)

For Éva, with thanks.
And for Gian, Carmel and Nalín.

Contents

Acknowledgments

We sometimes convey to our students—and others—that academic work is of the mind. It is of course, but writing *anything* is, and should be, also deep emotional work. We don't reflect the losses and the joys, and how we lose and gain our footing, in our academic texts. We write them out. And this book is no different, but the emotional work is there, and many of you will recognise it.

I'd like to thank a number of people who have read, argued and thought with me.

John Clarke, Snait Gissis, Jean-Louis Fabiani, Dan Rabinowitz, Alina Cucu, Engin Isin, Michael Saward, Istvan Adorjan, Don Kalb, Emma Cox and Florin Faje were generous in their readings of different parts of the text.

Ayse Caglar, Judit Bodnar, Sebastian Mehling, Anne McNevin, Peter Nyers, Anna Selmeczi, Carl Grundy-Warr, James Sidaway, Jef Huysmans, Rob Walker, Elspeth Guild, Didier Bigo, Helen Gilbert, Vicki Squire, Claudia Aradau, Harlan Morehouse, Anna Leander, Suvendrini Perera and Nevzat Soguk helped me think through and refine—directly and indirectly—many ideas in this book. Zsuzsanna Arendas is my coauthor for chapter six. I'd like to thank her for her work of course, but also her generosity in allowing me to republish our essay here.

The late Yehuda Elkana did more than most to create the atmosphere at the Central European University, where this book was written. My colleagues at the Department of Sociology and Social Anthropology have in the nine years I've been there helped maintain a challenging and stimulating intellectual atmosphere, and I do acknowledge that this book would have been very different had it been written elsewhere. Much of the book was first aired to students at my graduate seminar, "Colonialism and Post-Colonialism," which I've taught almost every year since 2004. I'd like to thank them for their thoughts and challenges.

Edit Kálmán gave me the book's title, and so gave it belated focus.

At Routledge, I'd like to thank Natalja Mortensen for her support of this project from the beginning, as well as Colleen Sharkey, Lauren Verity and Renata Corbani. Thanks also to Jenny Edkins and Nick Vaughn-Williams for putting this book in the wonderful *Interventions*, I'm honoured to be in such company.

A version of chapter six was originally published as: Prem Kumar Raja-ram and Zsuzsanna Arendas, "Exceeding Categories: law, bureaucracy and acts of citizenship by asylums seekers in Hungary", in Engin F. Isin and Michael J. Saward (Eds.), *Enacting European Citizenship,* Cambridge: Cambridge University Press, 2012.

There are others, those who helped write the margins of this book. Margins define, structure and provide space for the incidental, the minor, the passing—the things that succour and give meaning, and make every-thing worthwhile: Andréana Lefton, Ajang Farid, Siníva Sinclair, Krisztina Bradeanu, Raymond Switzer, Ash Nair, Anitha Rajaram, Vlad Naumescu, Edit Kalman, Ayse Caglar and John Clarke for talks, walks, emails, food, coffees and simply for accompanying me.

And my parents B. Rajaram, and Valsala Vasudeva Pillai: thank you.

And to Éva: this would not have been possible without you.

Introduction

This is a book about administrative government, which is a type of rule centred on devising and implementing regulations governing how we live and how we conduct ourselves economically and politically, and sometimes culturally. The principle feature of this type of rule is its technicalisation of questions and issues that would be political and moral: the important questions about how things should be arranged and for what purpose becomes a bureaucratic matter. There is a growing tendency to govern through depoliticisation; in this book I trace a genealogy of this type of rule. I am not interested solely in articulating power; indeed the assumptions about power that I follow in this book make it impossible for me to give an account of power simply as one-sided domination. I will rather emphasise that power is a social process, it is implemented socially, and the authority and terms of rule derived are tenuous, dependent on producing unitary meaning and direction to diverse political, social and economic relationships and practices.

Histories of the global south are rarely used to explain contemporary political structures or phenomena. This book uses histories of colonial power and colonial state-making to shed light on administrative government as a form of rule.

Administration increasingly sits in place of politics. Migrants and refugees in the European Union are governed by immigration departments, not even immigration or home ministries, that are not subject to day-to-day oversight. 'Good governance' programs in Iraq and other postconflict sites teach local authorities how to compete for investment while citizens are taught how to efficiently claim services. Politics becomes the efficient provision of, and claim to, services and not questions about how and why things are arranged so that some outcomes and strategies appear possible while others are beyond the pale. When administration sits in place of politics the performance of the political becomes more important. Ways of speaking, vocabulary and syntax and bodily and social comportment define 'politics'. This political theatre sits on top of, evades and represses problems about representation, justice and morality.

When administration sits in place of politics it stultifies. Politics is constrained but it is not always clear what it is that is constrained. Ideas about a different arrangement of things so that the politically possible and politically desirable can take new form certainly exist but they are made out to be irrelevant, irrational or utopic by the forces underpinning administrative government. The relative dominance of administrative government is contingent, it varies across time and space. Which is to say that aesthetic and scientific discourses are wielded by different parties in different spaces to establish the truth and value, and thus dominance, of administrative rule. There exists a general tendency to limit politics; the relative capacity of that tendency varies according to the strength or influence of dominant interests or classes and the capacity of people to resist their technicalisation and their environment's. Administrative rule is or was perhaps most dominant then where states and economically dominant groups are strong and their alliance relatively coherent, such as in colonies, or where that strength and cohesion appears greater than it actually is because alternative constellations are either incoherent or suitably repressed by discourses about their deviance, such as in postconflict Iraq. And it is also more dominant with respect to members of populations with little or no capacity to effectively counter technicalisation; this was the case in colonies and is the case with respect to migrants in the European Union.

This book will study how administrative government entrenches itself as a form of rule. The aim is to give an account of how politics become limited and issues of justice, belonging, morals and ethics become technicalised. The book is then an attempt to offer a partial account of how rule is established by limiting the right to the political. This is a historical and genealogical study and it begins with studying the implementation of administrative rule in two nineteenth-century European colonies.

I am not interested in articulating solely an analytic of power, and neither am I interested in pointing to resistance as an activity external to power. I think that power takes form in social processes and relations; it is bounded and enabled by history and space. Power is not then something that emanates from a single point, neither can it be said that it simply overwhelms a particular place. Following John Allen, I will argue that power is an effect of social relations (Allen, 2003). Rule and authority consist of a series of social relations that hang together tenuously. Rule and authority depend, I think, on the capacity to draw together varied economic and social relationships such that they refer to a dominating trope (such as nation or ethnic belonging, for example). This is tenuous because a multiplicity of histories and relations to space must be held in abeyance (and these can always rear up again). It is then the case that power is not an abstract entity outside of the social relations that constitute it: it *is* these social relationships. As such power is not to be studied as external force but as an effect of social relations bounded by time and place. This is not to say that there is no imagination or discourse of an external universality. This may be notions of progress or more concrete things like capitalism; these constitute ideologies that are used to (attempt to) direct and give meaning to social relationships.

'Resistance' then is not necessarily something 'outside' of power as social relations. As attempts are made to cohere and direct the meaning of social relationships so that authority over a place can be legitimately mooted, contest, negotiation and compromise occur as the multiplicity of meanings of a place, the relationships that constitute it and its relation to histories are encountered.

These movements can be made clear through close historical readings, or through ethnographies, and this is what I attempt to do here. I trace the development of administrative rule as a tenuous social process. Acts that deviate power or distort its meaning are not external to power (in chapter two I show how the terms of the colonial law on tenancy in nineteenth-century Bengal were reworked as they were received in social space so that advantage and gain could be had by locally dominant groups). I also show how subjects can creatively take advantage of the way authority, such as it is, is made by holding together—i.e. giving meaning to—different actors and institutions . Groups can seek to resurrect meanings and histories held in abeyance (chapter six explores a case of an asylum seeker in Hungary turning to the courts to emphasise the political and human rights dimensions of asylum, contesting the state's reading of it as an administrative procedure). A close historical reading of power and how it is developed points to it being an effect of social relations. The extent to which this appears coherent is the extent to which different social relations are held together.

It is in colonies, from the mid-nineteenth century onwards, that administrative rule was given its freest rein, by which I mean that the social process of establishing authority over space was most successful. Disenfranchised populations were organised into administrable blocs. Questions about the purposes or aims of economic arrangements were foreclosed and regulations governed the economic, and sometimes cultural, lives of people. This does not mean that administrative power simply bowled over space, rather it means that the process of asserting authority and meaning over space was dominant or could be effectively represented as dominant. Signs of dissension and of imperfect control could be read out through the weight of aesthetic and scientific representations (ranging from paintings and ethnographies to statistics and maps). A great deal of this was due to racial logic, and the sense that native peoples and societies had little merit in and of themselves. It would seem that a study seeking to understand the nuances of administrative rule would do well to study the colonial experience of trying to establish administrative authority.

But scholars have had difficulty with the idea that the history of government and social formation in Asia and Africa have things to say about other societies, indeed may have something to say about a form of rule that is important to modern forms of state- and nation-making and social formation. In a later section I engage with the perceived methodological difficulties of explaining contemporary forms of rule, including those present in the government of European societies, by recourse to histories of former colonies of the Third World (much of the strength of this methodological constraint lies in its implicit or explicit connection to a broader history of modernity and development that has Europe as its centre).

RULING THE MARGINS

Giving an account of administrative rule involves giving an account not of an instrumental and detached power of government, but of a culture and ideology that try to create patterns of legitimacy and illegitimacy, permissibility and impermissibility, the political and the technical. As such, administrative rule is not something that stems from a professional coterie. To be more specific, there is no such thing as a professional coterie, a group of detached technical experts, removed from social processes of contest and negotiation. Administrative rule is a dynamic culture and ideology, whose contours and essences vary across space and time. While variance must be presumed, it can be said that if administrative rule is culture or ideology then it is constituted by "social practices and social relations" (Williams, 1982: 29) and produces articulations and alliances between actors and institutions of varying fragility, and flickering moments of coherence and direction, but also contradiction. As an actually existing cultural state, administrative rule is contradictory as it should be; it is large enough to contain multitudes.[1]

Administrative rule may not exist anywhere outside of the messy projects that it seeks to implement (O'Malley, Weir & Shearing, 1997). These projects are not projections of expertise or detached bureaucracy: the bureaucrats and experts are invested in and related to difficult social formations; the projects that they attempt to realise are dynamic attempts to crystallise an intent, that often exists only in the upper reaches of imagination, against the contradictions of emotion and rebellion that characterise social formations.

Rather than an epochal account of dominance and hegemony, this account of administrative rule as culture or ideology puts emphasis on the interrelations through which it is constituted and so the focus is on a fragmentary and relational account of rule. An epochal account is one that describes rule in broad historical terms, not taking into account the process of establishing rule. My focus is on struggles to assert domination. There are 'internal' contradictions within a dominating culture or ideology as well as contests from the margins, whose recalcitrance is usually stalled for a time rather than wiped out altogether, which mean that power cannot be presumed but must struggle against counter-movements and even when realised can lead to identities, positions and relationships wholly unintended.

This means that while hegemonies can be acknowledged as dominant and effective at a specific space and time, the focus remains on the relationship of that which is dominant with the residual and the emergent (Williams, 1978: 122); between, in other words, the dominant and the marginal.

The residual—in Raymond Williams' sense—are the remaining traces of that which has been transformed by dominating practices. These are, for example, the remains of pre-capitalist economic and social systems whose effectiveness has been stalled but whose traces remain. These traces may become a means of constituting *emergent* relationships, positions and identities which can themselves crystallise into counter-hegemonic moments. Such emergent relationships, positions and identities—such as class identity for example—also arise as a result of the new dominating or hegemonic culture. As a dynamic social register, this culture or ideology contains, as I have said, moments of tension and contradiction that can be highlighted to form counter-hegemonies or that can lead to power playing out in ways unintended.

It is important to give an account then of the marginal, of the residual and emergent—actual or potential—that can appear from a certain height and perspective to have been defeated. The dominant and the marginal exist in relation, in a concrete and intentional way but also simply because of the way a dominant culture or ideology is produced. Concretely, the dominant culture or ideology exists in struggle and in relation to that which is deemed to be marginal. It is, in other words, premised on the production of the margin, and the peopling of that margin with the 'archaic', the irrational, the deviant and the other. It is through this production of the margin and the marginal—through maps and numbers—that we are able to discern the terms of domination, its essences and contours: what it is and what it excludes. Less concretely, but no less powerfully, a dominant culture or ideology is formed through interrelations between actors and institutions who are not static and enclosed beings but are variously scaled and articulated between the dominant, the emergent and the residual. A position, identity or relationship is probably never simply dominant or marginal, but constituted across a range of actual and potential connections; they mostly straddle the artificial line between dominant and marginal and are not easily enclosed into one category or another (at least not without ignoring temporality and change in order to make a dominant position appear entrenched and not likely to change over time).

Administrative rule, as I see it, is bent on ruling the margins, in the sense both of drawing that margin which encloses and excludes that which does not belong in the norm while also defining that norm, and of effectively governing emergent and residual positions, identities and relationships to prevent them constituting counter-hegemonic practices. A further feature of administrative rule is that the relation to the margin is based on technicalisation and depoliticisation—it is typically those at the margins of society who are subject to bureaucratic and administrative rule. But what is important is that these tactics and strategies of ruling the margin do not exist as isolated or abstracted toolkits to be pulled out when the marginal is encountered and then put away again. The strategies and tactics of governing the marginal emerge as a result of historical and social circumstance; the areas and terms of their deployment are not fixed. It is perhaps the most pressing feature of administrative rule that these tactics of depoliticisation and technicalisation are increasingly become a normal way of government: the margin is increasingly central.

Ruling, as in outlining, the margins is central to the processes of exclusion necessary for power to operate. It also produces an internal space that can be subject to government. Ruling the margins is also about keeping the emergent and the residual in check. It is here that the techniques of administrative rule are sharpened. Methods and politics of depoliticisation and technicalisation contain and regulate the relationship of the marginal to the centre. In the nineteenth-century colony, the marginal was central: native and indigenous modes of organising society, economics and politics were seen as dated, residual or threatening, and a large part of colonial government was spent on controlling these elements. It is increasingly the case that administrative rule, normally reserved for technicalising and depoliticising people and things at the margins of polities, has become centralised. The reasons for these are varied, but an account of this may begin with an acceptance that the tactics directed at the margin are not isolated and abstracted instruments, but formed in and through social relations.

ADMINISTRATIVE RULE AS SOCIAL PROCESS

The control over access to the political and what is politically possible or desirable is an increasingly dominant feature in the world today where more and more areas of government are ceded to experts and bureaucrats in response to 'crises' of one form or another. More and more people from different parts of the world find themselves and their environment technicalised and their right to contribute to ideas about justice and ethics limited (or, in the case of Greek citizens under their 'technocratic government', outright stopped). Under the terms of administrative rule, politics is professionalised and politics as the representation of constituencies—classes, interests, a population of some sort—is less important. While primarily perhaps a type of rule exerted at its fullest on the margins and on marginal populations (migrants, indigenous groups), technicalising administrative rule has had its resonances in the 'mainstream' (Newman and Clarke, 2009). Techniques of administrative, bureaucratic and expert, rule consigned to the margins of society and the world are increasingly becoming mainstreamed as means of dealing with crises.

Studying administrative government historically and socially is an attempt at understanding how its dominance is maintained and wielded. This dominance is not simply there, it is achieved—when it is achieved—tangentially and with struggle. This book is an attempt at reading an often abstract concept, 'administrative government', as a social process, involving cultural encounters and negotiations in the different processes of being devised, maintained and wielded. I study the policies and laws that are devised, maintained and wielded; these constitute the basis for rule. They give an account of a population to be administered and lay out how they will be administered. My study then approaches administrative rule in its operations and practice, not as an abstract or sovereign power. By sharpening administrative rule in this way, I am able to look at different social processes that constitute it.

The first such process is its *conception*. Laws and policies do not come into being without fuss. They are constituted in what may be called a relational field, where different and often acrimonious actors and interests claim an interest and expertise in the development of a policy. The policies that are the backbone of administrative rule are then not necessarily coherent, they are constituted by an uneasy alliance of otherwise conflicting parties: the particular nuance of any particular law or policy can change over time as the constellation shifts and different actors gain influence.

The *implementation* of laws and policies of administrative rule is the second social process. This usually has involved a prior laying of the ground, for example a cadastral survey to account for resources available. Such surveys are couched in a neutral and scientific register but they are cultural encounters where data about resources can be misrepresented or misrecognised or may be filtered by local registers that attribute borders and ownership in multiple and different ways. As they are implemented, laws and policies encounter local ways of understanding, and these are knowledges that are not easily subjugated. The spaces in which policies are implemented are not pliant and readily transformable spaces, but active social spaces constituted across multiple scales and with social arrangements, relations and hierarchies of varying durability and adaptability. Policies imagined at the centre are often taken up and reworked by the local context to become something other than was intended.

The *maintenance* of rule is the third social process. This can involve wielding a repertoire of statistics, maps and other data that prove rule (the unwieldiness of the local context can be thus domesticated). The collection and transmission of data is itself a social process (Asad, 1994; Appadurai, 1993) involving different cultural registers and the wilful attempt to contain that which tends to flux. The maintenance of administrative rule and its technicalisations are also made difficult by the contest present in the way policies and laws are devised. The presence of contrary opinions and interests in the relational field where policy is formed can be the basis for forming alternative constellations of interests that can question the way in which rule is maintained.

In examining the way in which administrative rule is a deeply complex social process, I hope to shed light on the undercurrents of this rule, of knowledges and ideas about a different way of doing and arranging things that have been subjugated and repressed but are still discernible. These are spaces of hope, they are maintained not because of their particular force or coherence but because of the incompleteness and tangentiality of rule.

Administrative rule can appear overwhelmingly dominant. It rests, however, on social relations that change over time.

ADMINISTERING CITIZENS AND SUBJECTS

Accounts of administrative government point to the regularisation and routinisation of techniques of managing polities aided by the quantification of people, space and resources; to the institutionalisation and taming of contestable concepts such as culture; and to the increasing number of issues and questions that fall under the remit of administrative law regulating decision-making rather than statutory interpretation (Farina, 1989; Rose & Miller, 1992; Weber, 1968). The consequences of these include the reduction of political decision-making to bureaucratic procedure, the ceding of decision-making to experts, and the increased role of the market in influencing the nature and intents of administrative regulation (Brenner & Theodore, 2002; Mitchell, 2002; Newman & Clarke, 2009). Administration is increasingly a dominant mode of government (Hoffman & Turk, 2006; Clarke & Newman, 1997; Newman & Clarke, 2009), meaning that it has been successful in making bureaucratic what should be political questions. This is most evident in the government of marginalised groups, such as refugees and asylum seekers (Costello, 2006; Guild, 2006). Administrative rule can lead to the depoliticisation and technicalisation of already marginalised groups and is a way of systematizing and organising resources and people in order to produce relationships and subjectivities that may be governed.

Societies however are not easily rendered technical. Administrative rule is not simply accomplished, it is negotiated and compromised. As Tania Li says, rule is a project rather than an accomplishment (Li, 2007a: 10). As a project, rule is something that needs to be continually established and re-established. The categories and rationalities of administrative rule are not coherent or static. The act of devising administration and policy is itself social. It involves balancing, recognising, misrecognising and ignoring claims by a host of different actors and institutions who feel they have a say in any particular field of policy. And then policy becomes intertwined with the social structures that exist in the sites in which it is implemented. Understanding rule as a social process means understanding it as a social phenomenon which at different scales and sites allow for different acts of agency which we cannot simply label 'acts of resistance'.

It is difficult to think about power outside of the social relations that constitute it. Communities are complex assemblages of actors and institutions in progress and they respond in various ways to attempts to solidify complexity into a mappable and governable whole (Li, 2007a). Administrative rule is an exercise of power that is received and responded to in social space. This power seeks to order communities and relations so that they may contribute to a particular enterprise, such as the pursuit of capitalism, and it takes form socially as a particular law or policy. This is formed in a relational social field, where different actors and institutions, usually those of the state, compete to influence that logic. In the implementation of a law or policy, it may become skewed, as local agents take and use it in ways unintended, or as they appeal to the less coherent, contrary or weaker points of the law. The production of governable populations and communities is often an aim of administrative rule, but communities are not formed by abstract policy but in the way in which power is received and responded to. One of the examples of this book is a study of the Bengal Tenancy Act of 1885, through which the British sought to create and protect a smallholding class of market-oriented peasants. But the categories and codes of the Act were implemented on agrarian space already riven by internal hierarchies, leading to a situation where those at or near the top of the hierarchy were often able to mould the Act to their purposes. Another example in this book is the government of migration policy in Hungary today; I show that migration policy is not coherent but subject to continual challenge in its conception and implementation by different actors who have an interest in the question and the relative capacity take part in policy formation. The competition between these institutions, primarily the judiciary and the immigration bureaucracy, makes migration policy a contested field. It is not always coherent in its implementation, with the technical management favoured by bureaucrats questioned by the more human rights approach of a national and European judiciary.

The implementation of administrative rule is a social and cultural process, where the terms of rule conveyed generate more complex social relations. One example in the book is the production and administration of a Chinese labouring class in nineteenth-century Kuala Lumpur. Colonial-capitalist systems of production did not entirely subsume 'traditional' and local modes of production. The Chinese labourer in Kuala Lumpur was at one and the same time a 'free' labourer under the law of the colonial state, in hock to various money lenders taking advantage of the new capitalist system, and finding that in many cases his creditors were agents of traditional clan associations. Capitalism—here the system of credit—was restructured by traditional elites who had the wherewithal to grab pole position. In addition to being exploited by 'traditional' authority, labourers also formed illegal associations, sought improvements in their situation, and found that the production process was intertwined with other 'traditional' modes of production. The aim of colonial authorities to cultivate easily regulated subjects led rather to an eruption of relations and exchanges on economic and cultural levels that the colonial state could not regulate, and at times was only dimly aware of.

COLONIAL POWER IN THE PAST AND PRESENT

Colonialism of the nineteenth century had many different aspects. In any study emphasis may be placed on cultural, political or economic consequences. To some colonialism was largely about the removal of the cultural ground on which people stood, replacing that with European norms derived from the Enlightenment (Chakrabarty, 2000). For others, the most important thing about colonialism was the incorporation of territories as a collective periphery to a capitalist world system, and the system's persistence following 'independence' (Wallerstein, 1974). To still others, colonialism of the period is understood through the metaphor of a politics of difference, where emphasis is placed on the struggle, negotiation and social encounters that animate attempts to establish rule and domination (Chatterjee, 1993; Bhabha, 1990).

In most colonies, but certainly not all, the mid-nineteenth century saw a turn of varying rapidity away from a purely exploitative rule with little deep intervention into social, political and economic arrangements (Mitchell, 1991; Dirks, 2001). It was in this period that colonial-capitalism sought to subsume not only labour but the means of production. There was a vast imprinting of colonial patterns onto space and society, meaning that how colonised populations conducted themselves economically, political and culturally became important: it was not enough to simply be in a culturally and economically subservient position (and to be exploited); subjects and relations to the colonial state and its preferred means of production were to be reproduced continuously by patterns imprinted onto space. Regulations and the institutions that conveyed them sought to embed in the fabric of colonial societies ideas of how to conduct oneself. An idea of productive and efficient labour was mooted, and contrasted with a native idea of work taken to be deviant or backward, and transmitted in laws and regulation as well as schools and other institutions. A durable system of government based on exploitation and differentiation was institutionalised. This did not occur with the same breadth and depth in different colonies or in all parts of colonies. Many colonisers had little effective presence beyond certain key urban centres or commercially important rural sites. There was a noticeable inculcation of a colonial order in the nineteenth century, but what this looked like, and how deeply it penetrated and how successful it was, varied across time and space.

A key characteristic of colonial administration was the attempt to institutionalise culturally specific notions about value and order in economic and political arrangements. This is not to say that there were 'European' or nationally specific cultures conveying order and value. Most notions of order and value were those of a specific class. Administrative rule meant that questions and debate about how things should be arranged were foreclosed, a technicalising and depoliticising bureaucracy administered colonies, meaning that political and economic arrangements favoured a specific class while concealing this bias under the cloak of expertise or civilisation.

Class rather than race was at times the dominant arbiter of rank and belonging. This meant that in many colonies at a particular juncture 'native elites' hobnobbed with Europeans; class affinity, which meant not only having money but also being able to culturally perform oneself satisfactorily, sometimes alleviated the terms of rule to which natives were subject. The arrangement was not static. Over time, the extent to which class trumped race, and in what particular field, varied. The Chinese *towkay* who won the contract from the British colonial government to build and run the railroad in Selangor, British Malaya, would find himself some twenty years later in a state of helpless rage when refused admittance to a first class carriage (Jackson, 1963).

The extent to which racial considerations trumped class considerations appears in part to be due to the extent to which colonial power needed inter-action with and assistance of native elites to establish rule and to rework a society's economic arrangements. Once power was more firmly established, racial logics reared their heads and native capitalist elites were not able to do many things that they had become accustomed to. This general condition also varied across space; from rural to urban and also from colony to colony. Not all colonies saw a significant sway between racial and class logics in determining the pattern of life and the terms of access that natives were granted. It does appear to be the case though that the simple description of colonies as being run through with a dominating and hegemonic static racial hierarchy is misleading; race and class, and sometimes religion and jingoism, intertwined, and each led to the alleviation of the forces of others, or at times the strengthening of other forces. It is generally the case, I think, that the nature of colonial rule cannot be described solely by one label or another; the terms of colonial rule were determined by the play of local and external forces which led to the relative dominance of race or class in specific policies directed at specific members of colonial society.

Colonial rule disproportionately benefitted a relatively small capitalist class. The genius and hegemony of colonialism was the way that it largely convinced poor Europeans, and sometimes mestizos, to see it as their project as well. This inculcation of groups that had no real benefit from the terms of rule maintained hegemony. The issue was in reverse for the leading native classes. By whatever form of doublethink, some could see themselves as part of the project of colonial rule while yet being refused access to rule.

Administrative rule in colonies is not an affair that can be explained sim-ply, nor can it be properly accounted for at a national or other generalised scale. The basis of administrative rule in colonies of the nineteenth century was a social formation complexly riven by articulations of varying durabil-ity along class, cultural and racial lines. The histories pursued here will seek to understand how rule plays out in specific places, but without suggesting that these places are sites conducive to a detached micro-history. The histo-ries pursued here emphasise that groups are located in a multidimensional spectrum, variously and to different degrees affected by racial or class logics with their relative position to the terms of rule changing as class or racial logics trumped. Variance can be accounted for by changes in local conditions as well as broader external forces that led to one or other group being able to achieve a level of cultural or economic dominance without the assistance of the other. Thus, generally speaking, European elites would dispense with connections to native elite when the means of production were more or less appropriated (but would again make connections when natives of lower classes needed to be controlled).

It would be simplistic to say that the European Union's management of asylum seekers and the CPA's administration of Iraq are manifestations of colonial power. Both have at a general level been identified as moments of colonialism (Hansen, 2002; Gregory, 2004). One is built on racialised exclusion from 'fortress Europe', the other involves one state seeking to reorganise and exploit another for economic gain. But following this logic any number of situations may be called 'colonial'. The term loses analytical purchase. It is the wielding of a technicalising and administrative power to depoliticise Iraqis and migrants in the European Union that may be connected to colonial administrative rule, but this does not mean that they are colonial situations. It means that they are areas where rule was wielded to restrict the access to the political, or to subsume the political to administration and bureaucracy, for reasons both economic and racial.

Legg (2007a) suggests that connections between rule in Europe and in colonies can be studied rhetorically but not historically. Points of connection may be drawn and specific modes of engagement may be indicated, but an empirical connection is, he argues, difficult to prove. Limitations on comparison might be because of a tendency to assert that colonial rule was exceptional or to make the boundaries between histories of rule in Europe and colonies unnecessarily rigid, as Frederick Cooper (2005) argues. My starting point is simple: because administrative rule had its fullest rein in nineteenth-century colonies, its workings are worth studying in order to understand the social process of implementing administrative rule in the present.

Another related impediment to comparison is the assumption in histories that rule was accomplished (full stop). The principle actor in the story is then a 'state' who rules subjects and society. It becomes easier then to point to differences between a seemingly coherent European nation state and the imposed bureaucracy that passes for a colonial state in most cases. An alternative story may say that rule, generally and everywhere, was difficult to achieve: it was and is an uneasy and often incomplete project (O'Malley, Weir & Shearing, 1997). This means studying the scope and extent of a state's dominance over any particular society and even over any particular terms of rule (it means studying the process of establishing rule rather than what are taken to be the symbols of that rule). As power plays out in space it becomes subject to attempts undertaken by different actors to direct its trajectory and relative force; the point of comparison between former colonies and European states is not then of differences between European states and colonial pseudo-states. This, as I have said, furthers the view of fundamental differences between Europe and the rest.

If we look at rule not as a teleological process culminating in a state but as a complex of cultural and social forces that seek to convey the terms of rule, comparison appears logical. The process of establishing administrative rule had its greatest scope in colonies. Methods of establishing colonial administrative rule by excluding or marginalising some groups from access to the political is central to administrative rule in the past and present. This is highlighted in colonies but obscured in a European history of the nation state that tends to stories of progress and growth with the individual sovereign citizen as both the focus and legitimator of the nation state (Brown, 2001). There are multiple scales of rule, both horizontal and vertical, rather than a single vertical line connecting a state and its subjects. Rather than focusing on states, I look at and compare the conceiving and relaying of laws and regulations intended to establish, fundamentally, access to the political and the nature of the political itself.

When it is relayed in social space, administration must deal with local forces that are not easily subsumed. Policies can be taken up and used in ways unintended; local actors are not simply pliant (Foucault, 2003). When it is studied in its functioning, in its movement and encounters across space, then administrative power cannot be reduced to a moment in the making of a coherent state. The relative difference of states in colonies and in Europe is not an impediment to comparison, at least insofar as the study is administrative rule as social process. It is only an impediment if administrative power is taken as static and contained in a sovereign (state); that is, when it is studied in its aspirations, and the stories it tells about itself, and not its operations.

A further constraint to using colonial histories of administrative rule is the idea that rule in colonies did not meet with the types of objection, resistance or manipulation that the making of the nation state may have in Europe. This is thought to be the case because 'native society' was overwhelmed, to the point of near abjection, by a much stronger colonising state. One response to this may be to clarify that this is not the case as a close reading of history shows. Colonial power did not simply overwhelm local social structures, neither was it ever always fully aware of the scope and persistence of these social structures; policies and modes of rule were *received* in social space, which implies actors and institutions who receive, and was not simply *imposed*.

A second response is more to do with methodology and continues the earlier point. A state can be the primary focus of analyses of power insofar as that power is understood as contained within it. If the aim is to study how power impacts in society then the way its practices play out in social spaces becomes important for understanding power and rule.

Thus far I have made three suggestions. First, that administrative power and rule is an increasingly important feature of the world at this time. Second, that a key feature of administrative power is its attempt to technicalise questions and issues that would appear to be political or moral in nature.

Third, that it is possible to begin such studies with histories of administrative rule in colonies. Underpinning these suggestions are ideas about power and the state and both their relations to space that need to be clarified.

POWER, STATE AND SPACE: TOPOLOGIES OF RULE

It is important to note that I speak of administrative rule, and power generally, as a social process. I seek to question the distinctions between inside and outside, local and global, that structure many accounts of power. The idea that power is a process of organising and ordering populations can obscure the connective relations, and sometimes the weaknesses in each of these connections, of the thing, territory, that is being made. John Allen (2011), following the work of the anthropologist Edmund Leach (1961), emphasises a topological understanding of power where power "composes the space of which it is a part" (Allen, 2011: 284), with the focus, to my mind, being on *how* the interrelated parts of a territory are connected (rather than how far or distant they are from power) in a weave or pattern. The onus then is on understanding how connections are made of new and extant social and economic relations within a space so that they may be aggregated into a territorial whole. Territory does not then arise as a deployment of an external (for example, colonial) power onto space, but neither is it the expression only of a distinct antagonistic relationship. Territory as a political and moral form emerges when a series of relationships are made out to have connections. Allen's study of power is then focused on how separation and distance are not "lines on a map, but . . . intensive relationships which create the distances between the powerful and not so powerful actors" (Allen, 2011: 284). I do use the language of proximity in what follows (e.g. 'local'), but I do so in order to show how a specific relationships in a space (e.g. a 'locality') seek to transform, with varying degrees of power, the meaning of that space.

It is not simply the case that power forms in place and that each exercise of power is disconnected from other exercises of power in a social formation. There may be attempts to ensure that the intentions of rule, as they are set out in policies and laws, are not subsumed to local contexts. The forces behind such attempts are not necessarily coherent or unitary. Rather than beginning with the assumption that there exists an ideological or normative position about how ordering takes place, I pay particular attention to how such positions are produced.

The ideology underpinning how 'a state' organises people and things in its territory emerges from social and cultural relations. The position of that state on how to organise a particular population is coherent to the extent that these relations have themselves been organised and hierarchised. The social relations animating how a state behaves are the contest between different actors and institutions that try to influence its organising principles.

The position of these actors is derived from structural conditions, the means of production, *and* the struggle of dominant groups to restrict the purposes and organisation of the means of production so that it may serve particular interests. This is not to reduce power so that its play is determined by economics. The relations that constitute systems of production are not only economic relations (the exchange between labour and capital). In part because of attempts to control how production takes place and for what purposes, the social relations that constitute a system of production are not simply economic; they may be racialised and ethnicised or heavily gendered (Hall, 1996).

I think that there is no direct mirroring of a system of production in the terms of rule; there is an intermediary stage where the norms and purposes of a system of production are packaged into rules and regulations. This is where the contests over how the state should organise, what sort of policy it should conceive of, occurs. Dominant social groups with different readings of the system of production, and different interests in cultivating or breaking down the system, try to influence policy in any particular area. This may involve competition over which group, or alliance of groups, may best assemble an influential knowledge-set from a mass of inchoate material about people and things (Steinmetz, 2007). Competition over the relative scientific merit of particular knowledges occurs, as does competition over the aesthetic merit of particular positions (by which I mean their positions on civilisational, moral and ethical issues). The relative purchase of different positions is influenced by the connections made between actors and institutions who wield power and those upon whom power is to be wielded (Li, 2007b; Newman & Clarke, 2009: 26–7). There are two types of relations that need to be analysed.

One is that set of relations between actors and institutions that have a direct say in the conception of policy, regulation or law (such as different government departments). These attempts to create a coherent policy occur in a social field; it is that complex social field *as well as* the policy itself that the subjects of rule encounter. Which is to say three different things:

1. First, different actors with different social norms compete for relative influence in the making of policy.
2. Second, the coherence of policy depends on an actor or institution, or an alliance of actors or institutions, dominating the social field of policy, making other positions less viable. It is not the case that this always happens; policy is not always dominated by a single perspective. Policy can also reflect different and contradictory positions, a reflection of the fact that no single perspective has been able to dominate a policy, or a social formation, with the result that other associated policies or informal practices but with contradictory aims impinge on the effectiveness of policy. For example, colonial employment law that sought to commodify Chinese labourers in nineteenth-century Kuala Lumpur

coexisted with laws that securitised Chinese labourers, and informal practices and discourses that emphasised the criminality and even sub-humanness of Chinese labourers.

3. Third, the process of connecting those who wield power with those upon whom power is to be wielded is, predictably, not straightforward. The extent to which subjects of power accede to the terms of rule can depend on the condition of the social field where policy is formed, including in particular the extent to which a single perspective has been able to dominate and structure policy. Even if policy is dominated by one perspective, marginalised perspectives and positions can be appealed to: they become sources of possible strength for resistance or evasion of policy when it is implemented on the ground. These positions may be excluded from policy on a particular matter but can be made out to be a part of the broader issues from which that policy has emerged (Ranciere, 2004). The example of migrants appealing to the judiciary in Hungary is apt. They make an appeal to a rights-based perspective on asylum that has been marginalised by the domination of a bureaucratic perspective but can still be seen as legitimate. The shadow of actors involved in the formation of policy, but temporarily subjugated, remains and can constitute grounds for questioning how policy is conceived and implemented.

The cultivation of a dominant policy on a particular matter involves an attempt to abstract that policy from the historical and social conditions of its emergence. Administrative rule involves the establishment of a clear and specific relationship of a population (and/or resources) to a particular policy and the rationalities and approaches it embodies. If that policy is able to hold in check the varied contests that I describe above, administrative rule is more likely to be durable. This is an attempt to solidify particular subjects, and their varied economic and social roles, into something graspable, and it is then to detach such subjects (or resources) from the social conditions from which they emerge. The dominant relationship and that which gives meaning to subjects or resources becomes policy. Subjects and resources are produced by the connections that are made between actors that wield power and those upon whom power is wielded. Thus, for example, colonial rule produced and gave meaning to 'labour' and to the 'labourer'. To consider colonial labour in the nineteenth century is to consider *only* something produced and regulated by colonial law and placed in a relation to a particular mode of production. This was a subsumption of local practices of employment and production, including the cultural norms towards ownership of the means of production and the scope of responsibility that 'employers' had towards 'labourers'.

The second set of relations is to do with encounters in places. The idea that power is decentred because it is worked out in the engagement in different places does not take into account the operational logic of power. Michel

Foucault identified in the modern system an individualising power, where subjects are taught how to conduct and govern themselves so that they may fit in with prevailing rationalities to do with culture and economy. Foucault also identified a totalising power, a biopolitics of managing life (Foucault, 1978; Agamben, 1998; Chatterjee, 2004). This is that power that produces and manages populations. It busies itself with the quantification and classification of groups, and then their administration. The individualising power that Foucault sees creates a citizen, a political subject whose consent is the basis of popular sovereignty. When policy is implemented it may strive to emphasise a totalising power, addressing groups as administrable populations. Those it addresses may however try to emphasise the basis of the policy or law which at its core involves an idea of citizenship, even if that policy involves the explicit declaration that it applies to groups *without* citizenship, such as asylum seekers. In the implementation of law and policy in different places we may see attempts by groups to emphasise the individualising and subjectivising aspects of a law or policy, to the detriment of its generalising and objectivising aspects. Different tactics may be deployed by authorities to lessen the likelihood of a law intended to generalise being contested on the basis of individualising power (and this is what I mean by the operational logic of power). One way has been the construction of a political infrastructure that restricts the exercise of political subjectivity to a series of technical appeals to government. One chapter in this book is on the Coalition Provisional Authority (CPA) in postconflict Iraq. The CPA's grassroots democracy initiative in Iraq forecloses questions about how things are arranged and for what purpose through a political infrastructure that recognises only technical appeals for material resources (USAid, 2008). The CPA sought to rework the terrain under which politics could occur, such that an Iraqi citizen seeking to perform his or her individualised political subjectivity, or citizenship, is caught up in a closed-off technicalising register of politics.

The 'state' is studied in this book in its operation; its rationality and interests can be discerned in the processes of making and implementing policies. While the terms of administrative rule tend towards the establishment of a 'state realm', a realm of professionalised politics, abstracted from society, studying the operation of the state shows its imbrication with society. The idea of an abstract realm of the state places that state above society and history; but looking at the operations of the state emphasises that it is a collection of different positions and contests that arise for historically determined reasons.

The role of the state in organising and attempting to direct terms of rule is important, but the state tends to be a collection of different institutions whose character and norms are formed in the contest over policy. The state that is encountered in different places is one that needs to govern policy as well communities and the multiple forms of allegiance that they may connect to. That is, the coherence of the organising force depends on the capacity of a dominating perspective to quell other possible perspectives. I show that the dominance of the immigration bureaucracy in devising asylum policy in Hungary depends on the results of an ongoing contest where the rights-based perspective of the judiciary (and nongovernmental organisations) is made out to be contrary to the interests of 'the state'. The appeal to an abstract state, and its interests, by the immigration bureaucracy may be an attempt to overwhelm the sociality of policy and power. By appeal to an abstracted state, the immigration bureaucracy sought what Gramsci called an 'integrated state' where the aims of political and civil society are in concert. The details and extent of this process varies, but much of the force of administrative rule depends on the extent to which the social process of making policy can be connected to and overwhelmed by an appeal to an abstract state realm.

In this section I have argued that power does not simply overwhelm local spaces; local hierarchies and relations respond to that power. This is in large part because what we understand as the organising logics and imperatives of power—its ideologies and norms—are contested from within. Different state departments, and civil society actors, with a say in policy formation tend to have different ideologies or norms. This makes the forms that rule takes—such as policies—dissonant, even inchoate at times. Policies intended to organise and order populations and resources are stalked by a shadowy spectre of rejected norms, ideas and actors; they may be appealed to by those at the receiving end of power, and in that way the aspirations of power may be distorted.

I argued that it is important to read this distortion alongside attempts to create a static and governable representation of society and of a state overarching that society. I do not argue that we should study power as disconnected and only in its local effects. I argue that the relation or dialectic between the local effects of power and an attempt or aspiration to centralise and generalise—to connect different local expressions of power—is important even if it is a struggle. Thus I understand ideology as something struggling to become coherent, to come to life and establish a hegemonic situation that would dampen the distorting effects of power as an effect of social relations. This is partly done by creating and maintaining alliances between different institutions of the state and society and it is done by promoting and cultivating a particular aesthetics that gives order and purpose to a society while also making illegitimate other imaginations of the purposes and ethical orientations of a society and of political life.

There is then a totalising power where the state appears as overarching and dominating society—rather than a part of it—and which can be played out on the more vulnerable and marginalised sectors of society, leaving a differentiated society where certain groups are more likely to be individualised by that power as sovereign subjects from whom the state derives its will and those who are subject to a totalising power, upon whom the state's will is imposed and organised. The differentiation and bordering of these two groups, and the way they relate to each other, is crucial. It may be the case that individualising and emancipation of some is formed only in relation to the totalising of others. The freedom of citizens is enabled by the restriction on the right of political participation of 'others'.

OVERVIEW

The cases studied in this book indicate that administrative rule is complexly articulated across different scales, institutions and networks of authority. Administrative government in this reading is formed and constituted relationally. Giving an account of administrative government requires a methodological approach that can focus on its relational and contestatory aspects, those dynamics of inclusion and exclusion and the circumscribing of the political inherent in wielding and embedding the technicalising power of administrative rule. The book approaches administrative government by studying the law from an anthropological perspective, by locating administrative rule within histories of nineteenth-century colonial rule and by studying the regularisation of scientific objects upon which administrative rule rests. Administrative government will be taken as a set of practices centring on the distilling of rules and regulations from law. Law, however, is not naturally static; it is subject to contesting interpretation. The stabilization of rules and regulations across different areas depends on the extent to which the contest over what the law intends can be contained. In this book I study the contests over the meaning and intents of the law and the limits of its employment as a tool of administrative governance. This interaction between the movement of law and the stabilizing forces of institutions of administrative governance constitutes then a dynamic structure within which administrative governance operates.

The second way in which the book approaches the relationality of administrative rule is by historicising it. The historicisation of power sometimes focuses on demonstrating the limits of a power that seeks to encompass all under a single or dominant rationality. But this focus does not explain the constitution and dynamics of power itself, it remarks only that it excludes some and includes others. This book takes administrative government as a project of incorporation where subjects and citizens are produced through the application and contest over the law. Colonialism as a project of incorporation through subjectification (Mamdani, 1999) is the entry point used here. Histories of the global south are rarely used to account for or explain political systems or social change. Colonial forms of government in the nineteenth century centred on the incorporation of subjects into a system of power that would lead to the reproduction of their attributed identities. This cycle of incorporation and reproduction was made good by a tight administrative gaze that described colonial subjectivity and allowed for agency within the terms of that description.

The third way in which I will try to unlock the relationality of administrative governance is by focusing on the cultural process of making scientific objects. The constitution of an object of scientific knowledge involves systematic practices of categorisation, refinement and regularisation (Daston, 2000: 3). Administrative government is based on the categorisation and classification through survey and statistics of resources. These resources, such as land, once stabilized in what they represent, become the basis upon which rule and government are built. The constitution of that resource involves processes of stabilisation and regularisation, such as land surveys, which claim to be neutral scientific operations but are actually heavily cultural expressions of power both in the meaning given to land and in the very process of conducting surveys (Appadurai, 1993). State- and nation-building is integrally intertwined with scientific quantification of data about groups and resources. The exploration of the contests surrounding the collection, interpretation and uses of the data is an important way of unlocking the stasis which administrative government would produce.

Underpinning all these studies of the analytics of power is a persistent sense of the possibility, and actuality, of contest and change. Power is a social process, and not an abstract nor automatic imposition onto a pliant space and people. It interweaves with norms, standards, procedures and moral economies in the spaces where it would flesh out. This perspective allows me to focus on the gaps and jagged edges of power and to think then the possibility of change. I end the book with a conclusion on rethinking the purposes of citizenship.

To be clear, I argue that power is not total nor can its aims be presumed to have been achieved. I am also not interested simply in the articulation of the structure and strength of power. I am interested in studying power—here administrative government—as a social process that is incomplete and compromised. The existence of spaces of incompleteness indicates moments and points of intervention; many of these points of intervention that I will outline in this book provide important breathing space—they effectively repoliticise issues that would be technicalised by thinking through how the management of resources and people are ethical questions. I am interested also in how such moments of political reengagement may provide an orienting point for articulating political and social change, in effect a reimbuing of ethics and politics into the political, and the book ends with a thinking through of the purposes and possibilities of citizenship, perhaps as a basis for a study that will follow this one.

Chapter One sets the basis for the empirical chapters by examining issues around administration, citizens and subjects and the project of ruling the margin. It develops the idea, outlined briefly here, of an individualising and totalising power, arguing that it is the wielding of a totalising population-centred power that is characteristic of administrative rule. I locate this power within a history of citizenship and the territorial nation state, focusing on the making of the postcolonial state. Administrative governance emerges as a form of rule in the process of making citizenship and deciding on its limits. Put another way, administrative governance operates at the limits of the political norm; it is a means of containing or preventing the political participation of groups considered not yet ready, or never to be ready.

Chapter Two begins the history of administrative government by looking at how the production of administrable subjects, an urban labouring class, was related to the rebuilding of Kuala Lumpur from 1880 to about 1912. Chapter Three studies the implementation of the Bengal Tenancy Act and the cadastral surveys on which it was founded as a means of producing a market-oriented agrarian society. Both cases look at how local power structures and norms respond to the implementation of law and regulations designed to achieve administrative rule. Local norms are not easily subsumed, and they can form the basis for reworking the intentions of government, such that the stipulations of policy or law are taken up and used in ways wholly unintended.

Chapter Four is a bridge between the two historical and the two contemporary (or near-contemporary) studies of administrative rule. I suggest in this chapter that what connects the two is the way in which administrative rule works by disqualifying individuals and groups from the political. So Chapter Three is an account of techniques of depoliticisation; I look in particular at what can be learnt from orientalist and ethnographic representations of 'natives' and native societies and make the case that this representation of people as being unfit for the political, essentially disqualifying themselves, continues to underpin and justify administrative rule.

Chapter Five is a study of the making of the Iraqi state by the Coalition Provisional Authority. This chapter focuses on how the CPA tried to establish a political infrastructure that would fundamentally and permanently change the terrain on which politics was to operate and to be recognised as such. The CPA's mooted political infrastructure would technicalise politics and the political, limiting political expression to the relaying of material needs. Chapter Six is a study of European Union asylum policy as it is transposed in Hungary. The focus here is on how policies are made, in what I have called a relational social field.

The book ends with a conclusion that tries to study the consequences of a fine-grained history and ethnography of administrative rule on how we conceive of politics and the politically possible. I think through the possibilities and desirability of thinking through the purposes of citizenship, beginning with the point that the connection of people and resources in a technicalised administration is a weak cultural process, rather than a robust abstract rule. I argue that thinking about the purposes of citizenship has tended to be foreclosed by a certain acceptance that politics is to do with the management of resources and the extent and scope that citizens—as individuals or groups—have access to it. Other ideas about the purposes of citizenship—and by extension the political—can be thought by thinking through the idea that power is a social process, replete with compromises and inconsistencies. I suggest that grounding what would be abstract administrative rule in messy reality may allow us to question the reduction of the political to the pursuit of self or group interest by citizens and the ceding of the responsibility of thinking the limits of moral and political community to the state.

NOTE

1. Paraphrasing Walt Whitman, *Song of Myself*.

1 Ruling the Margins

In this chapter I make the case that administrative rule is not exceptional, but an integral form of government that has existed alongside, and indeed enables, government centred on and derived from the consent of the individual citizen. My aim in this chapter is to (1) show that the norms of the political are premised on the depoliticisation of some and (2) that this depoliticisation is an integral aspect of the way individuals, resources, territories and states relate.

Administrative rule emerges, then, historically as a result of the organisation of community and politics; administrative rule is a part of a wider modern problem, and history, of government and not distinct from it. That history of government is taken by much of the scholarship as equivalent to a problem of citizenship: modern government is derived by delicately balancing a notion of popular sovereignty—government of the people legitimated by the people—and the agency of the individual citizen, which can disrupt the cohesion and purposiveness of a community of sovereign subjects. Popular sovereignty is then taken as the basis of modern power. The problem of government is a problem that stems from a European history of popular movement that culminates in the recognition of citizens as bearers of rights in a nation-state whose legitimacy is derived from that people. Outside Europe, citizenship—and thus nationalism—is a "derivative discourse" (Chatterjee, 1993; Chatterjee, 2004).

The history of colonial government to which much of the world's people have been subject is seen as a different problem of government, not to do with the broader and now dominant citizen-centred history of the problem of *modern* government. Colonial government was seen to be about the administration of subjects, individuals and groups with limited rights who did not have popular sovereignty, and of populations who were quantified aggregations and simplifications of society upon whom policy could be implemented. In this chapter I will argue that the citizen-centred problem of modern government and the subject- and population-centred problem of colonial administration are not distinct.

The enveloping of the history of government within a nation-state contains and restricts the history of how political subjectivity and its notions of ethics and responsibility emerged. My aim is to think through modern political community, and the omissions in that history, from the history of colonialism. What does the history of government look like if we see the problem of citizen-centred government and administrative rule as related rather than distinct?

CITIZENS, SUBJECTS AND GOVERNMENT

A population-centred governmentality has grown in the West in the twentieth century. States centred on welfare provision and resource management derive policy based on statistics about people and things. Statistically enumerated populations stand in for complex individual-centred citizens-as-sovereigns, simplifying government and changing the terms on which it rests. Rather than deriving legitimacy from the sovereign will of citizens, a state acts on the basis that it can "provide for the well-being of the population" (Chatterjee, 2004: 34). Administration becomes the dominant mode of government as more and more areas of public and personal life become ceded to experts who can understand what the numbers mean and what sort of policy would be best. Rule is characterised by a shifting set of alliances between institutions, civil society and experts undertaking projects of government, improvement and development (Rose & Miller, 1992; Mitchell, 2002; Li, 2007a).

The shift away from the problem of individual rights and common or communal interests in 'the West' is sometimes argued to have occurred as a result of 'neoliberalism' or the gradual extension of specific modes of managing economy to a generalised mode of governing society through abstraction, generalisation and depoliticisation. This growth of what may be a population-centred, rather than individual-centred, form of government is not, however, to be understood as a failure of politics. It is not the case that government centred on individual citizens, and beholden to their consent, has failed as the rise of economic epistemologies and methodologies take precedence in a professional government of experts and bureaucrats. The tendency of government to work on the basis of totalities—populations, rather than individual citizens—is an integral part of the way states, resources, territory and individuals relate.

Today, more and more individuals and groups are finding themselves—meaning a large part of their political and social lives—depoliticised. The border is encroaching into the middle, and it is in this way that contemporary government bears strong resemblances to colonial government.

The history of modern government includes technologies that individualise a citizen as well as a concern for managing and administering totalities. This is obscured by the dominance of histories of politics as the making of the nation-state (Cooper, 2005). These histories mean that the focus of academic work has been on the life and politics of individual citizens, rather than on those excluded from the political norm. It has also rarely been focused on the gap between the rights accorded to citizens and the capacity of different citizens to access those rights.

We have histories and accounts of politics that tend to territory, both in the sense of turning as a first recourse to territory to explain politics (enclosed by territorial borders) and fostering a methodological nationalism (Wimmer & Glick-Schiller, 2002). With territory as the basis for thinking politics, a number of questions about how and why the political has been foreclosed does not seem to merit discussion.

Ideologies—serving economic interests of a few—arrange and order space. These ideologies flower best when a number of their exclusions appear commonsensical, perhaps the most notable being that the noncitizen working-class members of a community should have different labour and family rights to those of citizens. Such exclusions speak to a cultural and moral sense of a nation, but they often serve to foster the economic interests of some (it's easier to employ people flexibly and cheaply if they have a lesser complement of rights). At the same time, and partly due to this lack of argument about the borders of the political, the way rights are distributed is filtered by the economic mechanisms, and their attendant cultural and social machinery, which arrange space and give it meaning. This results in individuals having unequal capacity to access bestowed rights.

This is where, often, culture and capitalism intersect. The capitalist mode of production carries with it classed, ethnicised and gendered ideas about labour and productivity. The forces and relations that influence production are in a dialectical relationship with dominant cultural forms and moralities and can reproduce racist or sexist norms and attitudes (Hall, 1996). An important outcome of this is that people have unequal capacity to act as citizens (Ong, 2000; Ong, 2006). Today when more and more citizens become subject to the exclusionary practices normally left at the border, overt and implicit racist practices or discourses can thrive (and this is another resemblance to colonial power).

The two principle consequences of modern government are (1) the way in which some groups are unable to access their rights because of embedded inequalities and (2) the exclusion of others from a notion of the politics at all. What can be tentatively said about this is that a politics of bordering within and without is central to the domination of territory by states. These are *politics,* and not strategies or tactics, governmental or otherwise, of 'a state'. As politics they point to the way political authority is intermixed with economic, social and cultural relations, perhaps most notably with capitalism.

The politics of the margin, of containing and restricting political legitimacy of noncitizens, does not exist solely at the margins. It is not a separate set of practices or ideologies that only come into play when instrumentally wielded at people at political or cultural margins. This is most evident when we see practices of marginalisation—of restricting politics—occurring within.

These politics of marginalisation and exclusion are evident in the way most spaces are neither orderly nor disorderly but strangely ordered, with unequal access to rights (food and housing are perhaps two of the most obvious) by those who have rights on paper, being the norm. This coexistence of two apparently contradictory but actually complementary and mutually constitutive political logics can lead to an individualising force of government fostering the citizenry rights of some, while a totalising force restricts or excludes the rights of others (citizens and noncitizens). There is little conceptual difference then between those most marginalised citizens within a polity and noncitizens 'outside'. The domination of administrative rule, premised on totalising accounts of populations, comes then when for different historical reasons (e.g. economic 'crisis') the politics of the margin becomes central.

The crux of the matter can be discerned by looking at how politics, the right to the political, is bestowed. This bestowal of the political is framed by a struggle to establish authority over resources, including land (Sassen, 2008). This struggle is marked by two factors. One is the singularisation of authority in a nation-state. The second is the arraying of resources so that they may be given meaning as national resources over which ultimate authority is held by a state. Resources are given meaning in ways that reinforce state authority.

The process of restricting the political to the articulation of claims for more resources to the state is imperfect at best. The concept 'governmentality' has been used to describe programs of rule that appear similar insofar as they involve techniques of standardisation and quantification that bring a population before a policymaker. This leads to accounts of an "insular and episodic vision of rule" (O'Malley, Weir, Shearing, 1997: 512), abstracted from how it was implemented and the social relations that constituted it. O'Malley and his coauthors say that this is to the detriment of being able to understand the important process of contestation that influences how a program forms, indeed it is to presume that a program can be considered outside of its implementation. It is to give a concreteness and abstraction to programs of rule that are historically unwarranted (as the authors say, many programs "only exist in their messy implementation" [512]).

Social change is made possible by groups able to question the terms of the political and there are ongoing movements to extend political community in different directions (McNevin, 2007). The crux of the matter is the capacity of individuals and groups to move away from the ethos that makes the rights-authority-territory nexus tight; a nexus that would establish two types of distinction when it comes to political personhood. The first distinction is that between the citizens and the noncitizens: there is a weak and universal right to the political as status that is bestowed to all citizens. The second distinction is that between the varying capacity of individuals or groups to either mobilise some resources to gain other resources or to question the terms of the political. This points to internal inequalities that make different citizens have differing capacities to command and enact the rights that may be due them (Isin & Saward, 2013).

ADMINISTRATIVE RULE AND COLONIAL POWER

I have argued that administrative rule had its broadest scope in colonies; this does not mean that native populations were simply overwhelmed and then ruled. Administrative rule in colonies involved complicated *projects* in which a belief that native societies were degenerating, backward and deviant were translated into practices of organising and regulating economy, society and identity. The *translation* of ideas or ideologies in colonies was not straightforward; it involved multiple points of engagement between native and colonial cultures and led to positions, relations and identities, and the struggles around these, that the colonial authority could not have foreseen.

A strand of literature on colonialism, taking its cue from Said's *Orientalism,* has it that an imaginative geography constitutes the 'orient' as a place where individuals have been unable to constitute themselves as political because the identity 'citizen' could not be formulated (cf. Isin, 2005). Political participation in the orient was not undertaken by individuals exercising a right to be involved in the public sphere as a rights-bearing agent independent of his or her role(s) in that society and its customs. The idealised sense of a sovereign political subject as citizen did not exist in the orient, but then it did not exist in the occident either. Engin Isin follows through on Said's argument about orientalism: the attempt to translate the imagination of absence set in motion practices and strategies of ordering and organising; through encountering and negotiating with these practices political identity was formed. Thus when Isin writes about the need to think through how subjects become citizens, there is an important historicised context to their action that he explores. Individuals do not simply move in a vacuum; their movement is propelled—but not, I think, determined—by the way in which projects of rule are messily implemented.

A focus on colonial histories can move matters beyond the study of the citizen as an individual sovereign subject. Acts of citizenship, by which individuals or groups seek to participate in the public and political life of a nation-state, are not the result of status granted or tolerated by a nation-state but historicised practices that emerge from the detritus of attempts at rule. Colonial histories are again important in shedding light on this process. The attempt at imposing an abstract vision of rule onto a disenfranchised and humiliated population was stark in colonies, more so than elsewhere. The tendency in what is now a minority of scholars, is to presume that that rule was simply achieved and to move on from there to discuss its consequences. A closer reading of history shows that these colonial projects of rule were not easily or completely achieved, they sometimes failed or were compromised in minor or major ways. The project of rule set in motion a series of interlocutions with 'native society' leading to the formation of stances and standpoints that provided a basis for articulating politics (Steinmetz, 2007).

Mine is a history of political community that does not begin with the status of a sovereign subject being granted. Moving beyond status, I focus on those struggles that arise from the meeting of different modes of rule (or different modes of thinking notions of government and subject) and suggest that acts of citizenship—acts of asserting oneself as a political agent—are ongoing means of asserting the right to public and political engagement in the face of ongoing attempts to contain this through administration.

The organisation of populations and resources always occurs for someone. Populations are not simply organised and ordered; as they are organised and ordered they are also arrayed in particular ways so that specific meanings can be attributed to them and specific types of actions upon them (such as policies) are encouraged, seen as more legitimate or logical than other options. Timothy Mitchell has described how colonial authorities exhibited native society; that exhibition was important not only in that a society was 'grasped' and placed before us, but also because of the way in which different images were juggled, arrayed and re-arrayed, so that particular meanings were attributed and particular policy interventions were made possible (Mitchell, 1991). The ordering and *arraying* of people and things did not simply legitimise intervention (by producing an image of lack or absence) but it also gave them a particular *future:* as resources conducive to certain types of exploitation rather than mere things. What we recognise as governmentality is not then, I think, a result simply of the outcome of a dominance of a particular scientific rationality—the need to count—but a directed counting.

CONCLUSION

To connect this idea to the arguments in the introduction, I suggest that there is a principle—perhaps an ideology—animating directions 'governmental' practices should take—but this principle is itself messily constituted, "written by many hands" (O'Malley, Weir, Shearing, 1997: 513) and so being a fodder for subjects encountering it to question its very terms.

In colonies whole hosts of people and things were counted, exhibited and arrayed in particular ways to mean particular things, policed, excluded or included, and—most importantly—administered. In the postcolony, Chatterjee argues, the consequence is that while everyone is ostensibly a citizen—they are recognised as such in constitutions and are talked about, endlessly, as such—many do not have the means to actually access the rights that are attributed to them. This is partly because the terms of colonial rule spill over, and some people are seen as not yet ready to become political, and it is because of this that a governmental, 'developmentalist' state overpowers them. Recognised as 'subjects', they are clearly political, says Chatterjee, but they are not a means of connecting the state apparatus with civil society in the way that individualised citizen-subjects are. There is a distinction in postcolonies between those who can access rights, and recognise themselves as rights-bearing individual citizens participating in the political life of nations, and those who are administered.

It only makes sense to think of there being two different forms of power, one focused on populations and the other on the individual subject, if we place greater than needed emphasis on the status 'sovereign citizen'. This is not to say that citizenship is not a status; it is—it can be acquired and held and disposed of and even transferred by blood or marriage. But it is also to say that having citizenship as status does not translate into *acting* like a citizen, seeking to engage with questions of moral and political directions. The status citizen can be a regulated and depoliticised entity, particularly if it has been so closely welded to the nation-state. This is perhaps most apparent in the externalisation of the question of asylum where it is seen as a problem of how to deal with 'strangers' whose exclusion is of a different order to that of the exclusion of people within. The status citizen can be used to limit political activity. But subjects are made by governmental practices seeking to organise and order for different purposes.

The orientalist imagination did not simply characterise a native population as equally lacking key attributes. Class interceded, and in practice, as I will show, a much more nuanced notion of native society competed with the general orientalist idea that these societies were simply and entirely spaces of 'lack' and absence. Colonial authorities competed to demonstrate ethnographic knowledge of native society or population, as Steinmetz points out, but that knowledge was not simply used to impose native policy on a pliant population. An orientalist or imperialist reading of society and its hierarchies made distinctions between sectors of population. An upper class was more likely to be subject to a more individualising power; a general body of the population—labourers of one sort or another—were more likely to be regulated as part of a nondistinctive population and with little scope for political action; and a third group was entirely outside that structure of government. This variegated reading of society led to different forms of rule and power operating within colonies.

It also meant that the agency of those subject to a more individualising power was related to and made sense of principally in terms of the marginalisations of others. If certain groups were conceived as more receptive to the modernising forces released by colonial power it was because they were differentiated from some or most of their fellows who were not. This set up a polity whose purposes and arrangements were formed in relation to presumed internal divisions.

Administrative power in colonies was marked then by two phenomena that will form the basis for this investigation. The first is the orientalist imagination of lack or absence, and the attempt to translate this into projects to organise and order society. The second is the sense that the colonial imagination did not simply see native people as equally lacking but created a society with internal hierarchies (Stoler, 1994). The purpose of the polity became then the realisation of goals of a particular group.

2 Class and the Colonial City
The Production and Administration of Kuala Lumpur

The British took over the direct government of Kuala Lumpur in 1880. At the time, the town was little more than a tin-mining village under the authority of a Chinese *kapitan*. By 1896 Kuala Lumpur would be the capital of the new colony, the Federated Malay States. The story usually told of the British in Kuala Lumpur is one that emphasises the rapid transformation to colonial modernity (e.g. Gullick, 1955). One consequence of these histories is that colonial rule appears abstract, somehow detached from social processes that it was able to overpower and transform. Colonial rule was not simply imposed; it was interposed amongst new and existing social relations. Rule was a social process; it was formed relationally by different agents relaying, engaging with, contesting or evading regulations and the new built environment. The social processes by which colonial rule developed influenced, perhaps compromised, the nature of that rule.

A primary aim of transforming the built environment was to manufacture a colonial public sphere, a space where the state and its subjects could interact. The new built environment and new regulations governing a range of issues from hygiene to proper business practice was intended to produce governable subjects, predictable relations and an abstraction called colonial society. 'Society' was perceivable in the connections forged between individuals and groups (Mitchell, 1991). The new environment emanated order thus allowing the distinction between modern and orderly behaviour and practice and deviant ones. More importantly the new environment was intended to stabilise social space and temporal flux. Subjects, their varied relations and the spaces they inhabited were placed under the administrative gaze of the state. Regulations ordered and stabilised society, making it predictable and manipulable. The story that is told here is that of how colonial administrative government as form of rule was made and the contradictions and struggles of this process. But the story remains straightforward (and abstract) only insofar as the will of colonial power is separated from its practice. If the practice of power is not separated from its intent or aspiration then we cannot see colonial power as distinct and above society, but operating within society. Colonial power was relayed by agents and actors in localities and neighbourhoods, it was an irremediably social process.

There were different logics guiding the attempt to rebuild and reorganise Kuala Lumpur. A key one was the urge to create the conditions for the ongoing production of surplus value and the permanent subsumption of precolonial labour and production to capitalist modes. Thus a key feature of the new environment and its regulations was the production, commodification and cloistering of a labouring class. The production of this class, and the different contests involved, is studied here, against the backdrop of building the town anew.

But the capitalist logic was not the only one in play, and it was not always dominant. A 'colonial-aesthetic' logic centred on the communication of a behavioural norm, to be embodied in a civilised and modern 'civil society' that could interact in acceptable ways with government, meaning that a particular way of comporting oneself in the public sphere was mooted. The aesthetic logic when turned on to Chinese coolies took on a frightening obsession with security and the threat to colonial order and economics posed particularly by Chinese coolies, who were represented as volatile and readily given to violence.

The colonial state in Kuala Lumpur was not a coherent or unified body, policy on any given issue was clarified and formed following contest and negotiation between different interested state institutions each of which tended to reflect different aspects or degrees of these three—and sometimes other—organising logics. These institutions, and their relative influence, varied over time but the primary ones were the Resident's office and the Public Works Department, often in cahoots and almost always conveying a capitalist logic; the Sanitary Board, emphasising modern development and hygiene; and the security-obsessed Chinese Protectorate. Because the colonial state at any given time and with regards any particular issue contained latent or actual contradictory logics, some classes were able to seek succour and protection; other groups found themselves doubly or triply marginalised, excluded or otherwise brutally treated.

Kuala Lumpur, the colonial city, was not dyadic or dichotomous; understanding Kuala Lumpur means avoiding the dual city frame dominant in studies of the colonial city (Abu-Lughod, 1965). This frame emphasises a site of power (the colonial town) and a site where power is exercised (the native town). This dyadic view must be qualified against the *politics* that occur in the town. The relationship between power and the city is most clear in the process of establishing rule and the way different agents and groups mobilise resources to effectively influence the trajectory, scope and degree of rule (cf. Castells, 1978). These agents and groups are not divisible into 'European' and 'native'. There were multiple different typologies of 'European', most obviously typified in the contest between different state institutions but also in the strong Christian-liberal trend, perhaps most clearly exemplified in the newspaper the *Malay Mail*, and in the divisions between planters and miners. These different groups or classes of Europeans helped constitute a contestatory relational colonial field. 'Native' groups were similarly varied, and not simply (or even primarily perhaps) in terms of the ethnic divisions often used to explain Malayan colonial society (e.g. Hirschman, 1987). For one thing ethnic categories were subjects of great work, and were probably derivative of wider economic activity (Kratoska, 1982). The 'native' groups comprised of people differentially positioned by the capitalist and aesthetic logics of colonialism. The two extremes were the Chinese business elite, who were barely different from their European counterparts in the first twenty years of rule, and the Chinese coolie labourers, who were gradually extracted by the colonial authority from traditional, precolonial structures of rule and made into 'free' labourers, meaning that they were commodified and administrable, existing as exploitable fodder for the tin mines around Kuala Lumpur. Coolie labourers encountered the state as a bureaucratic and security machine, seeking to regulate and control their movement and activity in social space.

From these and other social actors and factors arose a complex politics which influenced the development of Kuala Lumpur and colonial rule over it. In a brief sketch, these relations were influenced by (1) the attempt to create the infrastructure conducive to maintaining capitalist modes of production and the permanent subsumption of precolonial modes of production to capitalist ones; (2) an aesthetic logic that dismissed precolonial society as irremediably damaging and hopelessly inept; and (3) the meeting of capitalist and aesthetic logics in the way Kuala Lumpur was ordered and organised. Kuala Lumpur in 1912 was not obviously orderly, neither however was it disorderly; it was strangely ordered, meaning that spaces not only of inequality but of deliberate and sustained neglect (these were mainly workers' tenements) existed alongside broad avenues and quite stunning colonial buildings, amongst other trappings of the colonial modern. The operations of colonial government existed in the in-between spaces of order and disorder and their mutual interrelation.

Spaces of neglect did not simply hold the externalised 'other' that constituted the colonial-modern norm. Neglect was within and a part of the colonial modern. Boundaries between the colonial town and the native town do not make sense if externalisation and exclusion was not the aim of the colonial state: the aim rather was the controlled inclusion of labourers as pliant commodities without political voice or a role in the public sphere (meaning then also the controlled exclusion of labourers from the rest of social space). The combination of capitalist and aesthetic logics meant that workers were subject to dual narratives of commodification and securitisation (as dangerous habitual criminals barely held in check). Capitalist and aesthetic logics established the contexts in which colonial labour and employment regulations were made meaningful. Thus labour regulations that 'freed' coolie labour from customary authority led to claustrophobic surveillance and to tenements where workers could be cheaply housed but also kept apart from social space. The capitalist and aesthetic logics informed the public sphere, establishing norms about how to speak and who could speak, and tried to prevent the localisation of the public sphere.

The localisation of this sphere would mean the introduction of other norms about proper behaviour and comportment in that sphere, norms generated from localities and neighbourhoods rather than the general norms of the colonial authority. Other actors also tried to make colonial labour regulations meaningful, notably the Chinese reform movement sought to fill the authority gap caused by the freeing of labour. These new 'native' forms of authority sought to organise labourers into political subjects. The colonial capitalist-aesthetic logic tried to produce a cloistered, securitised and administrable class without the means of considering collectively their common relations to systems of production; new forms of native authority sought to give that class political purpose.

If the way Kuala Lumpur was ordered was driven by external contexts (the colonial capitalist-aesthetic logics), the tenements and poor conditions were also themselves generative of contexts (that is, of bases from which experience could be made meaningful and political subjectivity derived) (cf. Appadurai, 1996). The reform movement played on the living and working conditions of coolies and sought to use this as a basis for generating a politically-purposive class. In order to study the politics in this complex social formation I focus on (1) a petition sent to colonial government by homeowners protesting orders to demolish their palm thatch homes and (2) riots in Kuala Lumpur by the coolie, or labourer, class. The chapter begins with a history of Kuala Lumpur contextualising the shift from precolonial to colonial administration before moving on to study the rebuilding of Kuala Lumpur and its implications for the production and administration of an urban working class as commodity. While there exist histories of Kuala Lumpur, these have tended to focus somewhat uncritically on the role that British and Chinese social and economic elites played in the colonial development of Kuala Lumpur, a development that tends to be taken as a steady linear progress to modernity. I try to tell a history of working classes in Kuala Lumpur from the period 1880 to 1912. This means focusing on the details of social relations surrounding capitalist production, the way these were formed and relayed, and how they influenced the capitalist mode of production and colonial rule in Kuala Lumpur. Such a focus corrects a linear representation of capitalist development that overrides and subsumes social space. The nature of colonial rule, and capitalist modes of production, is influenced by local histories and class struggles. A history from the perspective of the working classes and the complex social relations in which they are located corrects the deterministic and linear sense of colonial capitalism simply overwhelming precolonial economies and societies.

KUALA LUMPUR IN THE 19TH CENTURY

At the time of the first census of the town with some claim to accuracy in 1891, 79% of the population of Kuala Lumpur were "Chinese", of whom 71% were Hakka. The total population was 43,786,[1] of which "Malaysians" were 14% and Indians 6%. Only 154 were Europeans (Butcher, 1979: 106–7). In 1880 the population was estimated to be around three thousand (Jackson, 1963: 119). Clearly the period between 1880 and 1891 had seen phenomenal growth.

Kuala Lumpur originated as a tin-mining settlement. The head of the settlement was the *Kapitan China*, a title granted to the headman of a Chinese community in Malaya by whichever member of the Malay nobility had most influence. The most important *Kapitan* was Yap Ah Loy, appointed in 1868 and staying in office until his death in 1885. So called 'secret societies' and clan associations played important roles in fostering community and in recruiting and disciplining workers. Mining workers were largely indentured. They were paid in arrears for work carried out and the amount paid was deducted against the cost of their travel to the Malay peninsula and their food and board. Gambling booths, brothels and opium dens were provided and run by mine owners where workers were encouraged to run up further debt.

The British, meanwhile, had established themselves in the Malay Peninsula in their Straits Settlements and from there sought to protect their interests by gradually imposing Residents to 'advise' sultans of the individual states on the Peninsula. Selangor, the state of which Kuala Lumpur was a part, accepted a Resident in 1874. By the end of the 1870s, the Resident had control over most aspects of political and commercial life in Selangor. The start of the 1880s saw the gradual formalisation of British rule, which would culminate in bringing together four Malay states to form the Federated Malay States in 1896, with Kuala Lumpur as its capital. Kuala Lumpur grew from a small mining village to the administrative centre of a new colony in about thirty years.

In 1880, the British moved the administrative capital of Selangor upriver to Kuala Lumpur from the port of Klang. Historians, taking their cue from colonial administrators, have tended to describe Kuala Lumpur in the early 1880s as a dirty and disorderly Chinese town. For Gullick, Kuala Lumpur was "a crowded and appallingly dirty village, swept by fire and epidemic disease in almost every year" (Gullick, 1955: 8; Jackson, 1963: 119). High Street was "a narrow, dirty, unpaved track, broad enough to drive a bullock-cart along but no more"; between High Street and the Klang River was "a mass of flimsy shanties of wood and attap, crowded together on either side of lanes only ten or twelve feet wide" (Gullick, 1955: 52; Butcher, 1963: 119).

Isabella Bird, writing of her visit to Malaya in 1879, had a different sense of Kuala Lumpur, calling it "the true capital, created by the enterprise of Chinamen". Klang, the state capital, where the British Resident served,

> . . . does not impress one favourably . . . [it] has a blighted look; and deserted houses rapidly falling into decay, overgrown roads, fields choked with weeds, and an absence of life and traffic in the melancholy streets, have a depressing influence. The people are harassed by a

vexatious and uncertain system of fees and taxes, calculated to engender ill feeling, and things connected with the administration seem somewhat "mixed".

By contrast, Yap Ah Loy's Kuala Lumpur is a place of industry and justice:

The leading man, not only at Kwala Lumpor (now the seat of government), but in Selangor, is Ah Loi, a Chinaman! During the disturbances before we "advised" the State [the Selangor Civil War; intermittent between 1867 and 1874], the Malays burned the town of Kwala Lumpor three times, and he rebuilt it, and, in spite of many disasters stuck to it at the earnest request of the native government. He has made long roads for the purpose of connecting the most important of the tin mines with the town. His countrymen place implicit confidence in him . . . by his influence and exertions he has so successfully secured peace and order in his town and district that during many years not a single serious crime has been committed. He employs on his estate–in mines, brickfields, and plantations–over four thousand men. He has the largest tapioca estate in the country and the best machinery. He has introduced the manufacture of bricks, has provided the sick with an asylum, has been loyal to British interests, has been a most successful administrator in the populous district intrusted to him, and has dispensed justice to the complete satisfaction of his countrymen. While he is the creator of the commercial interests of Selângor, he is a man of large aims and of an enlightened public spirit. Is there no decoration of St. Michael or St. George in reserve for Ah Loi? - So far, however, from receiving any suitable recognition of his services, it is certain that Ah Loi's claims for compensation for losses, etc., have not yet been settled. (Bird, 1883, n.p.)

Bird's representations of an efficient and orderly "Chinese village" teeming with enterprise would not be evident in the reports of the British authority from 1880 and it is lost in the standard historical view of the Chinese village. Gullick, for example, highlights dirt and squalor and—by extension—a disorderly and dysfunctional Chinese society, one that cannot govern the town properly, and calling out for replacement by British administration. In Gullick's history, enterprise, while admitted, is undermined by descriptions of filth and disorder: "the appalling and ubiquitous stench . . . streets were only twelve feet wide and they were always crowded and dirty . . . smallpox, cholera and other epidemics swept through Kuala Lumpur time and again" (Gullick, 1955: 18–19). There is probably significant truth to reports about the general squalor of Kuala Lumpur in the 1880s. In 1885, the Residency Surgeon was asked to undertake an examination of the conditions of what was taken to be the 'core' of the Chinese village, the Pudu neighbourhood. In a letter to the Resident, he describes being "struck with the horribly filthy state of the drains, wells, habitations and outhouses . . . especially the brothels" and writes "nothing possible could be done to improve them, short of pulling the structures down altogether and burning them" (MD 691/85 Sel Sec).

Kuala Lumpur was likely to have been a dirty town, but the emphasis on filth and disease meant an account of Chinese society as incompetent when judged before a more or less imaginary British norm and essentially incapable of managing the larger scale demands of integrating Kuala Lumpur into a modern world. This legitimised intervention.

Isabella Bird did not visit Kuala Lumpur, she stayed in Klang with the Resident and his family. Her reports of Yap's enterprise are second-hand. Bird lived while in Klang with the British Resident and appears to have heard of Yap and of Kuala Lumpur from colonial society in Klang. Bird heard tell of Yap's industry in clearing swamps and forests, building roads and establishing a large tapioca plantation. Perhaps the enterprise was more perceptible from distance, away from sensitive European eyes and noses and their tendency to equate—to *want* to equate perhaps—dirty streets with dysfunctional society, a problem with a people's mental order, that could be, perhaps had to be, replaced by an orderly colonial one.

A simple problem then with Gullick's emphasis on dirt and disorder is that others who visited Kuala Lumpur or encountered it in the general currencies and exchanges in Selangor like Isabella Bird, described a different town. The American naturalist William Hornaday, for example, writes that, "the principal streets are lined with Chinese shops, and are uniformly clean and tidily kept" (Hornaday, 1885). A second problem is that Gullick's (1955) account of Yap's chaotic precolonial Kuala Lumpur was intended to contrast with colonial Kuala Lumpur. But, as I write later, Kuala Lumpur under the British would be an extremely unequal town. There was an outer veneer of order concealing poverty and disease within, especially among Chinese labourers. In 1895 Kuala Lumpur was described as the "neatest and prettiest Chinese and Malay town", but in 1908 the newspaper the *Malay Mail* reported that Selangor, with Kuala Lumpur at its centre, was the "only country in the world" where death rates exceeded birth rates. Third, Gullick's dismissal of Chinese precolonial Kuala Lumpur is absolute and not in context. It dismisses Yap's Kuala Lumpur against an imaginary norm and does not compare it explicitly to other British or Malay towns of the period, for example Klang. Neither does it take into account the socioeconomic context of 1870s Selangor (this is despite the fact that Gullick wrote a fairly detailed account of the period). As Bird points out Yap's industry and judiciousness stood out: Kuala Lumpur thrived, Klang did not.

PRODUCING ORDER AND SOCIETY

Ambrose Rathborne, of Hill & Rathborne, the powerful British firm with a number of contracts for public works in Kuala Lumpur, published in 1898 a damning description of Chinese society; this was a description in favour of clearing the Chinese village and rebuilding it from brick and tile. Rathborne, a contractor, stood to directly gain from the rebuilding. Rathborne wrote in 1883, the British administration was three years old and the rebuilding of the town had just started. The Chinese core of the village was slated to be transformed, miners and labourers being moved out and thatched and mud houses being replaced by brick and tile. Rathborne's firm was an important provider of bricks in addition to gaining contracts for road building. Rathborne was close to the Resident, Frank Athlone Swettenham, his book is dedicated to him, and Hill & Rathborne have been described as an extension of the Public Works Department (Price, 2002). Rathborne was being enriched by the development of the town, and his dismissive depiction of Chinese society should be seen in that light.

> It was no unusual occurrence for a whole village, which had quickly sprung into existence owing to some great influx of Chinese miners to the neighbourhood, to be entirely devastated and laid waste by fire, a layer of ashes and a few badly-charred posts here and there being all that was left of what had been but a few hours before a flourishing little centre of trade. In the towns, of course, the destruction was on a bigger scale, and the opportunity was taken advantage of by all the bad characters to lay hands on and steal what they could; rioting and fighting also created a new danger, and made the confusion worse. . . .

The Chinese village for Rathborne contained an abject people:

> On no consideration would those inhabitants who were somewhat more remote from the fire help to extinguish the flames or open their doors, and the only way to gain an entrance was by bursting them in. As an instance of this, I have seen the roof of a shop catch fire from some spark that had blown on to the thatch unknown to the inmates within, who obstinately refused admittance to those outside endeavouring to enter, so that they might get on to the roof and put out the flames. Shouting and hammering were of no avail, and there was nothing to be done but to break in the door with an axe, when the Chinese occupants were disclosed crouching down and awaiting events in dumb stupidity, seemingly paralyzed by the dread of being robbed should they open their doors and by the fear that the fire after all might reach them. (Rathborne, 1898: 107–109)

In Rathborne's dismissive depiction the Chinese lacked any connective social, moral or cultural force that would constitute a functioning and cooperative collective. Part of this is attributed to the common Chinese mentality, a "dumb stupidity". Dystopic representations of native Kuala Lumpur contrasted with representations of the colonial government quarter, "pleasantly situated on the hills overlooking the town" (Rathborne, 1898: 106).

From 1883 to about 1890 much of the town was rebuilt out of brick and tile. Houses made from indigenous materials such as attap (palm thatch) were banned on the grounds that they were easily combustible and were replaced by "picturesque houses and shops, brightly painted, and often ornamented with carving and gilding" (Gullick, 2000: 143). As Kuala Lumpur expanded "an entire brick and tile industry [was] created to make the change possible" (Johnstone, 1981: 366). By 1887 there were 518 brick houses in Kuala Lumpur, only one of which was more than five years old. In 1889, indigenous materials were banned outright (Gullick, 2000); an industry was formed and housing became part of the colonial capitalist-modern milieu.

By the end of the 1890s Kuala Lumpur had a railway station, landscaped parks and gardens, imposing Moorish colonial government offices, piped water and a river whose course was slowly being straightened to prevent future floods. This is Ethel Hume's breathless take on colonial modernity in Kuala Lumpur in 1899:

> We bowled over perfect roads, past rounded hills with sloping swards, past fantastic palms and stretches of lily-covered water, where wreaths of mist shimmered steely grey in the starlight. "Joseph," I whispered, "this is fairyland". (Hume, 1907: 40)

But the claim of order and modernity was hollow and this became ever more a matter of public discussion in the early years of the twentieth century. Death rates, particularly among the coolie classes, were high. Tuberculosis ravaged overcrowded workers' tenements. Sanitation was extremely poor in many parts of the town and malaria was rife. Roads less than a decade old were buckling in the heat, dust and dirt and the availability of potable water was a perennial problem.

Regulations allowed the colonial state to manage things remotely. The regularisation of Kuala Lumpur's space created a sphere of interaction between the state and its subjects, a public sphere. Aside from regulations governing housing materials, from 1885 to 1899 a series of laws were passed governing space and society. Among these were laws regarding the upkeep of shophouses and brothels, the protection of women and girls, the use of weights and measures by shopkeepers and the employment of labourers. These were among the most important means by which the legal and financial geography of Kuala Lumpur was determined. These laws and regulations established legitimate and illegitimate behaviour and produced subjects, notably a 'free' working class.

INVENTING POLITICS AND CONTESTING PUBLICS IN PUDU

Most studies of the colonial public sphere are undertaken from a 'national' scale and from this rarefied height colonial rule can appear overwhelmingly dominant, meaning that it appeared that colonial government was able to comprehensively define entry into the public sphere and the terms of participation in it. But when we focus on how rule was constituted in localities, urban spaces for example, we see the difficult *struggle* of establishing domination. This does not mean that colonial rule was not dominant, in many cases it was, but it was dominant through struggle. A focus on struggle and interaction shows rule as an active social process. In the study following I describe colonial administrative power in topological terms (Allen, 2003). I aim to show how power was formed and encountered through a series of relations that sought to establish meaning over 'localities'. I do not say that 'local' contexts were autonomous of a general colonial power formed at a different scale, I am rather interested in showing how administrative power and rule was formed through relationships that sought to make places nearer or further away from power.

Pudu was located to the east just beyond the core of the town. Pudu was an economically and ethnically mixed area; the Selangor Secretariat Files of the period show economic and social interaction involving Chinese, Indian and Malay groups and individuals.[2] Coolies and better-paid natives, probably in administrative service, lived in the neighbourhood. Malay small-scale agriculturalists and Chinese pig farmers shared space (or vied for space) with gambling houses, brothels, opium dens, coolies in rented homes, individuals with title deed and out-of-work labourers. Indigenous building materials were still allowed in Pudu, and at the end of the 1880s, Pudu was something of a refuge, occupied by individuals and groups squeezed out of the core of the town by the rapid rebuilding.

As we have seen, in 1885 the Resident Surgeon described a part of Pudu in distinctly dystopic terms, citing the "filthy state of the drains, well, habitations and outhouses" and saying that "nothing at all could be done to improve them, short of pulling them down altogether and burning them". The Surgeon went on to warn of the contamination that may spread from Pudu: "faecal matter . . . is never removed . . . and should it escape into the river it does so in a concentrated form, heaving with septic germs". In a town where the availability of clean drinking water for all classes was always tenuous (*Malay Mail*, 16 August 1907), this fear had resonance. The Resident Surgeon goes on to identify another human threat, the presence of out-of-work, idle coolies: "there are many . . . hovels in this district which should be removed or burned down. Many of them are occupied by sick Chinese who, unable to earn an honest livelihood, live by stealing and begging. In one such hovel I counted 26 men". (MD 691/85 Sel Sec)

The Resident Surgeon's report on Pudu carries the imprint of the overpowering gaze of the state. The contexts of Pudu, the way in which locality is produced by ritual, repetition, negotiation and contest between residents, organising land and its use, and how all of these contribute to making local subjects (Appadurai, 1996), is simply overlooked by the colonial agent and Pudu becomes simply another in a series of filthy, unhygienic or simply troublesome native spaces to be "pulled down or burnt".

But Pudu in the 1880s was not simply an empty space, but a neighbourhood generated as a result of, in relation to and sometimes in spite of (Appadurai, 1996) a series of broader contexts, of which the new colonial power was primary. Pudu was a refuge, many of its residents were outcasts, people who did not fit modernising Kuala Lumpur. Colonial power was still somewhat distant, Pudu's separation from the core of the town meant that subject and class formation could develop in line with local historical and social forces.

The Pudu neighbourhood was a context in which local subjects were produced, but it was comprised not of a settled set of relations but of a series of contests; the neighbourhood was in process, animated by varying ethnic, religious and economic interests and imaginations which sought to determine its character and physical and moral boundaries. The processes of forming the neighbourhood were animated by greater contexts, religion, economics and colonial power. Malay residents petitioned the Resident for a *Khadi* court (where Muslim marriages were registered) the lack of which had led to "a great many" couples living outside of marriage. Many residents were in hock to moneylenders, usually Indians of the chettiar caste living to the north. Residents with deeds to title seemingly took great care to cultivate and care for homes, and there were also areas owned by absentee landlords and rented out to coolie labourers. In the 1880s Pudu was a neighbourhood where local social forces remained strong enough to provide a context for subject formation and a counter and basis from which to engage the state. The neighbourhood produced subjects who sought to engage with the state, through petitions on various matters, while clinging on to some vestiges of autonomy. In short, Pudu residents sought to engage with the colonial state, and its new economic and cultural terms, as local agents, formed by the contexts of the neighbourhood. The engagement with the state on different matters was an attempt at localising the public sphere, taking and seeking to use the terms of the new colonial state to seek protection and succour, but as residents living in a context not yet overwhelmed by colonial norms and authority.

The most striking of these engagements between subjects of the Pudu neighbourhood and the colonial state occurred in 1891 when notices put up ordering residents to tear down their attap homes led to a petition signed by some three hundred individuals. The colonial state had come to Pudu. The subject positions generated by the neighbourhood were to be overwhelmed as the colonial authority's reach and confidence grew and they sought to produce homogeneity and subject positions only in terms of identities provided by the state. The petition, and the brief exchange with the Resident that followed, was all the more striking for the seemingly naïve, perhaps strategically so, insistence by the Pudu petitioners on relating the terms and norms of the public sphere to their local contexts. They insisted for example on the norm of private property and this norm played out in Pudu as follows: they insisted on the right of ownership and occupation of land and to build on it in the way they chose (with attap). The state dismissed this, barely taking notice, and in doing so conveying that demands or appeals on the basis of the right to property required that that property be used and built on in certain ways. Land and property were didactic tools (Appadurai, 1993), and would produce subjects acceptable to the state.

The petitioners were a mixed group, some were coolies paying rent to live in houses; others were owners of land and houses, many of whom had taken out loans either to build homes or with their homes as security, and were likely clerks in the British administration. The notices were put up by order of the Sanitary Board, the first municipal authority set up in Malaya.

The notices ordered landowners to improve their properties in specific ways and in doing so indirectly asserted the overall right of government to establish and govern norms about land to the extent of demanding changes to privately held property. 'Land' was made meaningful by the way it was bought, sold, exchanged and built upon, which is to say that land was made meaningful in its 'publicness', in the way it was located in a relational web of regulations. The petitioners, in the very roundabout way characteristic of appeals by the colonised to colonial governments, question the 'publicness' of land. They question the way in which land is placed in a web of meaning and regulation governed by colonial norms and the right, authority and justice of the publicness of privately held land. The petitioners write:

> The memorialists have to lay before the kind and merciful consideration of your honour that it is extremely difficult on their part to demolish the houses at Pudu but according to the Legislation of the country they are compelled to do so the memorialists shall only pray that they may be duly compensated or as an alternative be given passes for them to quit the country and go to a better field such as the native states of India. (SSF 4505/1891)

The lead petitioner was Bapoo (sometimes Bapu) Mandor. 'Bapoo' is probably a derivative of 'Babu', used in British India as a prefix to the names of Indian clerks or other natives who occupied some type of interlocutory scribe position between British administrators and native society. Of the three hundred signatories, the very large majority are written in Tamil script, with a few in the Malay Jawi script, the Chinese script and a lesser number of names in Roman script. A number of the names are written by barely literate hands, some names are clearly written in the same hand, suggesting the use of a scribe for the illiterate, and a smaller number appear to be written by individuals with greater education as befitting a 'Bapu' or clerk. The 1880s saw the beginning of Indian indentured migration to Kuala Lumpur; the majority of coolie signatories were likely from the first batches of indentured labourers brought for railways and public works. Having been released from indenture, these workers were probably no longer housed and were left to find the cheapest alternative. The choices at the end of the 1880s for unhoused workers were crowded tenements or occupying land some distance outside the centre of the town where cheap attap could at that time still be used to build homes.

While asserting their loyalty to the British administration they request for passage to a *native-ruled* state of India, and not to British India, or the British-governed Madras Presidency where most probably came from. The request for passage away from British-ruled territory may be a roundabout way of expressing discontent.

> The majority of the memorialists have contracted debts by mortgaging their lands situate in Pudu to chetties and other money lenders to enable them to build their present houses. The memorialists have now to their surprise seen notices posted to very many places in English proclaiming that all the attap houses have to be removed or destroyed to the 1st mile. The memorialists have very humbly to submit this memorial and beg and pray of your honor as the head of this place to have sympathy on the poor memorialists the residents of this place.... (SSF 4505/1891)

There is a sense that the petitioners have been hard done by. They note that they contracted debts in order to build their present homes and they convey 'surprise' that these houses have to be now destroyed. In all like-lihood, this was not much of a surprise, certainly not to the petitioners working in government; the claim is rather a way of suggesting unwarranted intrusion into privately held land.

The petitioners were a diverse and unequal group. Amongst the petitioners were houseowners who complain of having "contracted debts by mortgag-ing their lands . . . to chetties [*chettiars*—traditional Indian money lenders] and other money lenders to enable them to build their present houses". Of coolies it is said that the rent they would have to pay "in any other place would be sufficient to meet their boarding and lodging in Pudu or in one of the Pudu houses". The coolies are silent in the petition; they are spoken for. The petition is written by the clerks and landowners. The petitioners were caught up by the new political, financial and moral geographies of colonial Kuala Lumpur. These geographies in the 1890s were however not clear. The landowning petitioners speak of their having been "given" land in the 1880s upon arriving in Kuala Lumpur, which they mortgaged and built houses on. They were more likely given the right to occupy and build on land either by the Kapitan or the British administration. They became bound to moneylending chettiars, a number of whom had begun settling in the northern part of Kuala Lumpur, taking advantage of the credit needs created by market economics and being able to exploit a situation where land title was as yet unclear. It is possible, but the historical record cannot confirm this, that many of the coolies who paid rent did so to other petitioners who mortgaged parts of their land to build attap houses. It is also possible that the coolie rent payers occupied land belonging to one Tamboosamy Pillai,

a leading capitalist, leader of the Indian community and a real estate specu-
lator with government contracts to bring indentured labourers from India,
and to whom reference is made in the petition.

The petitioners were caught off guard by the disciplinary weight attached
to their land, or at least claimed to be. Their right to land was the basis of
their legitimate participation in a public sphere; the regulation of land and
the demarcation of alienable property was a central aspect of the new colonial structure but ownership of land, however unclear the title remained,
meant acceptance of colonial cultural codes.

The majority of signatories are likely coolie labourers but they are spoken for and spoken about. They do not figure as agents in the public sphere.
The petition shows the uselessness of descriptions of fixed positions of rule
and of subservience between colonisers and colonised. To use such categories is to make much of vertical hierarchy in the colony between fixed
categories of people and less of horizontal hierarchy. There were shifting
and layered relations of rule and this furthers John Allen's topographical
idea of rule, that it was constituted by a series of intensive relationships
rather than a simple vertical encounter between those who hold power and
those to be ruled. Rule was not linear and unidirectional, played out on
homogenous bodies of the 'natives'. For the purposes of this petition, and
in response to the order by the Sanitary Board, diverse residents in Pudu
were pulled together, to represent a common identity and to present this
commonality as natural, regardless of their different social and economic
backgrounds.

The petitioners ask the Resident to "listen to their grievance through . . .
K Tamboosamy Pillai". The British regarded Pillai as the leader of the growing Indian community in Kuala Lumpur (Gullick, 1955) and he did appear
to have some leeway over the nascent Indian community, partly through
charitable works and temple building and partly, and less benevolently
probably, as creditor and landowner. Pillai first came to Kuala Lumpur to
work in the Selangor treasury, serving on occasion as Acting Treasurer. On
leaving the colonial administration in the late 1880s, Pillai, benefiting from
contacts made, received contracts from government to recruit indentured
labour from India. Many of the Pudu coolies were likely brought over by
him. The petitioners' reference to Tamboosamy Pillai was in part a strategic
and tactical move: it was an appeal to class and collegial solidarity existing
between British administrators and Pillai, their former colleague and business partner. It is also perhaps a way of noting that many of the petitioners
were financially bound to Pillai. He may have owned some of the land in
Pudu, including the coolie houses, and he may have brought over many of
the indentured labourers. Pillai was a moneylender and a capitalist entre-
preneur but he was also noted as a philanthropist and a temple builder
who was seen, it appears by the Indians themselves, as a leader of the community. This means that Pillai was taken as their interlocutor facilitating
exchange between the community and the British administration. Right

of participation in the colonial public sphere may have been given to individual agents, but in Kuala Lumpur in the 1880s the power of that agency to challenge administration was limited. Calling on Pillai was an attempt by the petitioners to increase the power and reach of their agency. While subtly complaining of the cultural demands imposed on them by landownership, the petitioners try to see if there is any advantage to be had in the intertwinement of culture, class and capital characteristic of colonial power at this time in Kuala Lumpur.

The petition came to little. The petitioners' agency had little power in the halls of administration and Pillai's influence was disregarded by the Resident, who would write a cursory note:

> Bapu Mandar and others are informed with reference to their petition that, as the Sanitary Board appears to have acted within its legal powers in ordering them, after due notice to remove their houses or rebuild them of permanent materials, the acting Resident is not prepared to interfere in the matter. (SSF 4505/1891)

And with that reference to the hegemony of law and administration, the matter ended. The tortuously put arguments about the justice and fairness of the demand that houses on private land be destroyed were ignored. The Resident did not seek to convince the petitioners about the justice of the Sanitary Board's decision. The rightness of the entire procedure is confirmed not because the Board's decision was just, but simply because the procedure had been correct.

In February 1892, a devastating fire coursed through the attap houses. Pudu was "totally destroyed". One man was killed. The *Straits Times* newspaper reporting on the fire smugly and somewhat cruelly noted:

> It is significant to observe that notice had been served on all the residents, by the Sanitary Board of Kwala Lumpor, requiring them to rebuild their house of brick, during the current year. The wisdom of this course may now be seen. (*Straits Times Weekly*, 24 February 1892)

RIOTS

The petition was an attempt to enter into the public sphere on the basis of subject positions forged in local neighbourhoods and contexts. A key issue was the 'publicness' of land, residents contested the right of the colonial authority to make land a didactic issue. How land would be used materially, and how it would be made meaningful, was a central concern of the colonial state in Malaya (Kratoska, 1982). The notices put up around Pudu were attempts to transform local practices of making space meaningful and to bring this into a broader colonial ambit. The state sought to organise and order land to bring Pudu into the general structures of subject production in Kuala Lumpur. The general attempt at creating a homogenised public sphere would continue, most notably in measures passed to homogenise the use of weights and measures in 1897. Put another way, there would be continued attempts to make good the abstract field of administration by detracting from the social and historical relations and geographies that constitute rule.

In 1897 the British administration in Kuala Lumpur passed a Weights and Measures Act to regulate commercial weighing of goods, replacing traditional weights and measures used in Chinese drugstores and jewellers. In response Chinese shopkeepers called a general strike, grounding Kuala Lumpur to a halt for two and a half days. Public traffic was halted and Chinese factory workers joined the strike. The *Selangor Journal* commented on "the immense influence that this small body of traders seemed to exercise upon all the business of the town" and speculated that one or more *towkays* were fanning, financing or even instigating the unrest (*Selangor Journal*, 1897: 225). Riots followed, their exact intent or origin uncertain. Shops were looted, food supplies destroyed, and there was at least one fatality (a looter shot by police). A deployment of Sikh soldiers quelled the violence fairly quickly.

The inability of the *Kapitan* to calm rioters further diminished his importance to the British. Frank Swettenham questioned in his annual report of that year the competence of Kapitan Yap Kwan Seng.[3] Upon his death in 1902, the Selangor government announced their decision to cease the office of *Kapitan Cina* as "the methods now adopted . . . for dealing with the Chinese render the appointment no longer necessary"(Annual Report of Selangor, 1902; cited by Butcher, 1979: 110). The intent of this was to announce the end of Chinese involvement in politics and administration. *Towkays* were to be purely business-minded and there would be no intervening authority between the British and Chinese labourers.

At the end of the riots, the Protector of Chinese, G T Hare, who would take a central role in the prosecution and banishment of leaders of the riot, published in Chinese a notice:

> And you, the Chinese of Selangor, are hereby to take note and warning that if instead of petitioning Government to redress any wrongs you think you have you enter into treasonable relations with unprincipled conspirators to oppose Government and try to intimidate its officers, you will be certain, early or late, to meet with condign punishment.
>
> Be loyal, therefore, to the Government under whose protection you live and whose justice you all recognise, and do not be again misled by lawless agitators . . . for punishment is sure to fall in the end on the wrong-doers and you will find yourselves involved in their troubles.
>
> A necessary notice. Tremble and obey. (*Selangor Journal*, 1897: 251)

Hare's apocalyptic language conveyed to a generalised population of Chinese that they were to understand themselves as colonial subjects. The invocation of a colonial justice that "all recognise" is performative: it enacts subjects whose political acts must be undertaken according to the rules, patterns and limits of colonial law and administration. The warning to the "Chinese" that they not be "again misled by lawless agitators" is telling. At stake for the British in the 1897 riots was not simply the way weights and measures were used, but the authority of colonial law and the threat to it posed by recalcitrant groups and contexts that produced subjects and positions other than those of the colonial state.

FREEING LABOUR

The response to the 1897 riots while ostensibly aimed at the rioting labourers, indirectly and forcefully addressed the Chinese *towkays* of the "better classes" and the customary authority that they represented. The British governance of the Chinese had depoliticised the *towkays*. The response to the riots was a reminder to *towkays* that their customary authority had been rent and that the British colonial power would not accept any counter in the public sphere.

The Chinese Protectorate was established in 1890. Its main duties were regulating employment especially of mining coolies, registering brothel workers and ensuring their standards of hygiene, managing 'vagrants' and the supervision of gambling and opium 'farms'. The Protectorate would grow by the end of the 1890s into a general surveillance machine with the Protector having the right to act as prosecutor in cases involving Chinese. In addition to his duties as prosecutor when cases involving Chinese went to court, the Protector also had the right to try and pass sentence without normal legal proceedings on Chinese who had disturbed the peace—rioted—or were proving themselves to be habitual criminals. The common sentence passed was banishment.

Three municipal authorities were important from 1890, the Public Works Department (PWD), the Sanitary Board and the Chinese Protectorate. With these departments, the colonial state administered Kuala Lumpur, meaning that the departments oversaw and enforced legislation and rules. The 'Kuala Lumpur' that was administered was a set of specific arrangements of people, places, resources and the relationships that connected them (it was an abstraction that made the connective economic and social relations constituted in place less important). Colonial economic and social arrangements were not simply organised in order to further capitalism, neither were they organised only to further marginalisation and racial hierarchy. Competition and relation between the three principle departments, and overarching these the office of the Resident, did more to decide how Kuala Lumpur was to be arranged than did subscription to any particular logic. Some histories of Kuala Lumpur outline a coherent and purposive colonial order. But the different priorities of key administrative departments led to contests over priorities. While by the end of the century Kuala Lumpur had wide boulevards and a very impressive set of colonial buildings, in the early twentieth century water supply continued to be intermittent, death rates especially from malaria, beri-beri and tuberculosis were worrying, and the general living conditions of the working classes was very poor. 'Vagrants', overworked and malnourished rickshaw coolies and starving out-of-work mining coolies competed for space on the streets with the more respectable of Kuala Lumpur's population.

The 1895 Labour Code (Regulation VI of 1895) formalised the idea of the free labourer who had certain inscribed and enforceable claims and rights before the employee while employed (but not when not employed). The free labourer was an individual agent in the eyes of the colonial administration with an individual right to contract out his (sometimes her) labour. Labourers in between jobs were vagrants and not well regarded by the state. The *Malay Mail* reported regular incidents of "Chinese" being charged in court with lacking "visible means of subsistence" and sentenced to a few months' imprisonment if a fine could not be paid (presumably it mostly could not or the defendants would not be vagrants) *(Malay Mail,* 3 January 1907). In producing the free labourer, the state extracted him[4] from customary authority. In the 1895 Code, the Protector is inserted in place of the *Kapitan Cina* as the overseer of contracts and of work. In effect the state was inserted into customary practices around labour and tin mining thus skewing the entire arrangement.

Under the terms of the Labour Code, the market was king in the making and terminating of contracts between employee and employer, there was no duty on the part of employers to keep on workers in lean times. The precolonial network of connections between clan associations, secret societies, mineworkers and mine owners which would ensure a position for the labourer that was not dependent on the changes of the market was rent by the state entering into the picture. Market relations would determine the organisation and functioning of tin mining with entrepreneurs, both labourers and owners, engaging as individual agents. With no customary or other enforceable bonds connecting the mine owner and the mineworker, there was little obligation to keep labourers on in difficult times. Riots or the threat of them in 1905, 1908 and 1912 coincided with low tin prices and mining coolies being out of work, with withholding of Chinese New Year bonus payments or the fear of any of these coming to pass *(Malay Mail,* 30 January 1908; *Malay Mail,* 8 February 1912).

By the end of the 1890s most miners in Selangor were hired as share labourers, or *laukeh,* meaning that they received no wages but had to pay a fixed percentage of the value of the tin extracted to the mine owners. This practice made for flexible hiring and was an advantage to the employer, but it also allowed a measure of freedom to the labourer and encouraged a certain amount of entrepreneurship. Many miners held shares in more than one mine but worked in one while leasing out the other shares. Presumably some shareholders did not work any of their shares, preferring to rent all of them out. *Laukeh* existed before British administration but the intervention of colonial law into the customary world of tin mining led to its multiplication and to the growth then of an urban 'yeoman' class.

The way the system operated, chiefly its individualising of labourers as separate shareholders, worked against the massing of workers with common relations to the production process. Class formation, that is the cognisance of common identity in relation to production, was disadvantaged by the conditions of production and employment and it was also actively discouraged by the colonial state in the form of the Chinese Protectorate. Perhaps in lieu of the production process organically creating conditions for the formation of a working class that could exert some form of agency, outside influence, particularly from elements connected somewhat distantly to Sun Yat Sen's reform movement in China, entered to fill an ideological vacuum. This led to the growth of a reform movement in Kuala Lumpur and Malaya, which concerned the British because of the threat, and reality, of riots between reformist and nonreformist Chinese workers.

Another attempt to fill the ideological vacuum would stem from secret societies and clan associations in cahoots with *towkays* nostalgic for the old order. The British authority sought to contain this development by trying to control centres of Chinese cultural activity. The Societies Act of 1909 legislated for the Protector to be a member of the supervisory committee in all Chinese-medium schools, Chinese societies generally, and temple associations.

This process of making a labouring class that would be subsumable to capitalist modes of production involved chiefly the establishment of an administrable group of workers that could be exploited without fear of political agency developing. This was done chiefly by strategies that sought to cloister workers away and led to their controlled entry as commodities into an economic sphere. This entire process occurred in social space and in direct relation to the town, its new order and material infrastructure, and to the social relations in it. It is this difficult process that I focus on now.

CLASS AND THE CITY

In rebuilding the town, the British confined workers to overcrowded tenements, generally the upper floors of shophouses whose shiny tiles and pretty aspect Governor Weld had been much taken by. These were 'free labourers' not at the time attached to a mine where some form of housing was usually provided, and, increasingly from around 1900, rickshaw pullers. At times of economic downturn the number of unemployed labourers increased. In 1908 the *Malay Mail* alleges some thirty thousand unemployed on the streets. The shophouses were overcrowded, insanitary and given to fire. "Wily landlords" made "fortunes out of the grievous necessity of the coolie" (*Eastern Daily Mail and Straits Advertiser*, 22 January 1907). In 1905 the Sanitary Board just about begged the Resident to tackle the problem of overcrowding. The *Malay Mail* reported that surprise visits by the Resident Surgeon had shown "sixty, seventy, eighty and ninety people living in ordinary shophouses, whilst in a three-storied house one hundred and eighty-two people were found. Even a small house on the Batu Road accommodated sixty-five people" (*Malay Mail*, 14 May 1907). The 1907 Resident Surgeon's report of colonial Kuala Lumpur had ironic resonances with the report of his 1885 counterpart, who was so dismissive of Chinese society in Pudu and its many failings, dangers and incompetencies. The Resident, arguing in favour of a cost-benefit calculation rather than a civilising mission, rejected the Board's request for new land to be opened up for building houses to the northeast of the town on the grounds that it would cost some three hundred thousand dollars and no more than two thirds of that sum could be recovered from the sale of the houses (*Malay Mail*, 14 May 1907).

The *Malay Mail*, a liberal voice until about 1912, was for periods a constant critic of the dominance of cost assessments when it came to native policy, calling for a systematic, proactive, benevolent European intervention to change the living conditions of workers. In 1907 and 1908, the paper undertook surveys of new outlying districts, a number of which had cropped up in the years preceding, as a consequences of new tin mines opening to the north. Two of the districts they surveyed, Ampang and Kepong, were to be centres of the 1912 labour riots. This is how Ampang is described in an editorial:

> the insanitary state of this township is really terrible and it is the same today as it was four months ago. Has any medical officer reported on this place. If not , for God's sake let the Government send somebody. It would be an evil day when the Chinese cooly could truthfully say "Nobody cares whether we sicken and die or not so long as the material progress of the country is maintained". (*Malay Mail*, 14 March 1907)

This is the newspaper's description of Kepong, a newly settled district to the North, opened without British permission:

> it is an extraordinary sort of place . . . the houses—if one may apply such a term to the hopelessly crazy structures that abound there—appear to be absolutely falling over one another in their frantic efforts to obtain air". (*Malay Mail*, 6 August 1908)

The *Malay Mail* was driven to distraction by the colonial government's refusal to undertake serious work to improve hygiene and living conditions in Kuala Lumpur and outlying districts. It gave prominence to the Sanitary Board's oft-rejected appeals for funding to undertake some improvement and to the Resident Surgeon's grim statistics on escalating death rates. As late as 1912, the Resident was prepared to reject a request from the Sanitary Board for a special provision of $5,000 for the disposal of sewage in Ampang. Death rates were high and increasing steadily. In January 1907, there were 246 deaths per month; by October 1911 the figure was 398 deaths per month (*Malay Mail,* 4 January 1912). In particular numbers of people dying from tuberculosis and pulmonary disease remained steadily high. The Resident Surgeon wrote urgently in 1912 that "deaths from pulmonary tuberculosis reflects the necessity for increased housing accommodation in KL" (*Malay Mail,* 4 January 1912). The majority of deaths from tuberculosis and pulmonary disease were among the rickshaw pullers. In his history of rickshaw coolies in Singapore, James Francis Warren writes that pulmonary tuberculosis, unknown in that city, and presumably Kuala Lumpur also, before the end of the nineteenth century, "was the characteristic disease of the crowded vermin-ridden slums of the rickshaw coolies" (Warren, 2003: 270). The medical data and surveys of the Kuala Lumpur Resident Surgeons emphasise repeatedly that tuberculosis was found almost exclusively in the crowded tenements where rickshaw pullers lived, their conditions then exacerbated by the lung-destroying immense physical work of pulling rickshaws.

Conditions for workers in the new Kuala Lumpur did not appear to be significantly better than in the Chinese dystopia that Rathborne and an earlier Resident Surgeon had been so dismissive of. The British by 1891 had banned outright the use of attap materials, insisting on the use of brick and tile to build permanent dwellings. This rule abandoned coolies to the market. Without the right to build houses out of indigenous materials, the Chinese labourers were forced into tenements and to pay rent that appears to have been exorbitantly high. The *Straits Times* commented in 1904 on this:

> The overcrowding in Kuala Lumpur is most acutely felt by the poorer classes while the rich are making hay while the sun shines. Not content with a big rent incommensurate with the cost of the building, the owners have imposed a clause on the tenant requiring a security in cash of three months' rent in advance. (*Straits Times,* 13 October 1904)

The coolie was also in hock to any number of other agents of the new capitalism. Even if he were able to avoid the now government-controlled gambling and opium 'farms', and save some money, the coolie had little recourse but to deposit these savings with shopkeepers. The shopkeeper paid no interest on that money: the coolie had to pay the shopkeeper for "acting as custodian of the deposited money" (*Malay Mail,* 25 April 1907).

The Resident, on advice from the Treasury and the Public Works Department, would generally (that is, not always but mostly) resist spending money on improving housing conditions and general hygiene in outlying parts of the town and in buildings housing coolie labourers until after 1912. This was because of costs involved and also it appears because of the way coolies were depicted in early twentieth and late nineteenth century Kuala Lumpur. Demeaning and dehumanising reporting of Chinese coolies appear in newspapers of the period, and they resonated with European popular depictions of the urban labouring classes of perhaps a few decades past. Despite its liberal inclinations, or perhaps because of this, the *Malay Mail* editorialised, "the coolie is content to live amidst surroundings detrimental to his health" (*Malay Mail*, 3 January 1907). In an editorial following the 1912 riots the *Straits Times* wrote, "when roused, the coolies are dangerous and there is only one way to deal with them. . . . We have to keep ever in mind that a vast proportion of the coolie population in Malaya is capable of hideous deeds" (*Straits Times*, 24 February 1912).

At the turn of the twentieth century, Kuala Lumpur was disordered, or perhaps strangely ordered. At the centre of this order were overcrowded tenements and the logic of aesthetics and capitalism that allowed for or directly gave rise to this permanent disorder within a scheme of order. The relationship between order and disorder created a dynamic from which identities would emerge; among these are those convulsions that may be the process of birthing a working class. Capitalism and aesthetics created a free labourer whose value was conceived of principally in terms of the production process and capital gain. The free labourer was subject to much slander about his criminal and subhuman characteristics or tendencies, and this was probably exacerbated by the presence of large numbers of labourers in the streets and not under the control of *towkays*. Letters to editors show that a significant sector of European society feared coolies and what they were potentially capable of. The Chinese Protectorate files show more concrete fears about the authority vacuum over coolies and particularly about the influence of the Chinese reform movement; the Protectorate sought to maintain a strong surveillance network over Chinese coolies because of this.

Social identities emerged from the relationship and interaction between logics and discourses of capitalism and aesthetics, and the bureaucratic practices they gave rise to, on the one hand, and the material conditions of overcrowding, starvation, disease and soaring death rates on the other hand. The emergence of identity was a process; its dynamics can be seen in the occurrence and response to riots.

SPACE, RIOTS AND ADMINISTRATION

The period 1900 to about 1912 in Malaya generally and certainly in Kuala Lumpur saw the rise of the influence of nationalist, anti-Manchu elements among the Chinese. The basis of this was support for Sun Yat Sen's reform movement in China (Yen, 1987). Night schools, drama troupes, reading clubs and public rallies spread that influence, the basis of which were the "illiterate masses" (Yen, 1982: 424), who were presumably read to.

In Kuala Lumpur the Chinese Protectorate viewed the reform movement with growing unease. In 1911 the Protector wrote to the Resident about the growth of pamphlets and books about the reform movement, writing that the literature could cause an "immense amount of harm especially to weak minded and ignorant people to the extent of forcing them to join [anti-Manchu associations]" (SSF 4435/1911). The Protectorate's management of this issue was guided by the continued representation of coolies as ignorant masses. The period from around 1900 to 1912 in Kuala Lumpur saw steady moves towards bringing coolies under the direct administrative control of the British authority. When Yap Kwan Seng died in 1902, the British did away with the office of the Kapitan. As administrative procedures and institutions were established, the authority distanced itself from Chinese *towkays*: there were to be no go-betweens in the relationship of government to the coolies.

While there were previously two mutually dependent elites, there was by around 1900 one that dominated (Butcher, 1982: 110). The 1895 Labour Code had signalled the end of support for the Chinese way of capitalism. The freeing of labour allowed it to be competed for and channelled towards British capital. The successful mechanization of tin mining by 1900 meant that British capitalists were finally able to gain a foothold in the industry. In 1907 gambling and opium revenue farms were taken away from mine owners, meaning that Chinese tin-mining *towkays*' capacity to turn a profit—and hold on to labour—even when prices were low ended. At the turn of the century, wealth was not so strongly concentrated in a few Chinese and British hands. The freeing of labour allowed new wealth to be made, among the Chinese and the British. One important consequence was that any remaining authority over coolies was dissipated and weakened as the coolies were employed, or not, according to market rules rather than traditional structures of authority and obligation or because revenue farms had enabled *towkays* to maintain coolies even in bad times.

One consequence of this was that 'free' labourers lived in degrading and unhealthy conditions. Another consequence was that secret societies and new reform movements buzzed around workers, playing on their discontent and feeding on the authority and ideological vacuum that had arisen. What was the extent to which class formation could take place, meaning the extent to which a political and moral purporsiveness could be given to workers especially in relation to their relative position in the new economy and its production processes?

In 1912 riots broke out in Kuala Lumpur, lasting for about a week. At least twelve people were killed, but possibly more as the fighting spread to tin mines and coolie lines surrounding Kuala Lumpur. The riots were chiefly between queued and queueless Chinese (the cutting off of queues, traditional Chinese pigtails worn by men, was taken as symbolization of one's

modernity and support for the reform movement). The riots appeared to
have started as fights between rickshaw coolies but spread to mining coolies
soon enough. The Protector called on rickshaw *towkays* to control their
coolies, but there was little influence left to be called upon. The *Straits Times*
of 24 February 1912 writes about the threat free labourers were thought to
pose:

> *The lower classes are less under the control of wise and cautious
> leaders.* . . . When roused, the coolies are dangerous and there is only
> one way to deal with them. They must be taught that the sole condition
> upon which they are allowed to live in a British possession or protec-
> torate is that they shall obey British laws, and as they are not a class
> that can be reasoned with the only method of teaching is prompt and
> rigours employment of force. . . . *We have to keep ever in mind that a
> vast proportion of the coolie population in Malaya is capable of hideous
> deeds,* that our imprisonment system has few terrors for men who live
> as comfortably in gaol as elsewhere, and that our death penalty . . . is
> not a very powerful deterrent. . . . Against the dangers arising from such
> a population the best weapons are rapidity and certainty of detection.
> (*Straits Times*, 24 February 1912; my emphases)

Depictions of the riots in the newspapers of the time and in an inquiry
that followed emphasised their supposed spontaneity, brutality and banality.
The Protector of Chinese in what was clearly intended to be a conclusive
statement about the meaning of the riots said that they were,

> . . . caused by crackers being thrown at people driving in rikishas
> [rickshaws]. Then rowdies began to pull Hokien [rickshaw] pullers'
> towchangs [queues] and later to cut them [off]. It was pure horse play at
> the start, *it was not a premeditated political movement.* Khehs [Hakka]
> and Cantonese rowdies dressed in European clothes caused the trouble
> at the outset and Khehs were said to have made the raid on the police
> station. (*Malay Mail*, 28 February 1912; my emphases)

The *Malay Mail* issues of February and March 1912 gave prominence
to panic-stricken letters from Europeans: "What would the people of the
town do if these rowdies some day took it into their heads to loot the whole
place?" (*Malay Mail*, 22 February 1912). One correspondent suggested ban-
ning and whipping of rioters as a preventive. The *Malay Mail*, themselves
a fairly liberal voice in the early years of the century, recommended that
the police shoot into the crowd because "to the uneducated Asiatic mind
lenience in Government is mistaken for weakness" (*Malay Mail*, 22 February 1912). The dominant representation of the riots was that they were the
inevitable result of an irremediably violent mass of people not suitably under
the supervision or control of government and given to spontaneous violence.

The Protector authoritatively and publicly underlined that the riot was not caused by political sentiments or exacerbated by the living and work conditions of poor Chinese: it was perhaps at the most a result of atavistic ethnic conflicts but were as likely to be a consequence of mere "horseplay".

One contemporary observer, however, was more acute, or at least more willing to say publicly what others, including the Protector, knew privately. H N Ferrer, a prominent lawyer in Kuala Lumpur who worked for a number of Chinese particularly in appeals made against the Protectorate's decisions, emphasised somewhat provocatively that the riots were both politically motivated and exacerbated by the British treatment of modernists and reformers in preceding years. He wrote this in a letter to the *Malay Mail:*

> Some time ago before the revolutionary movement had started in China and its representatives were being hounded out of the country by the Chinese Protectorate I did my best to obtain justice for them, but my efforts were entirely without success since as long as they were believed to be weak it was considered safe to harry and insult them. . . . Now the wheel has come full circle round. . . . (*Malay Mail,* 22 February 1912)

The intentions of participants in the 'riots' are unclear, but confidential police records of the time do note political activity of suspected rioters. For example, in 1914, one Sin Choon was arrested and summarily banished, without trial, by the Chinese Protector for his part in the 1912 riots. The arrest record takes note of Sin Choon's history of subversive political activity. He is acknowledged to have been a member of a banned reform movement, a strike instigator of tailors against their employees in 1909, and was charged with being a leader of the gangs that cut off rickshaw puller queues. Part of the reason why Sin Choon was banished was his history of organising labour.

The records of the Chinese Protectorate show a concern in the years before 1912 of the role that reform movements might play in fostering coolie unrest. In 1911 the Protectorate writes of reform movements "exciting the minds" of coolies "to the extent of forcing them" to join the movements (SSF 4435/1911). In 1909, following a gunfight at a Pudu Chinese temple, the Protectorate dismisses the haplessness of the leaders involved, but takes note of their capacity to gather a following among the coolie class and worries about a dissatisfied mob-in-waiting. Coolies were "bound to come under the influence of more capable peoples with definitely criminal aims" (SSF 3618/1909). The Protectorate's confidential files show a concern about how coolies outside of traditional structures of authority may be open to other forms of influence. The readiness of the Protector in 1912 to dismiss the riots as a spontaneous expression of atavistic ethnic animosity does not accord with the nonpublic, confidential concerns expressed in the Protectorate files in the years immediately preceding.

The Protectorate was concerned, privately, about the enactment of political agency by Chinese coolies. The reform movement, it was feared, would be able to give group identity and purposiveness to a class that the British hoped to remain an incoherent and flexible workforce open to the ready exploitation by capitalists. The British legislation was intended to make of the coolies a sort of exploitable underclass, simply available to capital without a perspective on, or agency in, the new economic schema. Whereas in the same period in the metropole political agency was slowly, and with struggle, extended to the working class, in the colony workers were to remain inchoate but accessible to capital and firmly under the aegis of the colonial state's administrative power.

The administrative power of the state was most evident in banishment proceedings. Banishment, forever or for a stipulated period, could sever a person's economic and familial connections, but it was a regular administrative procedure and not a step of last resort. In the two years immediately preceding the 1912 riots 112 individuals were banished, all without right of judicial appeal and all following a sometimes cursory administrative review by the Protector of Chinese. Following the riots, more than 200 were banished in two years. The Protectorate tended to see banishment as a means of pruning undesirable elements from the body of Chinese workers. It was an administrative tool used particularly on suspected leaders of the reform movement and on "habitual criminals" in order to ensure the continued pliability of the workforce (*Malay Mail*, 11 July 1907).

The Banishment Enactment of 1900 allowed for the arrest of any individual and for him to be held incommunicado until the Resident, or his appointed proxy the Protector of Chinese in cases involving Chinese, decided on his banishment. If decided upon, the banishment was either for a number of years or forever to a place decided upon by the Resident. A person banished from any of the Federated Malay States could not return to any part of the colony until the term of banishment ended. There was no provision for trial; banishment was an executive act of the state and was decided upon in the chambers of the Resident.

The Banishment Enactment placed on the defendant the burden of proof, "in every action so brought it shall be expressly alleged that the defendant acted either maliciously or negligently" (Federated Malay States, 1921). Beginning with the assumption of guilt and cloistering proceedings from trial allowed for a careless use of the Enactment. The records of the Chinese Protectorate show that suspicion and conjecture were often grounds for banishment proceedings. The formal record of the proceedings is an exchange of letters between the Protector and the Resident, with the Protector giving information on a case and listing individuals for banishment. The procedure is banal and the voice of the Protector dominates. The Protector gives background information, lists suspects and their suspected activity and recommends action. In 1909 following the Pudu temple gunfight, the Protector simply lists the priests of the temple, its business manager and others prominently connected as probable leaders of the unrest and recommends their banishment (SSF3618/1909). He goes on to recommend the banishment of other individuals, including one where the only reason given is that he shared a house with one of the accused. A priest was also recommended for banishment: "Hui Yong is a priest of the temple and harmless enough. He should however be banished as an example" (SSF 3618/1909).

In another incident in 1911, a schoolteacher wrote to the Resident to complain about the behaviour of the Protector who had apparently entered the school informally and threatened him with banishment. Asked by the Resident to respond, the Protector notes that the teacher sold books supportive of the Chinese reform movement and dressed far too well for someone on a paltry teacher's salary. The Resident then proceeded to call the teacher in and order him to leave the country before banishment proceedings could be enacted. This was an executive act of the state more or less without legal basis (SSF 4435/1911). The teacher's response in English is as follows:

Dear Sir,

I beg most respectfully to inform you that I am lieving your civilize Strait Settlement for HongKong and our China to-night.

I don't like staying any longer in so civilize place here, because I have no luck in myself.

I am obliged to say that my wife has got a son only four days ago, for which the voyage I hope that the God will bless us.

I have the honour to be,

Sir,

Your most obedient servant,

(signed) Tsang Fong.

Tsang Fong's initial letter of complaint sent to the Resident, which landed him in all this trouble, questioned the capacity of the Protector: "I am pleased to say that the Protector does not know what is the important things of any Chinese sign boards for any schools, shops &c, such so how can he to be a Chinese Protector".

Banishment proceedings were an opportunity for the state to develop its administrative capacity. For the Protector, it was an opportunity to assert his expertness as the authority on Chinese affairs and to extend his administrative reach. Tsang Fong's complaint provided the Protector an opportunity to raise the issue of the possible dangers to the British government of Chinese night schools. The Resident would agree to the Protector being on the governing board of all Chinese schools and to act as the Registrar of Societies (SSF 4435/1911).

Tsang Fong's letters were kept on file. The proceedings in camera that the file is an account of constituted a closed arena where the administrative capacity of the state was exercised, and thus developed, on subjects who did not have a corresponding voice. The interaction in the chamber sometimes became the basis for extending the administrative reach of the state. Tsang Fong's complaint contributed to the administrative control of Chinese schools. The nature of the proceedings is such that the responses, including such protests as Tsang Fong's, are automatically and bureaucratically archived but they have little or no weight. The proceedings and the Enactment served to sandbox away political agency. The entire process and the Enactment that backed it up turned political issues, interference in a Chinese school and the protests of a Chinese subject, into bland administrative issues. The archival and recording of Tsang Fong's letter served no particular purpose other than to add to the bureaucratic archive.

One of the individuals arrested under the Banishment Enactment following the 1909 Pudu temple gunfight was Yap Hon Chin, eldest son of the late Yap Ah Loy. That gunfight had occurred in bizarre circumstances. A group of priests had been holding a séance to raise up a ghostly army immune to British bullets. Yap Hon Chin was to be the new leader of free Kuala Lumpur. Yap probably did not know the full intentions of the priests but he seemed to have been flattered by the attention and duly turned up to attend the séance on the night of the unrest. Yap was arrested following the gunfight, but not charged and was released. whereupon he sued the Protector for wrongful arrest. The case went all the way to the Privy Council in London and ended with the judges stating that under the terms of the Enactment, "mere innocence has been laid down . . . to be not even prima facie proof of want of reasonable and probable cause" (*The Singapore Free Press and Mercantile Advertiser,* 19 December 1911). In other words, the subsequent release of an individual charged under the Act is not adequate proof that the state acted wrongly or without cause in arresting Yap and holding him incommunicado without charge. Yap had hoped to show that the state acted beyond its proper judicial powers but the court insisted that the state had the right to make arrests without trial or charge and it was in the end up to the defendant to prove that the state did not have reasonable or probable cause for acting as it did.

Yap's appeal all the way to London was similar to Tsang Fong's more humble complaints in that both were attempting to make political agency resound onto bureaucratic procedure. Their respective enactments of agency were attempts to portray themselves as subjects with rights as loyal subjects of the colonial state. However both failed to make any impact on state procedure. Political agency was contained within the procedure initiated in camera by bureaucratic procedure.

CONCLUSION

The British administration in Kuala Lumpur delegitimised customary practices of control and in so doing produced an urban labourer whose primary source of legitimation was the colonial state. This process went hand in hand with the rebuilding of Kuala Lumpur, which generated a moral and conceptual order, giving priority to colonial-modern notions of propriety and order. This reworking of the physical landscape lent ballast to attempts to devise a public sphere run through with colonial norms of a capitalist and aesthetic nature. The rebuilding of Kuala Lumpur was not guided by any single rationality. Evidence of tolerated disorder, in the form of squalor and overcrowding among coolie labourers, indicate that there was no single easily identified principle guiding Kuala Lumpur's rebuilding. The complexities underpinning the rebuilding are more evident if we investigate, as I have done here, the details of how people lived with and responded to those two signs of colonial power (labour regulation and rebuilding). Focusing on social relations means first of all suggesting that colonial power and capitalism did not simply overwhelm and transform space. Rather existing local structures and hierarchies continued to be important and the attempt to establish colonial power by producing subjects who could be administered led to the multiplication of social relations rather than their stymieing.

The urban development and politico-social character of Kuala Lumpur was guided by a contestatory politics where different actors sought to develop resources and mobilise populations in relation to the built environment. Whereas the colonial state sought to establish a labouring class directly accessible to capital but cloistered from social space and without political purpose, the new reform movement sought to give political purposiveness to a labouring class. Colonial rule, and colonial capitalism, did not simply transform local spaces and did not readily cause the real or even formal subsumption of labour and precapitalist modes of production to colonial ones. Local contexts and the relations and struggles that are generated from these remained important in deciding the trajectory and development of capitalist modes of production (and colonial rule generally speaking). The colonial state's quest to increase administrative capacity and to effect a controlled exclusion of labourers from the social norm was made difficult by the contexts in which regulations were imposed.

With respect to the principle arguments of this book, I have tried to show here how the town of Kuala Lumpur was produced as an object of administrative rule. Administrative rule was dominant in nineteenth-century Kuala Lumpur, but its domination was centred on the struggle to control or manipulate economic and social relations and their relation to the built environment. The case of administrative rule in Kuala Lumpur points, I think, to the way in which administrative rule was formed in attempts to manage diverse relations and to give these specific meaning. Such attempts were themselves not entirely coherent. The range of different municipal institutions involved in fixing Kuala Lumpur as a site of administrative rule meant that contradictory practices prevailed. Administrative rule in Kuala Lumpur was formed through the relation and contest between different institutions with each other, with the built environment and with subjects it would rule. This led to a form of rule that was often dominant, but also anxious and insecure, fixated on managing or containing real or imagined threat, threat that arose as a direct consequence of the contradictory logics operating in the relational social field of colonial administration.

NOTES

1. This is the number given by both Jackson (1954) and Butcher (1963). It may not however be accurate. The census report is queried by the superintendent of the 1891 census on the grounds that the period from 1887 to 1891 shows a decrease of some 20,000 inhabitants though the state's acting resident says that the 1891 census is the more accurate (Merewether, 1892: 28, 31).
2. An appeal by Muslim Malay groups for a mosque to be built; an appeal by Muslim Malay groups to the authorities to ban the keeping of pigs outside Chinese-owned homes in Pudu; and this appeal undertaken largely by Indian residents.
3. Yap Ah Loy's successor was Yap Ah Shak. On Ah Shak's death in 1889, Yap Kwan Seng was appointed.
4. Most miners were still male in the 1890s, but significant numbers of women miners were present. The regulation of sex work and the individualisation of sex workers was a way in which the Protectorate addressed Chinese working women.

3 Of Law and Land
Producing Peasants and Landlords in Bengal

This chapter continues the study of administrative rule in colonies. While the previous chapter focused on the production of a Chinese urban labouring class, impelled by the joint forces of colonial aesthetics and capitalism, this chapter looks at the attempt to form and regulate agrarian classes in Bengal in the late nineteenth century. This was also impelled by similar forces to that in Kuala Lumpur, but with some variations. A colonial aesthetics centred on the acquisition of knowledge, to an almost ludicrously detailed degree, seemingly for the sheer value of knowing and controlling; and capitalist logics centred on orienting agrarian practices away from 'customary' goals towards the market. Both these forces or logics centred on the making of discernible agrarian classes with clearly outlined rights and obligations to each other, to the land and to or before government. The colonial government's intervention into agrarian practices tried to extract wholesale the entirety of these relations, and all their informalities, hierarchies and complications, from their social and cultural contexts, reorganise all these relations and practices with the help of cadastral surveys, and place it back in local contexts.

The aim was to place agrarian practices, and the whole hosts of people involved in this, in a direct relationship with a state. That relationship would define and regulate what they, as subjects, should do and what they could not do with land and resources and with each other. Like the attempt to produce 'free labourers' in Kuala Lumpur, the aim was to override, dominate and delegitimise 'customary' rules and replace this with a colonial-capitalist administrative order.

Like in Kuala Lumpur, the British found that regulations could not simply impose and overwhelm 'custom'; regulations intertwined with existing and new subjectivities, orientations and ideas to produce outcomes and relations unintended, and often unknown. This situation in Bengal was even more stark, even more beyond the control—and even ken—of the colonial government, than in Kuala Lumpur.

In this chapter I study in some detail the Bengal Tenancy Act of 1885 and the cadastral surveys that it legislated. These surveys were intended to shed mathematical light onto Bengali agriculture so that agrarian practices and relations could be organised along capitalist lines and work carried out by orderly—meaning regulable, administrable and capitalist—subjects. The survey relied on information; getting information was, however, difficult: it involved engagements between very different cultures—that of the surveyors, their native agents, village record keepers, and the different agrarian classes. The many possible points of interlocution led, predictably enough, to much disagreement and deception.

This chapter then continues to study the difficult process of *translating* an aspiration to rule to actual rule. The production of the basis of rule—administrable identities and relations—was fraught and led to events and phenomena unintended that could only with great difficulty, and the help of a wilful faith in shaky statistics, be ignored.

CONTEXTS

The empirical material for this study are the annual reports of Surveyor-Generals of Bengal and India at the end of the nineteenth and the beginning of the twentieth centuries. These reports chart the progress of the Tenancy Act and the cadastral surveys that it legislates for. Cadastral surveys were conducted in two parts of rural Bengal. Cadastral surveys were systematically undertaken in western Bengal by1892. Eastern Bengal was subject to a systematic cadastral intervention only from around 1910 onwards.

The surveys sought to safeguard and make orderly the revenue relationship in rural Bengal, that is the payment of rent by *raiyat,* or peasants, and *zamindar,* problematically translated as landlord. The Tenancy Act wanted to make this payment regular, just and based on the mathematical principles attributed to land and agriculture by survey. Implicit in the Act was the sense that the revenue relationship between landlord and peasant cultivator was the most important agrarian relationship, that its ordering would be conducive to the growth of agriculture and that the best way to diminish the importance of local customs and make agriculture administrable was to gain control of and organise this relationship.

The British felt that this relationship had been made murky by intermediaries who influenced the flow of revenue and skimmed off it. These practices and the people undertaking them were deemed corrupt and illegitimate, in large part because the landlord–tenant relationship was seen as the basic order of agricultural relations.

The problem was that no amount of faith in mathematical principles or in the generative power of the revenue relationship between landlord and tenant could conceal that the social formations in which the Act and its survey sought to intervene was made up of diverse relations that interceded in that revenue relationship.

These relations were not, simplistically, 'native' or 'customary'. They were the consequences of increased capitalisation and marketisation, local, regional and global, as well as of earlier British attempts to organise agrarian relations along capitalist lines. Movements of capital and the fluctuations of the market had led to particular types of class formation, including the enriching of some *raiyat* who accumulated capital and bought up land, leading to the growth of landless labourers, and to the phenomenon of under-tenures. Such relations made access to finance important and the consequent growth of credit–debt relations. The revenue relationship was not, in any close reading, clearly the most important in rural Bengal.

A yeoman class of peasantry, *jotedar,* was an important actor in northern Bengal and parts of southern Bengal where these cash-rich peasants gained control of land and had other *raiyat* working for them and had control over farming tools and livestocks which they loaned out (Bose, 1986). *Jotedar* capital and landholdings meant that in practice *raiyat* worked for them and paid them rent; *jotedar* also had influence over *zamindars* who relied on them to get revenue (Robb, 1997). In eastern Bengal, *jotedars* were not a significant factor but the relationship between *zamindar* and *raiyat* was mediated by other types of creditors, most notably *talukdars* or middlemen who leased the right to manage *zamindari* land and collect rent from peasants. Such middlemen also acted as creditors to *raiyat* in the absence of a capital-rich peasantry such as *jotedars*. Agrarian conflict in eastern Bengal was also touched by a communal distinction: most (but certainly not all) large landlords were Hindu as were those who offered credit; the large majority of peasants were Muslim (Chatterjee, 1986; Ray & Ray, 1975; Robb, 1997; Bose, 1986).

The dominant tendency in the history of colonial Bengal has been to frame agrarian relations as a problem of revenue (Bose, 1986). This may have had consequences for explaining the structure of class relations and the development of agrarian relations and conflict and probably stems from the 1793 Permanent Settlement, the first British foray into managing agrarian relations. In the Settlement the British treated *zamindars,* who had been tax farmers on behalf of the crown, as landlords who had sole and dominant authority over land. In practice, *zamindars* had to cooperate with *jotedars,* yeoman peasantry, in any attempt to extract rent, or to assay the amount of rent. Further, increasing regional integration into world markets and the competitiveness that that demanded led to the growth of creditors who intervened in the revenue relationship between *zamindar* and *raiyat*, establishing not only a new layer of domination but a new volatility: peasant prosperity, and poverty, fluctuated not simply because of the demands of rent but also because of creditors. In northern and southern Bengal, the domination of a *jotedar* class had a similar effect in establishing credit lines (Bose, 1986).

Sugata Bose argued that accounts of agrarian society and change in colonial Bengal that centred on the revenue relationship were limited because they privileged something that was not clearly the most important relationship in agrarian Bengal (Bose 1986). Bose argued that the effect and pull of marketisation, and global capitalism, had greater effect over agrarian society and class formation than the revenue relationship. I think that while Bose is largely correct about the nature of hierarchical relations of domination in rural Bengal (while the data is not altogether present, corroborating evidence ranging from the difficulties landlords had in extracting rent and the mention of creditors in survey reports is strong), the material force of revenue, and the British insistence on understanding the relationship of revenue as most important, had crucial importance in influencing class formation and class relations. I study then how the complex social formation in Bengal, made up of varied relations of domination and exchange, responded to the intervention of the Bengal Tenancy Act.

In what follows, I study the cadastral surveys of the Tenancy Act as a means of bringing and refining colonial order and administration to a population and social formation already marked by other relations of domination. I study then the response of *raiyat,* and the social formation in general, not as individuals or populations unformed but groups caught up with a febrile capitalist system whose responses to the revenue relationship are formed by the pressures of market capitalism.

The reports of the cadastral survey make out that colonial order is being gradually imposed onto agrarian relations in Bengal. Such reports are representations of reality, the ethos or ideology underpinning it—the faith in mathematical order—read and give meaning to different relationships and situations encountered, legitimating or making more rational certain types of intervention. Reports are part of a wider spectrum of abstracting and dominating strategies employed by colonial authorities to create and maintain a repertoire or archive of information about a place (Appadurai,1993; Ludden, 1993). The report is a stabilising work. Like statistics they seek to regularise spaces and the relations therein (enacting thereby a concrete and delimited place for policy and government). Colonial reports however are not necessarily univocal. The annual reports of government bodies such as the Survey Office are intended to provide a narrative record of activities undertaken as well as a resolution of these activities. Thus the report contains ethnographic descriptions of the process of imposing the cadastral survey written by under-surveyors, and a sheaf of appendices, that are ultimately made comprehensible by the guiding conclusions of the Surveyor-General. This mix of more or less, but not completely, raw material and cooked conclusions provides an interesting description of the formation of colonial knowledge and the struggle to impose administrative rule on a confusing social formation. It also contains, in its unguarded moments, evidences of disruption in the survey.

Disruption often came from *jotedar* and estate managers—*talukdars*—whose landholdings or power and livelihood as creditors were in different ways under threat by the Act. The disruption led by these elites says much about the social formation in Bengal villages. The Tenancy Act was designed to order and sharpen the revenue relationship between *zamindar* and *raiyat,* it was to make that relationship subject to administrative law and regulation. But the relationship between *zamindar* and *raiyat* was murky, and *raiyat* appeared to have rarely had a direct relationship with *zamindar*. Rent was paid by *jotedar* or *talukdar* who extracted rent from *raiyat*. The Tenancy Act did recognise that the idealised relationship of a landlord to a peasant freely exchanging his labour was not borne out by facts on the ground: the Act legislated for a cadastral survey so that that relationship could be established between a *zamindar* with a clear idea of his holdings and a *raiyat* with a clear idea of the revenue he had to pay to use those holdings. The survey however was, as I will show, a complex cultural process involving interlocution between different classes and ample opportunity for local elites to skew its conduct or results.

While the Tenancy Act did have some sense of the reality of Bengal rural relations, it did maintain that the relationship between *zamindar* and *raiyat*—or landlord and peasant—was or should be the most important and delegitimised the intermediary role that *jotedar* and *talukdar* played. But their financial control meant that the terms of the Act did not readily reach *raiyat*. Also, the *jotedar* was treated as *raiyat* by the Act alongside less well-off members of that group, meaning that *jotedar* could derive benefit from the Act at the expense of less well-off *raiyat* over whom they held sway while also having its relationship with tenants, *raiyat* working on landholdings, made secondary to an imagined order between *zamindar* and *raiyat*.

AGRARIAN SOCIETY IN BENGAL

> *Quoad* land-revenue settlements, the Government is not to be regarded as a petty *zamindar*, but as a sovereign power (Phillips, 1886: 37)

Writing in 1878, Clements Markham, a historian of the different geographical surveys of India, is explicit about the social and political importance of revenue surveys:

> The Revenue Surveys of India are one of the bases on which the whole fiscal administration of the country rests. By their means the wealth of the various provinces is ascertained, as well as the food-producing capabilities, and their power to bear taxation. The surveys furnish the information comprised in agricultural statistics, *without which the statesman is deprived of the knowledge enabling him to improve the condition of the people,* to increase their means of subsistence, to avert famines, to add to the wealth of the country, and to adjust taxation. (Markham, 1878: 180; my emphases)

According to Clement Markham, statistics would enable "the statesman" to "improve the condition of the people". Statistics make populations and resources known, and they do so in a way that make them amenable to policy: surveys give meaning to people and things. Aside from cadastral survey, from around 1870 the government of British India gave increasing importance to censuses, ethnographic and geographical surveys and other enumerations of land, people and culture both large and trivial. India was being made 'known' and the quantification of the country made regions comparable. Statistics substantiated knowledge claims and allowed administrators to skip over the imperfections of knowledge apparent at local scales (Appadurai, 1993; Edney, 1997).

Revenue surveys, which included cadastral surveys, were a crucial part of a system of knowledge through which the land and its people were, first, discerned, and, second, made the subject of economic policy and also of pastoral government. They involve the assessment of the amount of revenue that can be feasibly gained from a plot of land. In Bengal there was a sense that information about agriculture pre-1885 was limited or altogether absent. The terms of the previous colonial intervention in Bengali agriculture, the 1793 Permanent Settlement, made agriculture in Bengal a closed book to colonial authorities: rental terms were to be decided between *zamindar* (landlords) and *raiyat*[1] (cultivators) in exchange for a specified amount to be paid by zamindar to government. In practice during the Settlement, rental terms were decided between middlemen who leased the right to manage lands from *zamindars* and between tenure-holding (meaning those with secure tenure) *raiyat* and landless *raiyat* or tenure-holding raiyat and sharecroppers. In practice, the burden of rent payment fell to the lowest class of *raiyat*. *Zamindars* were dependent on *jotedars* for the organising and employment of other peasants, *jotedars* were often granted the use of rent-free lands or portions of land.

The Settlement had set no limit on the amount of rent that could be imposed on tenants by *zamindars*. *Zamindars* and *raiyat* were left as parties freely contracting under capitalist conditions (Guha, 1996: 130). There were reports of drastic and overwhelming increases in rents and cesses for land improvements. This led predictably to increases in unrest and ejectments. H A D Phillips of the Bengal Administrative Service noted ruefully in 1886 as part of a general review of colonial administration in Bengal that "the *zamindars* have made far better terms for themselves than the Government was able to make for itself in 1793" (Phillips, 1886: 8). By the time of the Tenancy Act, the colonial government held to the idea that the Settlement had left them in the dark, bereft of knowledge and unable to satisfy the clamour at the end of the nineteenth century for neatly packaged statistics about land and people. B H Baden-Powell, of the Bengal Civil Service, complained in 1892:

> Agricultural statistics, which are available for other provinces, are wanting in Bengal. But even to enumerate the inconveniences, the difficulties under the tenant-law, and the endless litigation, that the absence of an authoritative record of subordinate rights may cause, would occupy more space than I can here give. In short, some day a district cadastral survey and a record of rights and rents must come; and the sooner it is commenced, the better it will be for the province. (Baden-Powell, 1892: 290)

By giving *zamindars* individual ownership rights , the Company state in 1793 had done away with or made subservient other claims on the land. Peter Robb notes that "common, overlapping or contingent rights . . . tended to be ignored or reformulated, especially as land measurements, court decisions and property sales gradually gave practical effect to formal changes" (Robb, 2002: 72). The Settlement reflected the univocity pursued by the British in its different censuses and surveys. Duality, overlaps and contingent rights and identities were anathema to clear colonial classifications. The *zamindar* while given control over land did not have the capacity to control the components that made land a commodity. Labour and access to markets were in the hands of *jotedars* or a class of middlemen contracted to manage land and extract revenue. (Robb, 1982).

Writing in 1886 Vipinichandra Rai notes:

> [The legal term] Landlord thus ranges from proprietors to under-*raiyats* who sublet; and being the correlative of tenant, there must be an equal number of grades of landlords as there are of tenants. And just as the payment of rent is not essential for being a tenant, so the receipt of rent is not, for being a landlord. It is sufficient if he could get rent, except for a special contract. A proprietor, *talukdar, raiyat* or under-*raiyat,* who does not let his land but cultivates or occupies it, is not a landlord. (Rai, 1886: 19)

Under the terms of the Permanent Settlement, capitalism did not simply overwhelm existing ways of organising agriculture. What occurred was the capitalisation of existing social relations. Existing relations of tenure, cultivation and production became market-oriented, leading to the bewildering array of tenures and under-tenures (Chatterjee, 1986).

The Permanent Settlement's introduction of colonial-capitalist logic onto agrarian relations in Bengal heightened and concretized some asymmetrical relations extant in Bengali agrarian society. Relations between landlords, middlemen (essentially revenue collectors and estate managers), *jotedars* and other *raiyat* centred on the extraction of rent from the lowest rungs of the *raiyat*. Where property was heavily partitioned into a number of subtenures and where *jotedars* were able to negotiate exceptions to rent payment over portions of their land, rent extracted from the sharecropping and labouring class of peasants tended to be high.

For their part, *raiyat,* particularly *jotedars,* responded to changes also through a partial adaptation to the new order and a folding of this order into traditional practices where possible. Peasant resistance to *zamindari* increases in rent occurred, gaining a momentum in the decades immediately preceding the 1885 Bengal Tenancy Act (Guha, 1996). *Raiyat* also responded to the capitalisation of land by participating in the market for cultivation rights. Such rights tended to be then leased and rented to an abject class of labourers or mortgaged. Creditors were often *jotedars,* well-off peasants, whose role as moneylenders added to their other economic roles of grain-dealing, employment provision and landholding and entrenched further their social and political position in Bengali agrarian society (Ray & Ray, 1975). *Jotedars* exercised strong economic and social clout in villages in Bengal. Their separate roles were heavily intertwined. As moneylenders, *jotedars* were able to ensure a supply of labour through the creation of a group of indentured labourers working off debts. Sharecroppers with access to ploughs but without seeds or grains were also given loans to enable them to work *jotedar* lands. Ensuring the cycle of patronage and indenture, labourers and share-croppers, without the means to store or transport their produce, sold this immediately after harvest when prices were lowest to the grain merchants, often the *jotedar* himself. The *jotedar* was able to transport produce or store it, often selling these to poor farmers for food or seed (Ray & Ray, 1975). Given this control over labour, *jotedars* wielded power not only over the labouring peasantry but over the landlord himself and were able to use this to their advantage in negotiating lower rental assessments on their land (meaning that the brunt of the rent was paid by people working their land). In the 1911 survey operations in Hazaribagh, Bengal, the surveyor writes of the structure of credit and the indenture that this can lead to:

> A *raiyat* whose ordinary credit is exhausted will borrow money from a landlord or well-to-do *raiyat* [likely *jotedar*] and engage himself generally by a written contract to work continuously for his creditor by way of interest upon the loan. The so-called loan really represents the price for which the man sells himself to perpetual service, because it is obvious that a man in his position can never repay the money. The Kamia agrees not to work for anyone except his creditor or master: his wife and children are also the creditor's servants. The purchase-money is generally from Rs 20 to 40, a strong man or a married man getting more than a weak man or a bachelor. It is said that the position becomes hereditary, the son continuing to carry the father's debt. The Kamia gets from 5 to 10 cottahs of land for his own cultivation and some payment in kind proportionate to the amount of work done by him. (Surveyor-General, Bengal, 1911: 14)

Into this febrile capitalism came the Bengal Tenancy Act and its cadastral logic.

THE CADASTRAL SURVEYS: MAKING A SCIENTIFIC OBJECT OUT OF LAND

Cadastral surveys were one of three types of geographical survey undertaken by the British in India. The other two were the trigonometric and topographical surveys. The trigonometric survey is famous because of Everest and Lambton's triangulation of India, a base that is used to this day for topographic work. The topographical surveys were used for outlining frontiers of states and kingdoms, and for outlining and making tangible 'India' as a subject of colonial rule (Edney, 1997). If triangulation was to reduce the physical and human complexity of India to a series of referential coordinates, then the topographical and revenue surveys were intended to bring back that complexity, contained and made legible within the cross-referential scales of the three surveys. The Calcutta Review described the work of the revenue survey, "to put sinews and flesh on the colossal skeleton which that survey constructs" (cited by Markham, 1878: 118). The three surveys provided an intermeshed scientific register that taken together would comprehend India across three scales. In his 1879 Report, the Surveyor-General would assert that "each rests on an accurate scientific basis, which may in all cases be accepted as practically perfect" (Surveyor-General of India, 1879).

Land in India could only be subject to policy so long as it was outlined and kept emergent as an object of scientific inquiry by rigorous scientific methods. Lorraine Daston argues that the constitution of an object of scientific knowledge involves categorisation, refinement and regularisation (Daston, 2000: 3). Categorisation is the bringing together of scattered elements under a coherent classification as similar objects. Refinement creates properties by which objects are included or excluded from specific categories. Regularisation involves the stabilisation of often unwieldy and complex objects, for example through statistical enumeration or survey (Daston, 2000: 6).

Land in Bengal was subject to different degrees of categorisation, refinement and regularisation. Certainly the terms of the Permanent Settlement where agrarian relations were left to the devices of *zamindars* and *raiyat*, left land as a material and scientific object somewhat murky. The Tenancy Act would subject land and the relations therein, that is—the materiality of land, to a more rigorous standard with its taxonomic categories outlining classes of peasants and labourers and subjecting them to regular survey and documentation of rights to land.

These processes of rendering an object scientific and emergent are forms of representation that simultaneously isolate a scientific object and assert the truth or veracity of its representation. Daston suggests that the process of articulating a scientific object is not simply contemplative but also empirical (Daston, 2000: 3). The materiality of colonial knowledge, sometimes reduced to a somewhat abstracted discourse by postcolonial theory, has been asserted by a number of scholars (e.g. Ludden, 1993).

The cadastral survey as outlined by the Tenancy Act involved four stages. The first stage was the demarcation of the boundaries of the village or *zamindari* estate being assessed. The second was the cadastral survey of internal fields and the writing of the record of rights (the *khanapuri* is the act of writing the record, the record itself is the *khasra*). The third stage was the checking of the survey and its records by the head surveyor. The fourth stage was the settlement of disputes and the finalisation of rent based on the *khanapuri*. The Bengal Tenancy Act placed potentially different elements (the diversity of agricultural society in Bengal) together in a single category, the cadastral survey refined that category and established a regularising statistical base.

In what follows, I will study what happened when the survey as a scientific agent of administrative rule encountered the complex social formations which it was intended to transform. How was the attempt to make administrable objects, subjects and relations received?

Agents of Rule

The terms of the Tenancy Act were relayed by a number of agents, both European and Indian. As relayers of rule, all these agents, but in particular the native ones, were the subject of much anxiety. Many agents tended to be embedded in local contexts. Their methods of measuring, counting and recording land and landholding had long reflected local relationships. These agents, the British worried, were likely to tamper or corrupt records to curry favour with local *zamindars* or *jotedars*. The colonial government then sought to train record keepers and native surveyors so that they would understand the magical objectivity of numbers. And if these native agents could be extracted from local contexts, they may—the colonial authority mulled in survey reports—become very adequate ways of killing off local customary ways of giving meaning to land. These record keepers and surveyors were trained to think and record land in the numerical imagination of their colonial masters, meaning that that land was taken out of local webs of meaning and made part of an emergent colonial state. But extracting record keepers and native agents, and land itself, from local contexts was a struggle, marked by evasion, deception and outright defiance.

The two main native actors here are *amins* and *patwaris*. '*Amin*' was a catch-all term in British India denoting an agent or helper of a colonial administrator. '*Patwari*' were traditional village record keepers. *Amins* would usually undertake the survey, working closely with the *patwari*. *Patwaris* were employed by surveys across India in their traditional duties of writing the *khasra* and they were also in some areas taught to undertake the cadastral survey.

The British felt that *patwaris*, largely drawn from the upper castes of the local peasantry, were too close to *zamindars*. H A D Phillips, a member of the Bengal Civil Service, wrote in 1886 that in the period immediately preceding the Permanent Settlement, "the village *patwaris* were made merely to keep just such accounts as the *Zamindar* wanted for his own purposes. In a word. . . . the *patwaris* [became] the bond-slaves of the *Zamindar*s" (Phillips, 1886: 284). Phillips' account of administration in Bengal was one of a number of accounts of the problem of government in the state circulating as a prelude to the implementation of the Tenancy Act. These reports, including Baden-Powell's cited earlier, assayed the problem of agrarian relations as a problem of native mismanagement, centring often on the incorrigible greed of the *zamindar* (Baden-Powell, 1892) and the incompetence of native record keepers or their collusion with grasping *zamindars* as well as the abjecting effects of these on the poor *raiyat*. These reports together constituted a tremendously powerful repertoire of knowledge from which policy was to be derived. Such policy was to target native actors, both *zamindar* and *patwari,* either removing them from the equation, or making their obligations and responsibilities clearly outlined in the administrative law of the Tenancy Act and then surveilled.

Such readings of *zamindar–patwari* relations were however motivated by a particular colonial aesthetic. The sheaf of expert reports on agrarian relations in Bengal made out that British intervention was motivated by a concern for order, to be brought out by the magical properties of numbers, and for a desire to "improve", in Markham's take, the lot of the people. The will to improve (Li, 2007a) centred on taking land and the relations that surrounded it out of local contexts and investing it a particular idea of 'publicness', as we saw in Kuala Lumpur around the same period. Land and landholding was to be conceived in broader upscaled norms, part of an Indian colonial administration and the aesthetic and capitalist logics that dictated how that land was to be regulated and used.

A *patwari* sometimes would not record the cultivation of a part of a wealthy *jotedar*'s land, allowing it to be cultivated tax-free. The British saw this practice as fraud "perpetrated on the zamindar or the state" (McLane, 1993: 55; Baden-Powell, 1892: 629) and failed to understand the social context in which this occurred. By allowing for tax-free lands, this practice allowed the collection of surplus as a hedge against poor harvests. The system contributed to the establishment of the class of *jotedars* and allowed for the maintenance of demand for labour, and thus supply of food, during lean times. McLane argues that the system of allowing *jotedars* to keep some land tax-free was essential for the maintenance of the village as a whole during lean times (McLane, 1993: 55–56). It also allowed for the control over labour power on the part of the *jotedar.*

In order to mould the *patwari* into a servant of government, the Tenancy Act outlined the specific duties and responsibilities of the *patwari,* including sanctions if he failed to carry these out. The Tenancy Act outlined two types of cadastral survey for which *patwaris* were responsible. The first was the large survey undertaken at the time of revenue settlement. The second was during the interim period (which varied across India and in Bengal itself) between settlements when *patwaris* were expected to keep an up to date record of any changes in fields, including enhancements and leasing.

Schools for training *patwari* were set up, along the lines of those in place in other parts of India. These were reported to have had mixed success. Surveyors in the Central Provinces speak dismissively of the training of the *patwaris:*

> The amount of knowledge of surveying and the thousand and one details which go to make up the acquirements of a good executive officer of any

grade can hardly be gained in a fortnight or three weeks, which was the
average time spent in the survey class. . . . Their work has been classed
as equivalent to that of slow second class *amins* . . . this plan of teach-
ing *patwaris* does not seem a very promising method of introducing a
better style of surveying into the central provinces. *The men in many
instances are too old to learn new ways, and are wedded to methods and
customs which cannot be swept away by the fiat of the legislature, or
by the exaction of heavy penalties.* (Surveyor-General of India, 1885:36;
my emphases)

The anxiety about the capacity of the *patwari* too wedded to "custom"
to learn new ways is a concern about the embeddedness of this office in
local contexts. The righting of the *patwari* record, the establishing of a clear
and factual numerical record of landholdings and land relations, was seen
as necessary to impose a coherent structure of governance and of revenue
lines. *Patwari* records were to be a simple reflection of numerical facts on
the ground.

What was effectively being done was the establishing of the terms of
engagement between a *sovereign* state and its subjects. The statistical regulation that would present a 'true' picture of conditions would remove, in
theory, mediators between the state and its affairs and it would allow the
state to exercise, indeed *make,* its sovereignty. Agricultural relations were
to be standardised through surveys and the work of the *patwari,* meaning
that they were not to be left to the sway of norms and hierarchies in local
social formations but should instead reflect 'true' conditions on the ground,
as represented by numbers.

The appropriation of the village records, the local archive institutionalising and memorialising land relations and obligations, to serve the ends of
the revenue survey, and more generally of colonial law, was intended to code
and organise local reality in terms conducive to administrative rule. In the
terms pursued here, such appropriation was intended to move away from the
complications of intensive local relationships that structured power. Colonial presence intruded onto social formations and sought to restructure it in
ways that would guide its future development. The British understood well
that archives have and constitute a particular rationality. They do not merely
reflect reality, their logic organises and legitimises prevailing terms of rule.

The chief of one survey party in the Central Provinces wrote in the season
1885–1886 of the difficulty of maintaining this archive:

In any village, I invariably enquired for the year in which the *patwari*
visited the place. He had probably been three or four times since last
settlement, but on enquiry if he had ever been into the fields, the answer
was invariably 'No'. In fact he wrote, i.e., copied out, the old papers
in the village, with certain fancy additions. (Surveyor-General of India,
1887)

Where the *patwari* was seen as corrupt or incompetent, the British would use *amins* in their stead. *Amins* were portable interlocutors of empire, providing a fairly cheap and relatively efficient way of conveying the goals and ethos of colonial rule to native society. They were not a part of local society. The British used *amins* from elsewhere in Bengal and in some cases from outside Bengal.

As intimates of colonial rule, *amins* were a much-discussed office. The level and tone of this discussion in the survey reports instrumentalise and racialise *amins*. In an early survey of a district of Bengal in the season 1879–1880, the chief surveyor writes that *amins* and "Bengalis generally . . . while possessing good abilities were disinclined to use their talent . . . except with the one object of getting pay for doing nothing; they hated the strict supervision of the Survey Department. . . . Much labour was lost over men who absconded or who were found to have only pretended to learn [how to conduct a cadastral survey]" (Surveyor-General of India, 1881: 34).

The cultural intimacies between the *amin* and his British supervisor are here transmitted as a clash between British endeavour and Bengali sloth where a story is told of the attempt to impose British technical rigour and *amin* resistance or subversion of this. The corruptibility of the *amin* is mentioned in a public document giving notice of the procedure of the cadastral survey under the 1885 Tenancy Act: "The *amin* is a paid servant of Government and all persons are warned that it is a criminal offence . . . to offer a bribe to any *amin*. . . . No person has anything to gain by bribing an *amin*" (Survey Office, Bengal, 1894).

The *amin*, however, was a useful corrective against the *patwari* who was sometimes too caught up in local practices to be able to usefully convey what the British wanted. In the survey season 1889–1890 in Chittagong district in Bengal the chief surveyor reported difficulties in employing locals to doing the *khanapuri*,

> . . . their chief aim seemed to be to get allotted to them the record writing of villages in which they had some interests, so that they might falsify the records to suit their own purposes . . . it is a mistake to employ local *amins* [i.e. *patwari*] for this work, and believes that it would be far better to get men from other districts, who can have no local interests at all. (Survey Office, Bengal, 1891: 30)

The cadastral survey was a cultural process that required entering into and transforming local societies and the way they dealt with issues of land, ownership and production. The agents of the survey added a further dimension. The Tenancy Act was not simply imposed; it was conveyed by a material but yet cultural process, the cadastral survey. Tracing how colonial rule was conveyed materially allows us to look at the complex and uneven surface where rule was supposed to be imposed. The terms of rule were almost necessarily compromised; the way it was conveyed and the agents who conveyed it meant that it involved an ongoing process of cultural inter-action, with much room for negotiation, contest and evasion.

CONVEYING THE TERMS OF RULE

> We can talk of it and write with indifference of it, but, to the tenants of an estate, a sale is as the spring of a wild beast in the fold, the bursting of a shell in the square. It is the disturbance of all they had supposed to be stable. (Henry Ricketts, 1850; cited in part by Baden-Powell, 1892: 640; and in part by Mookherjee, 1919: 69)

Colonial power was not outside of society, it did not fashion administrable communities from afar nor out of thin air. It was deeply intertwined and imbued with societies in the different local contexts in which it operated; and this is made clear in the way the Act was implemented.

The Tenancy Act had three aims. The first was the imposition of some sort of visible order to remedy the murkiness perpetuated by the laissez-faire Permanent Settlement. The second was the extension of rights related to the law on private property to cultivators, and the third was the individualisation of the cultivator as an autonomous agent with an individualised relationship to the law and to the state. I study the first two aims in one section before examining the third.

Ordering and Extending the Law

Bengali agrarian society was to be ordered by transforming the local archive of land rights, the *khasra,* by cadastral survey. There were two problems with this aim: how to extract the *patwari* from his ties to *jotedars* and *zamindars;* and, second, how to make sense of the complicated, and at times downright bizarre, ownership structures that had resulted from the Permanent Settlement's capitalist system of land ownership without regulation. In particular, the *zamindar* tendency to simultaneously treat land as a capitalisable commodity and as a cultural entity distributed by dint of patronage relations led to a daunting web of tenures and under-tenures. The surveyors in the Chittagong district of Bengal survey of 1889–1890 report,

> the record writing . . . presented peculiar difficulties, owing to the numerous descriptions of tenures and under-tenures, the immense number of tenure-holders and the thousands of . . . estates, which have been still further split up by sales. . . . Purchasers and heirs have neglected to register changes in the [Government] *khewats* [statements of accounts and liabilities]". (Survey Office, Bengal, 1891: 30)

The unregulated alienation of land had left cultivators in an insecure position. An 1859 Rent Act had given limited rights to tenure-holders who could prove continuous cultivation of a plot of land for twelve continuous years. They were called 'hereditary cultivators' and retained rights even after a plot was sold. Cultivators who could not prove continuous right of occupancy were reduced to the position of "mere tenants at will" (Phillips, 1886:12). The latter class were subject to a different protocol of rent assessments and were easier to eject. Given the way records of rights tended to be maintained, it was difficult for a cultivator to prove continuous cultivation. One consequence of this was the creation of a pool of landless labour who migrated across Bengal hiring themselves out as temporary labourers to the more well-off peasantry. This is then the freeing of labour, the creation of a pool of potential workers, not tied to any particular structure of custom and is in effect the creation of a rural proletariat. It effectively was the creation of 'free labour' serving the needs of a nascent 'free market'.[2]

The British wanted the *khasra* to reflect the enumerated holdings and rights of different individuals. Ordering and normalising were social processes with exchanges between different vocabularies and 'moral economies'. Resistance to rewriting the local archive and the meanings attached to it occurred. Such resistance should not be understood as that of groups of people wholly autonomous to British systems of ordering. It was not, in other words, the resistance of a romantic indigenous tradition to the devilry of colonial systems. Resistance tended to come from well-off peasantry and middlemen leasing the right to collect revenue from *zamindars*, both of whom had been able to take advantage of the terms of the Permanent Settlement. Hereditary cultivators, in particular those who had been able to accumulate capital and land (*jotedars*), folded the enriching capitalist logic into 'traditional' structures of land relations. The survey reports speak of the tendency of these groups to "tamper" with the *khasra,* noting that there existed groups of hereditary cultivators (*patnidars*) and middlemen *(ghatwals* or *thikadars)* in wrongful possession of land. (Surveyor-General of India, 1891: 63–4). The reports also record that survey operations were obstructed "by the deliberate uprooting of survey marks by the *patnidars*" (Surveyor-General of India, 1892: 7). The 1911 Survey Reports in Hazaribagh, east Bengal note:

> The most exacting landlords were generally found to be the *thikadars*. . . . Many villages are given out on short temporary leases; on the expiry of each lease the rent of the *thika* is raised. The *thikadars* have no permanent interest in the village; their only object is to recoup their outlay and make as much additional profit as they can during the five or six years of their incumbency. Accordingly each successive *thikadar* must raise the rates of rent; and the system imposes a cumulative burden upon the tenants. The system is at its worse when the *thikadar* introduces a

dar thikadar for the exploitation of the village and the profits of two professional middlemen have to be extracted from the tenants. Again as the profits of a *thika* are from two sources, (a) the rent collection, and (b) the cultivation of the *manjhihas* (landlord's privileged land), there is a strong combination of the landlord's agent with the *thikadars* to extend the *majhihas* by seizure of the best rice-lands in the village. The ousted *raiyat* regards resistance to this combination as hopeless, and in fact his chances of success in a suit for recovery would be very small [because of the corruption of the *khasra*]. (Surveyor-General, Bengal, 1911: 14)

This representation of *thikadars* besides being an important summary on the nature of this localised, hybrid capitalism, also emphasises the idea that the *raiyat* bears the brunt of a bewildering, many-levelled persecution. To rewrite the *khasra* is not only then to organise agrarian relations according to clear boundaries, it is also the activity of the colonial administrator as saviour helping those poor *raiyat* persecuted by the local system. With this assumption, the British made it clear that the native raiyat was persecuted by a native system that was incorrigibly and immanently corrupt: succour needed to come from the outside, the native system could not reform itself. The description of the nefarious *thikadars* is counterbalanced with the hope that the correcting of the *khasra* will improve this situation:

It is hoped that the settlement operations may put a check to the further extension of this system of tenures; many of the *thikadars* are finding that when the legal rent of the *raiyats* is recorded in place of the rent which they have been exacting, their profit on the *thika* is exchanged for a considerable loss and are anxious to escape from their contracts: the *raiyats* are not likely in the future to submit to enhancements which they know to be illegal; . . . and consequently the profession of *thikadar* is likely to be less attractive than at present. (Surveyor-General, Bengal, 1911: 14)

The problem of the *khasra* was a problem of vocabulary and the imposition of a "discursive hegemony" that would order the "taxonomies, legitimacies and meanings" of local social actions and processes (Dirks, 1997: 199). The more well-off and articulate peasantry objected to the British imagination of orderly agrarian society. The relayer of this vocabulary was the imported *amin*. In order to redress the *patwari*'s failings (his embeddedness in local society), *amins* were often imported in by the survey. The Surveyor in the Burdwan Khas Mehals in Bengal notes gleefully in 1891,

records were written in Urdu or Hindi by upcountry *amins* and were [only] translated into Bengali in office . . . unqualified approval of this system [was expressed] as it will be much more difficult for the natives to tamper with the original *khasras* when written in a foreign character". (Surveyor-General of India, 1891: 63)

The writing of the *khasra* in a neutral language of Hindi or Urdu connected local structures to a more abstract, and dominant, order. The writing of the archive in an alien language emphasised that the meaning of the archive was not anymore to be determined locally and that its truth was to be adjudicated by the British.

The British worked on the basis that underpinning the obtuseness of land and property structures lay coherent and enumerable borders that could be recorded. In the Central Provinces, faced with persistent dissimulation by cultivators, a survey party devised a list of indirect enquiries to ascertain tenure:

> I devised the *"fard tarikat"* or list of enquiries, indirect enquiries, into every man's tenure . . . here all difficulties vanished; *the naked truth, regarding tenures . . . became apparent and the work progressed.* The battle of *khasra* writing in the Central Provinces was won". (Surveyor-General of India, 1887; my emphases)

The presumption that there was a "naked truth" that could be got at with the right type of questions was a feature of the different censuses and surveys in India. Much time during the ethnographic surveys and the population censuses, particularly the early ones in the late nineteenth century, was spent devising questions that could bring to light essential properties of identity (Risley, 1891).

The early surveys of the Tenancy Act did not have a standard practice of information gathering. The accepted practice was to demand attendance on the *amin,* or, where he was trusted, the *patwari,* by cultivators and landlords who were required to point out borders and state the recent history of land cultivation. The survey was a social encounter between two, or more, groups, often at cross purposes.

The Surveyor-General of India writes in the season 1889–1890 that in Bengal surveyors were "met with the usual want of co-operation on the part of the inhabitants, which has been more or less the case wherever work has been carried out in Bengal" (Surveyor-General of India, 1891: 5). A survey party in the same season noted "the unwillingness of the cultivators to attend when called on to do so" and this "passive opposition" is attributed to "the Bengali's love of ease and leisure, and in the case of the richer tenure-holders, to pride of purse and love of litigation disposing them to despise attendance on the *amin*" (Surveyor-General of India, 1891: 29).

Opposition to the survey is dismissed as the response of a lazy native. This depoliticisation of resistance is challenged by evidence of ongoing and organised opposition to the survey. Another example from a different region in the same survey of Bengal notes that the richer class of peasants "displayed a determined spirit of opposition to the survey operations . . . it appears that a regularly organized opposition was created by them. . . ." (Surveyor-General of India, 1891: 32). In yet another district, the surveyor notes that the *jotedars* "were on the whole inimical to the survey and were very unwilling to help in any way, except under compulsion" (Surveyor-General of India, 1891: 40). Lack of cooperation was one strategy, direct subversion was another. In 1891–92, surveyors note the "deliberate uprooting of survey marks" by *jotedars* (Surveyor-General of India, 1893: 7). The surveys consistently note also the feeding of wrong information by *jotedars* to *amins*.

The Tenancy Act and its cadastral surveys had difficulty organising Bengali agrarian relations. Feudal relations influenced the local record of rights. The stated intention of the Act was to provide rights of cultivation to the lower classes of the *raiyat*. However the Act reflected a faith in the capacity of survey, of enumeration, to uncover a distinct and measurable truth about land relations. Record keeping was undertaken in a local context where *jotedars* and other influential gatekeepers were able to mould the survey and the Act to their advantage. This led to the further consolidation of the economic and social position of *jotedars* and the marginalisation of other cultivators reduced to the position of landless labourers or sharecroppers. The reordering of land and relations surrounding it, given that it occurred in a situation of complicated hierarchies that could not be simply done away with, meant that local elites were able to use the terms of the Act to further increase their economic power. Those whom the Act had depicted as being exploited by native systems, the different classes of *raiyat*, were, as I will continue to show below, generally furthered in their exclusion and marginalisation by the Act, and not necessarily helped by its imposition.

Individualisation

The Tenancy Act placed local peasantry in an individualised relationship with colonial law. The survey and the Act itself were intended to break through the murkiness of land relations which served the interests of *zamindars, jotedars,* middlemen and others who were able to profit from the Permanent Settlement. The Act worked to isolate the *raiyat,* extract him from the web of feudal relations and identify in him a *corpis juris*, a rights-bearing self.

The Tenancy Act established that there would be no intermediary between the state and the landowner or cultivator. The extraction of the individual, and hence the governance of agrarian relations, from customary practice in Bengal created a modern political subject whose principle tie was to the colonial state. Whereas the world of custom was seen as a world whose norms and structures were decided and derived from the dictates of a tyrannical collective, European law was represented, in opposition, as the sole means by which agency and autonomy could be derived (Dirks, 1981). It was hoped that the Tenancy Act, in giving cultivators right over their bodies and land, would lay the basis for an entrepreneurial capitalist agriculture (e.g. Rampini & Finucane, 1889; Finucane & Ali, 1913; Baden-Powell, 1892).

As we have seen, the imposition of colonial law failed to establish this class of individualised smallholding agricultural entrepreneurs. The corpus of rights did not exist in discourse alone; it was established on materiality. This materiality was the cadastral survey, the process of measuring, negotiation and contest that would uncover who owned what, who tilled what, who rented what and who had the right to remain and the right to land. Colonial law then was not only discursive; it was not merely inscribed but enacted in the material landscape of agrarian relations. It is insufficient to say that colonial law provided a grid or pattern upon which life was to be lived. The law was enacted in the materiality of agrarian landscapes where it was contested by local structures. As I have shown, the record of rights and the cadastral surveys upon which the record was based, did not offer the law a straightforward channel of intervention into agrarian relations in Bengal.

If the record of rights was to provide the basis upon which the law was to operate, then the inability of the British to influence that record in any comprehensive way meant that the law was enacted in ways unintended. *Jotedars* and *zamindars* tended to appropriate rights, identities and political subjectivities intended for poorer cultivators (Chatterjee, 1986). Rather than increasing individualised entrepreneurial agrarian capitalism, the Act contributed to the furthering of semifeudal structures in Bengal.

The rights generated by the Act constituted a framework of recognition and of adjudication but these were either appropriated by *jotedars* or *zamindars* (Chatterjee, 1986) or were found to be simply impotent (they could have little transformative effect on material conditions). In the 1911–12 survey of the Dacca region, the surveyor suggests that the *barga* (sharecropping) system is a method employed by *zamindars* to prevent the application of the terms of the Act (the *khasra* is amended to show that cultivators have not worked on land for a continuous period of 12 years thus leaving them as sharecroppers). The surveyor's recommendation that a relevant article of the Act not be brought to the knowledge of the sharecropper is testament to the power of feudal relations in Bengal:

> There is not the slightest doubt . . . that the *barga* evil is increasing and extending rapidly and that landlords have discovered in it a method by which to avoid the provision of the Bengal Tenancy Act. If no *khatian* [account of individual cultivation rights within the *khasra*] is opened for the *bargadar*, we fail in our duty of recording his rights as a tenant; if a *khatian* is opened for him, he is promptly ejected and risks the loss of his means of livelihood. . . . No attempt has been made to advise the *bargadar* to apply for commutation under section 40, as it would merely result in his prompt ejectment. (Surveyor-General of Bengal, 1912: 14)

Section 40 of the Tenancy Act legislates for the provision of money payment to sharecroppers instead of a share in crop or seed (Rampini & Finucane, 1889). The surveyor here suggests that both the recording of a sharecropper's cultivation rights and the introduction of a basic measure to alleviate his condition would not be advisable given the structure of feudal relations almost thirty years after the Act was first passed.

In a document written in 1881 (before the Tenancy Act but following the 1859 Rent Act), written and published by "Abhay Charan Das, a *Ryot*", a flavour of the way that *zamindars* are able to use the terms of the court to establish further their feudal hold over cultivators is given. The author describes himself as "a *ryot*" but it is written in English, Das is probably a pen name of a reformer.

> There are several causes of the inability of the *ryot* to protect his rights through the Courts of Justice. The first cause is his ignorance, the second his poverty, the third the great distance of the Courts of Justice from his house, the fourth the delay of decision, the fifth of the very great difficulty of getting witnesses, and the sixth and last the terrible vengeance of his zemindar. Here it ought to be remarked that the Courts of Justice are nothing but a plaything in the hands of the rich. The zemindar and his agents are thoroughly acquainted with their ins and outs. Besides he has his . . . pleader in the Court to plead his cause, while the poor *ryot* has neither the knowledge of it, nor the means to advocate his cause. First of all, he must have to pay for a stamp paper; then he will have to pay to get his petition written out. The power of the zemindar . . . being omnipotent, there must be not only very great difficulty in inducing witnesses to give evidence, but also he will have to pay them at least double the usual fee. As he gains his livelihood solely from the cultivation of his land, so he cannot spend several weeks or months, which much elapse before the decision of a case, in attending the Court, without doing great injury to his crops. He will have to defray the lodging expenses not only of himself, but also of his witnesses in addition to their fee. Moreover he cannot expect success without bribing the Amlahs of the Court. . . . And for all this he is not at all sure that he will gain the case. Suppose that 'by some extraordinary chance' he gains it. But what will be its consequence? He will be marked out by his zemindar as a victim of his terrible vengeance, which is sure to be wreaked on him on the very first opportunity. During the absence from his house, his rice is almost sure to be cut, his cattle driven, or his house plundered. As if these are not sufficient to allay his passion, civil and criminal suits, which had existence nowhere except in the fertile brains and forged documents of his zemindar and his agents, will be heaped upon him, till the poor fellow is forced to leave the village as a consequence of his rashness in contesting the demands of his master. Or if he dares not punish him in this way, the latitude of appeal allowed by the Civil Code is resorted to by him

as a legal means for making him feel the consequences of incurring his displeasure, till the poor fellow is reduced to beggary by the expenses of litigation, is forced of his own accord to do whatever his master bids him. (Das, 1881: 93–4)

The power of landlords in eastern Bengal is noted in the 1912–1913 survey where the surveyor in the Mymensingh district, the largest district in Bengal, notes:

> . . . the big landlords have been found to be the worst offenders against the section of the Bengal Tenancy Act limiting the enhancement of rent. Indeed their power is such that the tenants, when their rents have been reduced by the department to that legally payable, have even filed objections asking for the record of the rents they were paying. (Bengal Surveyor-General, 1913: 3)

The legal recognition of the cultivator as an autonomous agent under the law does not make him so. The Mymensingh surveyor's depiction of the landlord's ability to force his tenant to make a claim against the tenant's interests points to the limits of the law. Das' description of the legal process indicates the limited capacity of the poor and uneducated tenant to enact his rights as a legal subject. The Act's presumption of an autonomous individual able to make claims on the basis of inscribed rights does not take into account the contexts within which rights are to be claimed.

In Dacca again in the 1912–1913 survey, the survey officer notes the sway of the landlord over his estate and the sheer difficulty of considering cultivators as autonomous agents under the law:

> Illegal enhancements are prevalent to an enormous extent, evictions are rife without recourse to the courts, . . . and illegal cesses are levied: the right of inheritance is denied; illegal confinements and other corporal punishments are resorted to, in order to crush refractory tenants. The tenants are kept in check by a rod of iron and to such an extent to do they live in a state of dread and awe, that it was with the utmost difficulty that evidence could be gathered for the purpose of preparing a true record-of-rights . . . but it seems that the age should now have come when the courts might protect and not crush the oppressed; that age, however, is inconsistent with the wealth of landlords and the venality of the local preservers of the peace. (Surveyor-General, Bengal, 1913: 5)

Colonial law is not simply or overwhelmingly imposed onto local spaces, it is filtered and used by extant power brokers for their own sake. That that law may be appropriated by existing hierarchies of power points to the restricted capacity of law itself to uncover and alleviate conditions that it names as unjust. It points also to the way that law may be used and appropriated, creating conditions and temporalities (feudalism) unintended.

CONCLUSION

The Tenancy Act fabricated persons and things. The production and administration of subjects and objects of rule and the terms of their relation to an overarching authority (such as the state and its law) is an intimate cultural process (Li, 1999). The production of subjects and relations to administer is not undertaken by an abstract power which sits atop and overwhelms society. In the colonial setting the production of administrable subjects involved a dynamic and dialogic relation between native and colonial epistemes, social structures and social mechanisms. The domination claimed by colonial states because of the existence of a structure of rule (courts, revenue agents, police) was illusory: it had purchase to the extent that contests, usually at 'local' scales, were ignored or suppressed. Colonial rule was made up of dialogues and contests; it was not simply imposed and it did not simply overpower existing terms of rule.

The Permanent Settlement and the Tenancy Act both attempted to place a capitalist framing onto agriculture in Bengal. In doing so, both attempted to produce and succour a specific class. The Settlement focused on a landlord class, the Tenancy Act focused on recovering a class of market-oriented 'free' peasants, meaning that they were to be liberated from customary hierarchy and, with attendant regulations and administrators in place, be more properly engaged in a free and contractual exchange of their labour for wage under market conditions.

However, the vaguely historical deterministic formulation that colonial power would lead to the subordination of local moral economies and material and cultural control over land, resources and their exploitation does not take into account the specific localised and historicized struggles that determine how social formations interacted with capitalism and colonial administration. The point is not to argue that capitalism did not dominate in Bengal—it did—but it is to argue that this domination was not complete or efficient; administrative rule was in colonies often stumbling and awkward, run through with compromises and a lack of knowledge because of the recalcitrant 'local' (cf. Chatterjee, 1986: 172–3).

When the cadastral surveys of the Tenancy Act interacted with social formations and with capital, the result was not, and could not have been, predetermined or perfectly influenced by the colonial authorities. The Permanent Settlement assumed that peasants and landlords would relate to each other under mutually beneficial market conditions. They did not: the veil of the Settlement allowed landlords to increase rents and cesses, or additional payments ostensibly for land improvements, and to eject those who did not or could not pay. The Tenancy Act was designed to help succour these tenants and was certainly partly motivated by a string of riots and disturbances. The terms of the Tenancy Act Bengal were appropriated by *jotedar* or a class of overseers, estate managers and professional middlemen: precisely those who controlled credit arrangements with *raiyat*, their debtors. The Act did not simplify; the Act did not create readily administrable bodies of tenants with a clear record of rights, and landlords with definite parcels of land. The Act and the capitalism it sought to refine were received in social space, and transformed by the struggles therein, contributing to class formations and patterns of domination and subservience unintended by the British.

The Tenancy Act, through cadastral surveys, established in law a written record of plots and boundaries that were connected to written records of tenancy and ownership. Access to information was a key aim of the Tenancy Act, as was the establishment of an organised structure from which information could be easily and continuously derived. The cadastral survey was intended to order and organise the relationship between cultivator and so place both land and social actors in a direct relationship with colonial government, leapfrogging customary norms and practice. By creating conditions where information would be continuously generated and passed upwards because of the stipulations of the Tenancy Act, the colonial government effectively sought to create predictable patterns in the future development and growth of agriculture in Bengal.

The cadastral survey was an instrument designed to overwhelm and marginalise local knowledge and local records of rights. The aim was to move away from the intensive social and cultural relations through which power was constituted. The survey was intended to standardise records about land boundaries and land use. Surveyors were fixated on the question of how the local, and unreliable, aspect of information could be controlled or eliminated. While the Act ostensibly sought to protect the rights of a sometimes romantically conceived smallholding peasant or *raiyat,* it did so without fully taking into account the control over economic and social resources that *jotedars* had in large parts of Bengal and their capacity to influence or corrupt the work of the cadastral surveyors. It similarly did not take into account the role of middlemen who had leased the right to manage estates, nor of *patwari* or village record keepers. Most of all the Act did not take into account how all these actors, and more besides, were caught up in local webs of customary practice, or if they did the British appeared to think that these could be swept away by colonial law (they could not, at least not entirely).

What do we learn about administrative power from the study of the Tenancy Act? One insight is that the struggle of the state to move away from local geographies is fraught. The colonial state in Bengal tried different strategies to make the social relations in specific places inconsequential. The state tried to remove the *khasra,* or record of rights, from its specific meanings, and the relationships that gave it meaning. The record of rights was to reflect an 'objective' mathematical logic and not customary relations or 'moral economies'. *Amins* and other agents of colonial rule replaced local *patwaris* as recorders of rights. This attempt to displace the social relations that constituted agrarian relations, and power, in Bengal was confusing and beset with difficulty. The cadastral survey, which was to convey the mathematical logic, became a convoluted cultural process. The survey did not displace the relationships that constituted agrarian Bengal, rather it seemed to get caught up in this. Rather than a scientific instrument to abstract and generalise about space from a distance, the cadastral surveys, and the record of rights that ensued, became a series of relationships through which administrative power was conveyed but also negotiated, evaded and resisted. In this chapter then the principle lesson for my study of administrative rule is that the claims to abstraction should not be taken as given. In the next chapter though I show the power of representation, a power that can often dismiss or ignore the reality of power as a series of social relations, but usually only temporarily. An account of the persistence of challenge, or simply of power's, inefficiencies is important to understand social change. That which is ostensibly marginal matters. In other words, it is important to understand domination and hegemony relationally. If we are able to give an account of the marginal alongside the dominant then we are better able to understand how hegemonies exist only in relation to other possible ideas about how to arrange society. We are also able to argue that hegemonies are processes that must always try to detract and make marginal other possible presents and futures.

NOTES

1. I use the term 'raiyat' when describing this group in my narrative, but stick with 'ryot' when it is used in my source material.
2. I thank Alina Cucu for this insight.

4 Representing the Margins
Colonial Art and Photographs in the Service of Depoliticisation

Achille Mbembe argues that one of the most important aspects of colonial rule was the way it was entwined with a civilising mission (Mbembe, 2001). Colonial rule was not the simple administration of people and things. Rule was exercised on the basis of a strange mixture of disgust, religious or capitalist fervour, fear and desire (for improving others, for native women—sometimes men—for material wealth). Colonialism as a project of rule was "written by many hands". I have shown the fear the British had for the unemployed coolie, their disdain for native systems of controlling labour and desire for the wealth that such systems obstructed, and their packaging of this whole project of rule as a means of achieving civilisation, progress and order. Others have shown the intertwinement of rule with sexual desire (Proschan, 2002; McClintock, 1995), with misogyny (Hayes, 1996) and with an everyday disproportionate and harrowing violence (Taussig, 1984).

Perhaps the key argument of this book is that administrative rule—the technicalising away of questions about how things and people should be ordered and for what purpose—is a project centring on marginalising or excluding certain groups from politics: administrative rule, in the past and the present, is a way of restricting access to the political and it is based, in one way or another, on an accounting of who deserves to be political. This is an accounting that reflects economic and cultural interests of dominant groups.

The restriction of the right to politics that underpins administrative rule is clearest in colonies. On the face of it, it may appear less apparent in contemporary cases of administrative rule but a number of scholars have tried to show the intertwinement of administration and depoliticisation. In their studies of development programs in Indonesia and Lesotho respectively, Tania Li and James Ferguson both focus on the making of an intelligible field of intervention for policy makers and how this "renders technical" complex social reality, producing "trustees" and subjects who are to be administered by experts (Li, 2007a: 7; Ferguson, 1990. The results include (1) the growth of an "anti-politics machine", in Ferguson's memorable phrase, a voracious assemblage of experts, trustees and bureaucratic techniques that consign more and more aspects of social reality to administration; (2) a distinction between those who are more likely to be in a primarily administrative relationship with a state and those who have room to act as citizens—i.e. to act politically in ways that appear not to be foreclosed by administration; and (3) the technicalisation of the political itself: political practice can be depoliticised, for example when politics centres on articulating development or consumer needs to a government of experts who figure out how best to meet those needs. In this type of political infrastructure, citizens are claimants to material resources; they cede the power to determine *how* ends are to be met to teams of experts (Newman and Clarke, 2009). It is not easy, of course, to depoliticise politics in this way. The infrastructure or channels of political practice are not easy to control or limit. In postwar Iraq, the Coalition Provisional Authority attempted to do this by creating assemblies to foster 'grassroots politics'. Citizens were welcome to address their resource or development needs to these provincial assemblies, but how these needs were to be met was determined by a wider 'neoliberal' context. It is important of course, and this is central to all the cases studied in this book, that there was and is a gap between the aspirations of administrative rule to code and restrict politics on the one hand and reality on the other hand. People did not remain within the categories set for them.

The issue in this chapter is *not* whether administrative rule was and is an attempt to restrict access to politics. A number of scholars have argued that this is the case across different contexts and I do so also in the next two chapters of this book. What may be useful is rather an attempt (1) to articulate the techniques by which certain groups are made out to be unworthy or unfit to undertake political practice and (2) to argue, based on the first articulation, that there is something to be said about the connections between the marginalisation and depoliticisation of some groups and the economic, cultural and political domination of others.

In this chapter I explore the connections between administrative rule, of the past and of the present, and cultural denigration. I have argued in the previous two chapters that denigrating native societies and their economic and cultural systems was an important condition of establishing, however imperfectly, colonial administrative rule in rural Bengal and Kuala Lumpur. I will show in the two chapters following that this method of disqualifying groups from the political is central to justifying and perpetuating administrative rule today. Administrative rule is justified by discourses and representations that disqualify groups from the political. One important bridge between colonial and contemporary administrative rule is then the persistence of tactics of depoliticisation. Indeed administrative rule as I describe it requires this type of depoliticisation.

THE AESTHETICS OF ORDER

If colonial administrative rule rested on quarantining away the discussion of how, and for whom, people and things have been ordered then a primary way of accomplishing this was to make some expressions of order sacred.

The ways things were organised were not to be taken simply as one among many possible ways of ordering, but as order itself, or progress itself (Mitchell, 1991). Making a particular idea about how, for example, a town was to be organised sacred rested on denigrating other possible ideas of the order and purpose of a town as antinomies.

Edward Said's seminal *Orientalism* (1978) has dominated accounts of how native society and ways of knowing have been denigrated. The organisation of people and things is sometimes understood as a secondary or different expression of power to 'orientalism'. The power of organisation is cold-bloodedly repressive and dominating, seeking to count, classify, survey and describe subjects and resources so that they may be regulated. Administrative power, in this reading, dominates for a purpose, for government, whereas orientalist denigrations of native society occur because of the civilisational and moral superiority of 'the occident', and not in order to achieve any particular project of order or improvement. The distinction between the two is important because it allows us to distinguish expressions of power that emerge from different historical and political circumstances; but saying that both emerge from specific historical contexts is not to say also that they remained distinct practices occurring at different times or in different places.

I have shown already how administrative power was rooted in 'culture'. The surveys in Bengal involved interlocution between different cultures: there was never any such thing as objective knowledge extracted by surveys from social milieux nor any attempt by colonial administrators, as far as the Bengal surveys go, to seek knowledge free of prejudice about Bengali agrarian society in general, and the *zamindar* and *raiyat* in particular. But the interesting thing about colonial administrative rule was not that it sought to build on the dismissive and denigrating 'orientalist' representations of natives (in paintings for example) nor even that administrators were connected to and replicated the prejudices of orientalists (though they were of course). The most interesting thing about colonial administration was that its method adopted and furthered the vicious orientalist perspective to the extent that under certain conditions and with respect to specific groups, denigration was intertwined with government to the extent that rational administrative goals were under threat.

I have argued that not all subjects of colonial government were equally excluded from what we may describe quite loosely as politics. That is, to different degrees, different groups were more able to escape the suffocating administrative relationship with the colonial state. This is partly because of class, dominant natives were the natural allies of colonisers particularly in the early period when they were finding their feet. It is not the case then that administrators simply and without compulsion fell in with orientalist dictums about native society; they seemed to have done so, often though not always, because it was economically opportune to do so. This also helps account for the way certain groups were able to avoid a wholly administrative relationship with the state. The colonial state did not, then, simply distinguish between Europeans and natives. Colonial power, including administrative power, was not simply imposed equally onto natives; that power was graduated, it fleshed out differently on different bodies depending largely on their relative value economically as well as culturally.

In what follows, I look at three sorts of representation of natives in the colonial period. One is painting from the orientalist genre, the other is documentary photographs and the third are photographs for identification and surveillance purposes. I study these examples as an entry point for discussing a complex process of denigration of natives. My aim is not to investigate in detail the different types of representation, paintings and photography that I indicate nor to give a comprehensive account of genres. My aim is to open a discussion to show how the denigration of natives through aesthetic representation proceeded in step with their depoliticisation and with their objectification as units of administrative government. A second aim is then to lay the ground for the argument that this type of cultural or civilisational denigration of specific groups as not yet ready to be political continues to be harked at in different ways in contemporary instances of administrative rule. The connection between colonial and contemporary administrative rule is the persistence of tactics of cultural denigration that makes it easier to disqualify specific groups from politics.

Three Representations: I. *The Fanatics of Tangier*

Eugene Delacroix's *The Fanatics of Tangier* (1837–38; figure 1) is particularly evocative in comparison to his other well-known crowd scene, *Liberty Leading the People* (1830). Wild men, arms flung upwards, seem to break through a crowd; a child runs in fear, a man is trampled. Delacroix has arranged the light to focus on the five men at the front, barely in control of themselves, and the child they seem to be pursuing. The painting arranges actors on a stage; we focus on the five as the main participants in this chaotic frenzy, while at the backdrop their leader sits atop a horse holding the green flag of Islam.

Delacroix explained *Fanatics:* "their enthusiasm excited by prayers and wild cries, they enter into a veritable state of intoxication, and, spreading through the streets, they perform a thousand contortions, and even dangerous acts" (Delacroix, 1838; cited by Sharp, 2009: 22). Is Delacroix's painting a record of the strangeness of others? Europe may be the invisible but orderly contrast that gives meaning to the painting, recognising a procession as chaotic and fearful, rather than the liberating and emancipatory tones of *Liberty Leading the People* (it may also, equally, be that it is interpretation that frames *Fanatics* in relation to a ghostly European vision of order).

Delacroix's painting is recognisably a part of a wider repertoire of orientalist images. The analysis of orientalism has been expanded but also limited since Edward Said's seminal text, which used a Foucaultian and Gramscian

Figure 1 Eugene Delacroix. *The Fanatics of Tangier* (1837–1838). Minneapolis Institute of Arts.

perspective to argue that orientalism was an act of acquisitive power. It is important however that the acquisition, or denigration, of the orient was not necessarily inherent in the individual work of individual orientalists. orientalism took on a sharper edge when it was the backdrop to intervention and to projects of reordering native society and economy. The different constituent parts of orientalism came to be arrayed with each other to form a repertoire that could be wielded to claim knowledge of natives and native society and to justify native policy including the exclusion and neglect of some groups.

There have been two persistent critiques made of Edward Said's argument about orientalism. John MacKenzie has argued that Said reads homogeneity and purposiveness across orientalism that is actually difficult to discern. This is perhaps particularly the case with 'orientalist' painting, a category that brings together a variety of different periods and perspectives on the 'orient'. MacKenzie also argues that Said's reading of orientalism as a dominating system of power has led to a selective interpretation of orientalist painting, with those representations of the orient as in one way or another deviant and uncultured before a western norm becoming dominant. Orientalist painting also, like other paintings, were not simply interested in the representation of 'truth'; they were extensions of a theatrical imagery and imagination, where a culture of the fantastic already present in nineteenth-century European cultural life found further form, and were explorations in painting and style that extended the remit and boundaries of European art (MacKenzie, 1995). MacKenzie's critique is important in recognising the diversity of perspectives among orientalists, and in pointing to the diversity of reception that 'orientalist' art had, but he perhaps understates the acquisitive effects of orientalist painting. The acquisition of the orient was not done only through the depiction of ignoble men or willing females but by recording and describing oriental culture and society: this constituted knowledge of that society and contributed to the sense that local social formations contained no relevant mysteries and could be grasped and be a subject for colonial policy.

The second critique made of Said's *Orientalism* centres on the differences and connections between representation, reality and production of the orient. Said's *Orientalism* concentrated more on the representation of the orient, to the extent that it becomes unclear what the ontological difference between the orient and its representation is (Isin, 2005). The question of the reality of the orient, and how it may be approached, becomes clouded in a framework that emphasises the productive force of discourse (Turner, 2000) where the aspirations of power are not associated with an examination of how discourse becomes operative in social reality. David Ludden (1993) argues that it is important to understand the materiality of orientalism if we are to take into account how orientalist discourse influences colonial government. George Steinmetz (2007) argues that colonial administrators vied with each other to demonstrate the superiority of their ethnographic knowledge of the native and thus influence native policy. Engin Isin (2005) studies the struggle between occidental and oriental subjects and perspectives in social space over the production of the political. Ludden and Isin emphasise that orientalism needs to be studied in its material and social effects, which means for me a focus on the social processes of producing the orientalist imagination of the native and native society.

I explore throughout this book the attempt to produce in government and policy a denigrating imagination of native society. The argument centres, like Isin's, on the production of political being and the exclusions, disenfranchisement and marginalisation that this includes. The focus in the study is what happens when administrators attempt to concretise imaginations of native society into policy, often in order to pursue specific economic arrangements.

The intent of Delacroix in painting *Fanatics* is, in the grand scheme of things, largely unimportant; what may have been important was the transformation and generalisation of a specific account of native society, with all its varied intents and contexts, into a basis for dismissing the political capacity of native society. In the same way, the eroticisation of other orientalist paintings, such as Jean-Auguste-Dominique Ingres' odalisques, became generalised away from the contexts of specific work into an account of native women with real and violent consequences. The attempt was to group together varied forms of orientalist art and literature to make the orient at once available and immediate but also exotic, ripe for government but a form of government centred on denigration and racial difference. Whatever the motivation, the orient was made available. These interventions could take the form of ecstatic pleasure-seeking (Proschan, 2002) or a cold-minded will to improve; or it could lead to a strange intertwinement of the aesthetic and government where orientalist denigrations of native social formations was a useful referent to justify narrow economic interests as 'civilisation' or 'order' or 'progress'.

Three Representations: II. Felice Beato and the Mutiny

> As there is now scarcely a nook or corner, a glen, a valley, or mountain, much less a country, on the face of the globe which the penetrating eye of the camera has not searched, or where the perfumes of poor Archer's collodion has not risen through the hot or freezing atmosphere, photography in India is, least of all, a new thing. From the earliest days of the calotype, the curious tripod with its mysterious chamber and mouth of brass, taught the natives of this country that their conquerors were the inventors of other instruments beside the formidable guns of their artillery, which, though as suspicious perhaps in appearance, attained their object with less noise and smoke. (Samuel Bourne, 1863; cited by Chaudhary, 2012: 85)

Colonial photographs, like colonial statistics, are ways of laying bare, of making something known but at the same time exotic and strange. The photographer, at once present and absent, provided a fixed perspective from which to derive meaning and made distant events, places, things or people immediate—graspable—and strange (Mitchell, 1991).

Photography from the middle to the end of the nineteenth century was finding its way in Europe as a tool of reportage, of recording reality and making an inventory of possessions. Photographs were attractive to institutions and commercial media interested in the truthful representation of people or things. The invasive camera was sharp and clear, entering nooks and glens and bringing people out of hiding to record their truth. State institutions, intrigued by the possibilities of this technology, became interested in the standardised production of true identity. Alongside statistics, photographs became instruments of establishing identity, and made one officially recognisable before state offices, in the form of identity papers (Landau, 2002; Maxwell, 1999). Photography was also used for documentary and photojournalistic reasons. As records of events or cultures, photojournalism communicated a story.

The Italian photographer Felice Beato arrived in India in 1858 soon after the end of the Mutiny.[1] Beato's time in India was personally enriching, the

Mutiny received wide coverage in the British papers and his photographs were bought up. One of his photographs, "Interior of Secundrabagh after the Slaughter of 2,000 Rebels," (Figure 2) depicts the aftermath of battle in Lucknow. At the foreground are skulls and bones of an enemy defeated, scattered around the courtyard some five months after battle. Beato had had the bones dug up and placed in the yard (Chaudhary, 2012). There are natives in the background in oddly laconic and disinterested poses, perhaps for purposes of scale and to draw attention to the ruins at the background. The resulting photograph was miscaptioned in London, stating that the photograph was taken on the same day as the battle (Chaudhary, 2012: 77).

Beato was a pioneer in the field of war photography. He would later follow British regiments in China to battle in the Second Opium War and was probably the first photographer of corpses. As Beato constructed this photograph, he tried to reveal a dramatic authenticity about the Mutiny. Reconstructive photography was not uncommon in colonies. In the quest to record and reveal truthfulness and authenticity about native society many encounters were staged. Sometimes they were quixotic, even whimsical,

Figure 2　Felice Beato. *Interior of Secundrabagh after the Slaughter of 2,000 Rebels* (1858). The Anne S K Brown Military Collection. Brown University Library.

stagings of hunts—for example—that never took place (Landau, 2002); at other times they were violent attempts to reveal a 'truth' about events or about natives, before they were changed by the encounter with Europe and modernity. In 1865, the head of an orphanage in the Andamans described a photo of his charges who were taken on tour and exhibited in Calcutta:

> At the studio of Messrs. Saché and Westfield. where several gentlemen—strangers to the Andanmanese, were present when the photographs were being taken,—we encountered positive difficulty, in inducing them to group themselves, stripped of their European clothes. That difficulty overcome, however, it was remarkable to observe how quickly they appreciated the fact that they were required to keep steady, and how willingly they did the best they could, when undergoing an ordeal, which is disagreeable even to those whose vanity it is pleasing. (Homfray, 1865; cited by Falconer, 1984)

There are three dominant ways of interpreting colonial photography. The first is to find in such photography a racial and gendered perspective, where the visual representation of natives as savage "helped to sustain imperial expansion" (Maxwell, 1999: ix). Seeing and recording natives as savages is not the same thing as imperial expansion (Landau, 2002) but images of denigrated natives helped vindicate imperial expansion and formal disenfranchisement and influenced the moral basis of the relation between coloniser and colonised. The second interpretation is to understand photography as an interface for documenting and revealing social reality but with the capacity to transform "what counts as reality" (Chaudhary, 2012: 80). In framing portions of reality, photography, like statistics, privileged particular slices of that reality (Mitchell, 1991) and these were made out to be representative of a greater whole that was absent from that photo but alluded to and fairly comprehensively accounted for (Appadurai, 1993).

Photography held the keys to truthfulness and permitted generalisation about social reality. Like statistics, photography became a way of grasping a sequential, systematic and historically and socially located truth about events that eyewitness accounts, including painting, in all their specificity and subjectivity could not lay claim to. The techniques of photography and statistics obscured the violence that went into making a society and a population visible, or at least made it difficult to focus on that violence because of the promise of a deeper and wider instrumental truth useful, indeed necessary, for government that these techniques allowed. Also obscured by this promise was the dynamics of how reality was not simply apprehended but constructed by these techniques. These are sometimes explicit constructions, like Beato's recovery of corpses in Lucknow, but they are more often painstaking and concealed. The cultural processes of the cadastral surveys in Bengal, for example, are more or less impossible to fathom simply from the numbers.

The third interpretation of colonial photography is, then, to see it as an instrument of government, where specific ways of representing reality came to be standardised. These representations brought to light not simple events as such, but standardised truths about populations and resources that could be comparable across different areas. This quest for standardisation in truth through photography is the subject of the next section of this chapter.

Eugene Delacroix's representation of fanatics was a very subjective one: it could lay little claim to a systematic account of fanaticism and its danger to order. We are little closer to understanding fanaticism after Delacroix, which in the nineteenth century meant little closer to grasping it as a problem that could be solved by a state. Delacroix's painting is brimming with life, and with danger; it is a chaotic painting. Felice Beato's photographs of Lucknow are of equally dangerous people, but these people are now dead and the danger has passed. Delacroix's uses the contrasts between vibrant colours and still and moving figures to create a chaotic scene at the centre of *Fanatics*. Beato's photo privileges stasis; in comparison to Delacroix's painting, the danger is not present or active. In Beato's image it is easier to give meaning to an event; the Mutiny was vicious, but it had passed and all that remains are the ruins.

Photography extracted a manageable and generalisable knowledge of native society, dampening somewhat the fear and anxiety of rebellious natives and laying the ground for extensive government of populations and resources. Concealed within photography, and statistics, are cultural processes that help determine how things and people are to be represented. These processes are more explicit, perhaps, in orientalist painting. The cultural frames that influence representation and what counts as reality are more obscured in the generalising truth-telling techniques of photography and statistics, though they remain not too far under the surface of both, as I have shown in the study of surveying in Bengal and as will be highlighted again in the next section on anthropometric photography in the service of the state.

Three Representations: III. Maurice Vidal Portman's Photographs of Andamanese

Ethnographic photography was a means of producing natives, but in the midst of colonial rule and the complicated contexts that this gave rise to, there was increasingly little evidence of a 'pure' native lifestyle. The ethnographer cum administrator cum photographer, and Maurice Vidal Portman saw himself as all of these, tried to document what were described as disappearing cultures, of which Figure 3 is an example. Portman produced a number of such anthropometric portraits. As Protector of Aborigines in the Andamans, Portman had ready access to people to photograph. Andaman culture was disappearing. Certainly the active missionaries would have encouraged them, or cajoled them, to be clothed (in a specific sense of what

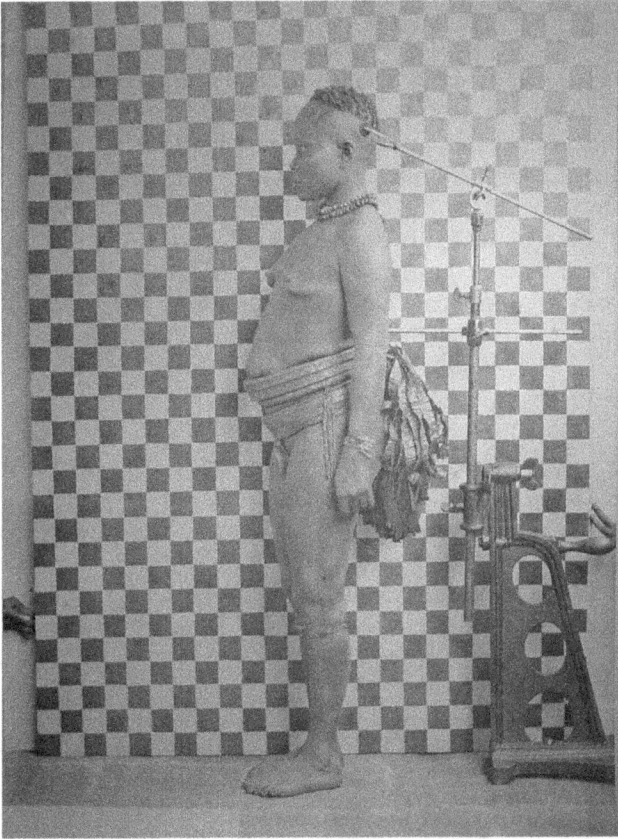

Figure 3 Maurice Vidal Portman (c. 1893). *Andaman Islander.* Copyright © Trustees of the British Museum

this meant). The people on the islands also were not well-served by colonial progress; at the time of Portman's portraits the Andamanese were dying in large numbers in the face of colonial rule and Indian migration.

Portman's anthropometric photographs followed a template designed by J H Lamprey some thirty years previously, with the addition of startling gizmos to hold limbs up in unnatural poses or to keep backs straight (Sen, 2013). People were removed from their normal contexts and environment, but still strangely clad in 'customary' dress, placed against a backdrop of two-by-two-inch squares and photographed. The photos show a native being actively possessed by neutral and neutralising mathematics, but the native remains an anachronistic figure 'primitively' clad against a modern mathematical grid.

The production of a pure native body required work; women and girls may have had to be stripped of their clothes (as I noted earlier). The native body was not then simply there to be grasped: it had to be first created, before then being dominated by the scientific grid. Portman's photographs were commissioned by the British Museum, at his initiative, "having regard to the approaching extinction of the race" (cited by Falconer, 1984). The project probably began around 1890, and by 1894 fifteen volumes had been produced, eleven of photographs and four of medical details and measurements.

Portman claimed not to have had much difficulty in getting his subjects to pose for him (though perhaps it is telling that his anthropometric photos are mainly of women and young children). Portman was by turns deeply protective of his subjects or punitive—hunting down recalcitrant 'tribals' (Sen, 1999; Sen 2013). One of Portman's former charges related his experiences to a European traveller after Portman's death:

> He had lived for many years with a former Chief Commissioner named Portman, and had learnt the Christian theology, the English language, Hindustani and time sciences of photography and piloting. He told me he had not liked his time in the settlement—'No fun, and always sickness', he said—yet Portman had made pets of the Andamanese, and given them bicycles and champagne, relieved by occasional beatings. (Clifton, 1911; cited by Falconer, 1984)

Portman's photographs are an example of a wider standardisation of the people and things that were to be governed. His volumes published in the 1890s are a late addition to the genre with William Wilson Hunter's *Statistical Survey of India* and Watson and Kaye's 1868 photographic record *Peoples of India* the first manifestations of a quest to lay bare the hidden reality and truth of people and resources in British India. Yet the initial push, in India at least, to survey and surveil was a record of multiplicity with little attempt at standardisation, of the meanings for example of 'tribe' or 'caste'. Portman's photographs were made possible by this type of pioneering work but Portman was as much interested in the possibilities for standardised comparison and government as he was in the scientific record of variety. It is with Herbert Hope Risley's 1907 *Manual of Ethnography for India* that Portman's work resounds. Risley standardised the ethnographic surveys of India, allowing for comparison of 'culture' across great spaces by using a few standard categories. Portman's work resounds with that; his was an attempt at standardising that focused on wielding a dominating mathematical gaze over the naked bodies of people to govern. Nakedness, and sometimes the concerted removal of clothes of women, Phillipa Levine (2008) argues, is a way of consigning photographed natives to an ahistorical state, outside of time. No longer part of Christian teleology, they are objects of colonial modernity. Consigned to the body in the case of the Andaman Islanders meant actively denigrating indigenous customs as a viable perspective on the world around and a basis from which to enact agency. Andaman natives become problems of the state, problems that a modernising colonial state had to deal with. And deal with it they could: the overarching and somewhat sinister gridded background is reassuring to the administrator; these islanders can be understood alongside other deviant races.

The anthropometric photograph was then a way of presenting a problem. If photojournalism like Beato's was a step up from Delacroix's wild fanatics in that it killed them off, photography like Portman's went a step further making not simply knowledge but a standardised depiction of populations that government could deal with. The quest for knowledge centred then on the reduction of people to their bodies, which were standardised by a mathematical grid; in Risley's case key categories standardised 'custom'. This certainly happened in Europe also, but not in the generalised and alien terms that it did in the colony: whereas Europeans like Weber's peasants were to be incorporated into a system that was said to be for them, natives for the most part were to be integrated in (or excluded from, or both) an alien system. Whether in terms of stripping them naked, or denigrating the customary means of regulating employment in Kuala Lumpur or agriculture in Bengal or simplifying custom into standard categories of 'religion, tribe and caste', colonised natives were stripped of an inherent basis for being considered political. The extent to which such agency would be given back by colonial government varied, the point is that it was to be apportioned by government.

From Delacroix to Portman, via Beato and Samuel Bourne, we can observe a process of acquiring and instrumentalising native society. The control over native societies and bodies may have centred on the search for a figure that would be representative of a wider whole. Such figures were often imagined or actively produced. In Bengal, a relationship between *raiyat* and *zamindar* that rarely existed in its pure form was the basis and justification of the Tenancy Act. Manageable native orders, that could be reduced to legislation, seemed to hinge on making static a fluid 'native society'. The relationship between *raiyat* and *zamindar* did not remain as imagined or as legislated for; it changed as the agrarian relations in Bengal responded to wider economic and cultural developments. The production of a static agrarian society marked above all by a revenue relationship between only two distinct parties was a struggle and involved a great deal of work; the cadastral survey was a means then of concretising this imagined relationship.

There was no robust boundary between aesthetic denigrations and administration. Portman's photographs highlight that, and the point is more substantially made in the two preceding chapters. We saw that in Bengal and in Kuala Lumpur, the ostensibly objective—even scientific—bases of administrative rule was run through with cultural assumptions about the other. These assumptions influenced how policy and rule were developed; things that were ostensibly contrary to the aims of rational administration (for example the existence of spaces of neglect in Kuala Lumpur) prospered and the denigration of native custom led to their easy repackaging into basic and understandable parts: the *raiyat–zamindar* relationship was insistently seen as the dominating relationship by administrators and in the precepts and regulations of policy. The complex politics and social relations of agrarian Bengal were passed over.

POLITICS

The trouble with Said's *Orientalism* as a means of describing colonial power is that it describes a native space and moral economy overwhelmed by a daunting repertoire of images. David Ludden has argued that if we look at the materiality of colonial power we pay attention to how the discourses of orientalism have to be translated into material and social forms of exercising, deploying and institutionalising power. In translation, discourse becomes wrapped up in and compromised by social formations. This idea, of the way power is imbricated in the places in which it seeks to make itself known, is—of course—central to the ideas I am pursuing in this book.

Colonial art was itself received in social space and understood as ways of describing a relationship between native as subject and colonial authority—colonial civilisation—as ruler. There are limited examples of interlocution taking place in the production of colonial art, interlocution that occurs within the frame and logic of colonial authority but nonetheless seeking to question the depiction of natives as overwhelmed by colonial power. In what follows, I examine the interlocution through painting of two takes on one event, the arrest of Diponegoro, a Javanese prince. The Javanese version in particular is an attempt to recode politics and native history into an event depoliticised and overwhelmed by the history of colonial state-making by the Dutch version.

Commemorating Empire: Two Representations of Diponegoro

Diponegoro was a Javanese prince, commemorated now as an Indonesian national hero. Passed over for the throne, he led a rebellion against the court, i.e. his family, and its Dutch allies, precipitating the Java War (1825–1830). The *Subugation of Diponegoro* (Figure 4) was duly painted by Nicolaas Pieneman, an artist fairly well regarded for his heroic depictions of Dutch history. In *Subjugation* Diponegoro is being summarily pointed to a coach that will take him to the port and then out of Java by General De Kock, who had arrested him. De Kock towers over the scene, but he is a benevolent figure; there is no anger or viciousness, but a firmness that pliant natives appear resigned to. Diponegoro's followers show no sign of resistance, they mill about in a resigned sort of way before Dutch power. The man himself is placed on a lower step than his arrestor and he seems as resigned to obeying the Dutch. The entire painting is apiece with the infantile or puerile depictions of natives, in particular before the masterly and manly General. Above

Figure 4 Nicolaas Pieneman (1835). *De onderwerping van Diepo Negoro aan luitenant-generaal Hendrik Merkus Baron de Kock, 28 maart 1830, waarmee de Java-oorlog (1825–30) werd beëindigd* [The submission of Diepo Negoro to Lieutenant-General Hendrik Merkus Baron de Kock, 28 March 1830, which ended the Java War (1825–30)]. Rijksmuseum, Amsterdam.

it all a Dutch tricolor waves gloriously. Pieneman had never been to Java, his painting is based on a drawing from someone at the scene.

Pieneman's painting was a work of imagination where a certain code or template determined the way the painting would look. Edward Said argued that nineteenth-century art was marked by a latent orientalism; orientalism as a code to decipher native society was engrained into the being and sensibilities of any occidental who approached the orient. What could be said about something in the orient tended to reproduce and normalise images that denigrated the orient before the occident. These reproductions were not necessarily explicit in the content of the painting—like in Delacroix's *Fanatics*—but were subtle touches that framed the meaning of the painting. Such touches were normalised codings of images; they were expressions of deeply ingrained meaning. For Pieneman, who had never been to Java, it can be assumed that the centrality of the Dutch general as the main actor, the principle place of the Dutch tricolor, the obscured faces of natives and the lower placing of Diponegoro were all normal and commonsensical.

In 1856 Raden Saleh, the Dutch and German trained Javanese romantic, painted *The Arrest of Pangeran Diponegoro* (Figure 5). There is little doubt that Raden Saleh had seen Pieneman's painting. In 1829 Raden Saleh was sent by the colonial government to Europe for further artistic training, and he would remain there until 1851. Raden Saleh did the circuit of European courts, and found particular favour at Saxon-Coburg-Gotha, where Lady Canning, lady-in-waiting to Victoria and the wife of the first viceroy of India, wrote this in her diary when she was visiting with her queen:

> In the Gd. Duke of Baden's rooms I saw one of the works of the Java Prince Ali who lives in Coburgh like a tame monkey about the house. Ld. Aberdeen was so taken aback the first day to see this black in his Turkish dress instead of handing us coffee, take some to drink himself. (cited by Kraus, 2005: 273)

In spite of Lady Canning, and the general presence of empire in what could be said or thought about him in Europe, Raden Saleh did not seem to feel entirely out of place. He gained some fame for his portraiture and landscape and felt particularly welcome amongst the German nobility. After twenty years in Europe he returned to the Netherlands Indies, in the strange position of being more versed in European culture and better educated than the majority of the Dutch rulers. He would die a torn man, not quite a part

Figure 5   Raden Saleh (1856–7). *Die Gefangennahme Diepo Negoros* [The Arrest of Pangeran Diponegoro] Museum Istana Jakarta.

of either native nor Dutch society. But before his death he took on the arrest of Diponegoro in a startling attempt to reframe the event from a sign of Javanese capitulation.

In *The Arrest of Pangeran Diponerogo* (1856), Raden Saleh intersperses a scene of Dutch triumph and Javanese defeat with coded meanings not readily discernible to European eyes. The meaning of the painting is given by the relation of two nations, Holland and the emergent Javanese—or Indonesian as later nationalists would have it. In Pieneman's painting the setting is also a nation-state, but only one. De Kock is at the centre of the painting, underneath a resplendent Dutch tricolor and flanked by upright soldiers in uniform. By contrast the Javanese are careworn and subjugated; if they had a state, nation or a means of politics it had been defeated, shown for the farce it was before the controlled and benevolent might of De Kock and the Dutch. Raden Saleh's painting shows a clash between two nations and so two ways of giving meaning to history. The differences in the two paintings in how the two nations are placed and frame the meaning of the event are sometimes subtle, other times troublingly disquieting to the Dutch, who could sense something not quite right but could not place a finger on it.

The centre of the painting is not De Kock but Diponegoro, who stands aggressively before his Dutch captors, who look uncomfortable about the whole business. Unlike Pieneman's painting, there are no invisible lines magically separating natives from Europeans. In *Subjugation* de Kock and his soldiers stand apart, there is space between them and the natives. Raden Saleh crams everyone together. The Dutch abandon their separation and distinction and the superiority that space gives; they also tellingly abandon their orderly ranks: Javanese squeeze between them and they are not centralised in one part of the painting.

Rather than dismissing Diponegoro with a pointed figure to the waiting coach, De Kock is shown making what looks like a gesture of invitation. The faces of Diponegoro's people, the Javanese, are clear; they have expressions, unlike the vague outlines of Pienemaan's natives. Other elements of the painting are subtle insertions of Javanese semantics. De Kock and Diponegoro are placed on the same step but De Kock is to Diponegoro's left, the woman's side—the inferior place (Kraus, 2005). And De Kock's and his officers heads are disproportionate, larger than they should be. Some critics have dismissed this as a mistake by the painter, an odd conclusion to make given Raden Saleh's skills. To Javanese eyes, the large-headed Europeans would resemble *rakshasas*, demons of India and Southeast Asia (Kraus, 2005).

One of Said's most useful interventions is to cast orientalism as a systematic and politicised repertoire of power. Its representations create an illusion of truthfulness. While it would be problematic to cast the notion far and wide to encompass in orientalism representations of the East Indies, Said's insights do lead to an important means of analysing the mechanics of making truth. Pieneman's painting uses devices that give meaning to the arrest of Diponegoro in terms of a triumphant and masterly Dutch colonial power and order. Said's intervention may however presume that orientalism, or a structure that determines truth-telling in relation to empire and imperialism, is caught in a specific and limited web of intertextuality.

Representations of colonial society and history may perhaps exist in an interlocutory web that includes more than just other like-minded paintings (the logic and force of Pieneman's painting comes from its connection and references to other orientalist and imperialist representations). Raden Saleh's painting of the arrest is altogether different. The web of meaning that representations of empire cast, whether termed 'orientalist' or not, is not cloistered or controlled but may lead to responses and reflections on the part of the orientalised. This is interesting because it points to a moment of politics, of contesting the devices of representation and how they give meaning and endow truth. It is this moment of politics that in turn indicates perhaps the politics involved in transforming an orientalist or imperialist sense of native society into a set of analogous structured and systematic policies of domination and control. This is what I have explored in studying the gap or ruptures between the aspirations of colonial policy makers in Kuala Lumpur and rural Bengal and the politics that mediate how policies play out in specific spaces.

CONNECTIONS

What connects administrative rule in the nineteenth-century colony and the contemporary period? If administrative rule is an attempt to contain and restrict politics, and who is to be counted as political, then it may be argued that it is contemporary attempts to make out that such-and-such a group do not deserve politics, or are not worthy, or simply logically are not political. In the two chapters that follow I look at the restriction of politics in Iraq by the Coalition Provisional Authority and the restriction of asylum seekers in Hungary to an administrative relationship with the state. In both cases, prefiguring and vindicating this is a denigration of the right to be political and to be counted as political.

What do we learn about contemporary forms of administrative rule by looking at colonial history? The important first point is, as I have argued, that it is oversight of a most vulgar kind that refuses a genealogy of administrative rule that is begun from a part of the world and a period where administration had its freest rein on the basis that European histories and those of the rest of the world are disconnected. Second, it is in colonies that administrative rule had its freest rein because colonial authorities were able, incompletely as I have shown, to depoliticise colonised populations, their resources and how these were to be exploited and shared. The technicalisation of that which would appear, on the face of it, to be deeply moral and political questions about how things should be was centred on an articulation of who was deserving and not of the political. Third, then, underpinning administrative rule was a technique of derogating and dismissing native ways of thinking and doing politics, something that I have highlighted in this chapter with reference particularly to orientalism. I will emphasise in the chapters that follow that an aesthetic denigration of the right of certain groups to the political was central to the establishment of administrative rule. In Hungary, an ethic derived from the conflation of politics, citizenship and the state refused asylum seekers political agency. In Iraq, a very straightforward orientalist discourse on the limited political capacity of overly "emotional" Iraqis with a propensity to have allegiances to multiple sources of authority (religion, kin) justified the building of a new political system that would restrict political agency to the expression of material need to the state (there was to be no discussion of ethnic difference or ethnic representation for example).

The conclusion that I draw from this, and that will operate as the starting point for my two remaining case studies, is that administrative rule needs a population that has been made out to be unworthy of the political. Allied to that, the process of making unpolitical involves derogation: a basic capacity to do and have politics is put to question. In Iraq, as I will explore, this was rooted in 'expert' accounts of Iraqi society commissioned by the State Department. In the management of migrants in the European Union, and specifically Hungary, their depoliticisation is an outcome of a more generalised connection of politics to the possession of national identity (citizenship).

NOTE

1. Many scholars, including Chaudary, now prefer 'Revolt'. I prefer 'Mutiny', to emphasise the power of colonial readings of complex events.

5 Mapping Iraq
Publics, Politics, Experts

This chapter is about the making of the Iraqi state following the American-led invasion in 2003. In the aftermath of the war a network of cartographers, military units, bureaucrats, statisticians and auditors sought to organise and order, to make a sense of the physical and social landscape of Iraq. One outcome was a "state effect" (Mitchell, 1991), another was the production of a public who were to serve as audience to the state and its governance, as auditor of that governance and as an entity that could be governed in particular ways (and not in other ways). People and things were organised and categorised in ways that pointed to a cohesive unity that could be achieved even in the face of atavistic and divisive ethnic affiliations sometimes taken to be dominant in Iraq. Maps and statistics produced and represented this cohesion establishing certain narratives about people and things in Iraq and how they may be best governed. Such representations served to assuage the anxiety about Iraq being essentially ungovernable and doomed to falling apart into ethnic ghettoes. Perhaps most importantly the technicalisation of Iraq as a space conducive to administrative rule depoliticised oil. The focus came to be on technical questions of exploiting resources rather than ethical questions over ownership of resources and the right to rents. In this chapter I explore the nexus between the social and political production of space as a site of governance and the physical transformation of space through survey.

In what follows I study the work of the Coalition Provisional Authority (CPA) that was set up to run Iraq following the invasion and on the work of a group of military surveyors tasked with undertaking Iraq's first universal geographical survey. Both processes of knowledge-making, social and physical or scientific, involved the creative production of knowledge by the arraying of things—people, resources, land—in meaningful ways and then the interpretation of what this is intended to convey. I will argue that the political system that the CPA constructed was based fundamentally on the scientific resolution of the meaning of physical space undertaken by surveyors. This knowledge allowed for administrative government and led to a political structure focused on the identification and provision of public services, a technical politics that would allow the ethnic affiliations to be trumped. Politics was the technical assessment and provision of services.

Where dialogue and contest occurred it was in the form of outlining needs that needed to be met. This technicalisation of the political was made possible by a scientific resolution of physical space and an attempt by the CPA to similarly resolve social space by promoting a particular moral and conceptual order that emphasised certain types of political behaviour while diminishing others.

It is important that the technicalising of a national space in Iraq was tied in with oil. Land surveys created the effect of a unitary nation and made Iraq, and its resources, a technical problem (how do we extract and share resources?), rather than a political problem (how do we adjudicate between claims of ownership over oil resources?). The technicalisation of 'Iraq' enabled policymakers to think of a national public rather than of a divided and problematic society with differing ideas about rightful ownership over resources. This move was then crucial to opening the Iraqi oil market for international investment.

MORAL ORDERS AND STATE EFFECTS

A central aim of the Coalition Provisional Authority was to create the conditions within which individuals could act as political subjects within a properly ordered moral order that would contain ethnic division. Its first Regulation, concerning the Authority itself, states:

> The CPA shall exercise powers of government temporarily in order to provide for the effective administration of Iraq during the period of transitional administration, to restore conditions of security and stability, to create conditions in which the Iraqi people can freely determine their own political future, including by advancing efforts to restore and establish national and local institutions for representative governance and facilitating economic recovery and sustainable reconstruction and development. (CPA, 2003a)

The onus then was not simply the material transformation of space. It was the creation of a moral order that would govern or direct the way people conducted their economic, political and social relations. Imagined in this process were notions of society, public space and publicness: expansive notions that would incorporate individuals into particular patterns of being and relating together and to others.

> Historically Iraq is a difficult nation to rule. By nature people are extremely emotional, insistent and individualist. In the last four decades they have been ruled by force, fear and humiliation. Considering these factors they have been mislead [sic] by the regime and become isolated from the rest of the world. What we need to do is concentrate on how

to educate Iraqis to be good citizens and how to insert values of public interest, work ethics, and individual rights. (Future of Iraq Project,
2003; n.p.)

In a memorandum dated 28 January 2003—two months before the
invasion—and titled "Civic Education" the State Department's Future of
Iraq project team wrote,

> The new regime's objectives, such as building a nation, establishment
> of civil society, and democracy, should be all clarified. *People should
> recognize what they have been missing in the past.* Iraqis should be
> taught to share responsibilities in serving the community and not to
> expect the government to be the sole provider of social welfare . . . they
> have to be able to take initiatives and be active in making changes and
> creating a better nation. . . . Ordinary citizens have to be trained to
> express their differences without being emotional. They should learn
> to work as a team and collaborate with others. All education programs
> should start with training people how to think, analyze, conceptualize
> and make a decision. They should learn to not only be implementers but
> creators, initiators, and producers. (Future of Iraq Project, 2003; n.p.,
> my emphases)

The Future of Iraq project was marginalised in the lead up to and immediately after the invasion by Donald Rumsfeld and other civilian leaders at
the Pentagon. However the CPA did gain access the Project's two thousand
pages spread across thirteen volumes; the CPA's policies on local government and the economy resonated with the project's. In addition, a number
of members of the CPA appointed Iraqi Interim Governing Council were
members of the Future of Iraq project team.

The Future of Iraq team clearly had a sense of a moral and conceptual
order to be conveyed to Iraq and Iraqis. This order was based on an argument that Iraqi culture lacks fundamental qualities necessary to develop and
maintain a thriving democratic society. Notable is the sense that Iraqis are
individualist and divisive; nation-building is high on the agenda. The depiction of Iraqi political culture in terms of what it lacks before a presumably
well-endowed American or western one has clear resonance with orientalist
thinking of the eighteenth and nineteenth centuries. Not least in this is the
association of a cultivated rational mind with the west and the dismissal of
Iraqis as emotional (Said, 1978). A notable consequence of this then is the
licence given to dismiss or diminish in importance existing moral and conceptual orders. Iraqis needed to be educated to become good citizens within
a national state, they need to be made aware of what they have missed.
What this meant is outlined in some detail: the good and democratic Iraqi
would be a decisive, nonemotional initiator of development and democracy
and take personal responsibility for his or her well-being. The cultivation

of this mental world creates broader and generalisable patterns of activity that become associated with the terms *democracy* and *development*. Society is recognised here then as a networked group of individuals who have a common trajectory and means of achieving that trajectory (and this is the core of nation-building). It is the cultivation of this society, rather than individuals, that bears a lasting imprint. It allows developmental goals to be identified and a comparative assessment of relative development (one section of the memorandum mentions differences in capacity between rural and urban dwellers). A new moral economy is set in place against which notions of political, economic and social conduct is to be developed. This is the establishment of a national-scale society, one that would elide and contain divisive elements. As will be noted, the way this was done was to decentralise the state and political power but with a framing political structure that would limit the scope of claims made on ethnic grounds. This political structure would be what I refer to as technicalised administrative rule: the articulation and provision of public services.

Associated with this is a resolution of the physical space of Iraq. This means subscribing to the idea that Iraqi space has been adequately and scientifically tamed into being a distinct and boundaried information-bearing space where resources could be counted, allocated and generally made known and distributed. As I will note, the plans for the development of local governance and of national development emphasise the geographical data that can be derived. The state would be a derivation of these practices of making known: existing as an effect of processes that arrange people and things. Geographical surveys quantify resources allowing therefore for a political structure aimed at exploiting and distributing these resources, creating a connection between individuals that is based on a shared way of making claims and operating in public space that trumps local conditions and affiliations. As I have noted, a key consequence of this was the depoliticisation of oil, its ownership and distribution of rents to be had.

SURVEYING SPACE

In December 2004, the United States' Army 175th Engineering Company arrived in Iraq with a mission to provide general geospatial engineering support to "Operation Iraqi Freedom". Their remit was to make maps and undertake terrain analyses and geodetic[1] surveys to assist both military and civil operations. In the course of their work, the 175th Company "realised" that Iraq lacked a networked spatial reference system. Previous survey work by the British (1915) and the Poles (1975) were undertaken for specific projects; survey data was thus segregated and could not be joined to form a continuous network "that would benefit the nation at large." (Yenter et al., 2005). The 175th Company applied for money from the military's Joint Acquisition Review Board (JARB) and was granted almost US$400,000 to establish what has come to be known as the Iraqi Geospatial Reference System (IGRS), basically a networked system of six continuously operating reference stations (CORS) that would provide real time geodetic survey data throughout Iraq.

In a paper written for the professional journal *American Surveyor* led members of the survey team describe their work as central to the "development" of Iraq (Yenter et al., 2005, n.p.). Survey control stations form the basis of the modern actuarial and statistical gaze that enables cadastral records, the mapping of resources, and navigation systems. The CPA's governance structure gave a central role to local government, who were tasked with the provision of adequate public services (CPA, 2004a). The actual development of local governance capacity is the responsibility of USAid, who have contracted this out to a private company, Research Triangle Institute. Central to the development of public investment is the provision of geospatial information and knowledge about how to interpret it; training in the use of GIS information is central to the development of the RTI's Local Governance Programme (USAid/Research Triangle Institute, 2008). The uses of GIS in local government is by now common practice the world over (O'Looney, 2000); it aids the measurement and utilisation of land and contributes to the efficient delivery of public services, though there is a strong body of critique about the epistemological and ontological implications of local government relying on GIS which emphasises the instrumentalisation and technicalisation of politics (for a summary see Elwood, 2006).

The parcelling of land, the measuring of surface space and the enumeration of the resources or productive capacities of land are amongst the ways that development is expressed spatially. The IGRS makes land something that can be effectively acquired, manipulated or exploited in order to attain developmental goals. Duly surveyed land imparts on space a culture of number, a sense of land as something divisible and parcellable. This "culture of number" constitutes an active referential archive with both a technical and symbolic power. Technically, land becomes reduced to a series of utilitarian coordinates and is then eminently divisible. Symbolically, the culture of number instituted has significance beyond utilitarian demarcation of land: it encourages a particular modern imaginary centred on commodification and the consequent change in a series of social, economic and political behaviours and practices. Duly surveyed land is a fundamental building block of a system of perception, or a political cosmology, based on imposing a hierarchy of uses and of belonging to space.

The breaking down of land and resources into component parts is followed soon enough by its reassembling. The purpose of the survey work is to know space, to know Iraq as the sum of its constituent, duly surveyed and mapped, parts. This founds a basis for thinking Iraqi space as a known and integral domain, one that at its very outset carries with it particular disciplinary functions. The 175th Company's survey thus provides the basis for the functioning of a managerial and overseeing state, one that is located within a wider modernity that establishes the functionality of land.

Cartographic representations and enumerating strategies, such as cadastral or land surveys, are fundamentally about articulating territory and knowledge about territory. The processes of counting and representation allow not merely occupation of a space, but also its dominance by a particular set of rationalities. Ways of counting, enumerating and representing space are ordering mechanisms that give knowledge and thus allow for the possibility of contact and government. Dominance ensues insofar as other representations and enumerations of space and peoples may be read out or delegitimised. The actuarial and cartographic representation of space and peoples do not in themselves lead to dominance. Such dominance is enabled and maintained to the extent that alternative readings can be elided. Such elision is at least partly enabled by the ballast of numbers and maps and their reference to objective science. It is also enabled by the delegitimation of alternative readings on the basis of their association with activities beyond the moral pale.

Spaces have moral or aesthetic claims attached to them; these serve disciplinary functions and derive directly from processes of mapping and enumerating space and resources because such processes also demarcate ownership of land, a hierarchy of belonging to land and a hierarchy of how that land may be legitimately used. Actuarial and cartographic representation of space also tie subjectivity and agency to space; that is, it makes these spatially dependent. At a broad level, the process of rendering space knowable is also a process of articulating borders that mark the end of political community and the civil patterns that enable and regulate political agency and subjectivity. At a more intimate level, the actuarial and cartographic processes create differentiation within spaces in terms of their functions and the forms of political, economic or social behaviour appropriate. Agency and subjectivity change in accordance with spatial variations.

Actuarial representations promote a political technology that unites disparate bodies and spaces under a collective rubric (Feldman, 2005). They are a means of doing away with the immediacy, risk and complications of everyday experience. Actuarial representations abstract and generalise events, phenomena and people, thereby bringing them into a roughly comparable plane and onto a generalised semantic register where meaning can be gleaned through the exercise of expert knowledge. By actuarial representations I refer to statistical representations, such as land or cadastral surveys: these are risk-reducing instruments. Statistical representations remove spaces and practices from the immediacy of social relations, allowing for government undertaken at a distance. The elision of immediacy is an attempt at removing the unpredictable; it organises and structures space and resources in ways that minimise risk and unpredictability.

THE COALITION PROVISIONAL AUTHORITY

The Coalition Provisional Authority (CPA) replaced the Office of Reconstruction and Humanitarian Affairs (ORHA). ORHA had been established to oversee Iraqi reconstruction in early 2003; the CPA replaced it in May 2003, quite suddenly and perhaps as a response to the escalating violence in the early postinvasion months. The CPA ceased operations in June 2004. During the thirteen months of its operation, the CPA issued twelve 'Regulations' and one hundred 'Orders' in addition to 'Public Notices' and 'Memoranda'. Regulations are "instruments that define the institutions and authorities of the CPA"; Orders are "binding instructions or directives to the Iraqi people that create penal consequences or have a direct bearing on the way Iraqis are regulated, including changes to Iraqi law."[2] The CPA involved itself in three broad areas: economic reconstruction, the promotion of good governance and the promotion of public security. It had broad executive and legislative power.

The origins of the CPA are unclear. A report by the Congressional Research Service in 2005 could say only that there are competing, though not necessarily mutually exclusive, accounts of its origins. It is unclear if the CPA was a federal agency, and if it was not then it is unclear by what right it acted as an administrative body on behalf of coalition powers or the United States (Halchin, 2005). Whatever its origins or legitimacy, the CPA administered the occupation with a brief to ready Iraq for sovereign rule. This meant establishing political and legal institutions by administrative fiat and limiting political discussion (Chandler, 2004).

By investing executive power in an administrative bureaucracy, the American action had clear parallels with colonial policies of the nineteenth century. Colonial bureaucracies created governable subjects by detaching natives from their local milieux and reforming them, through education and legal regulation, into legal entities recognisable and governable under colonial law. Frederick Cooper for example has shown how in Kenya through the imposition of a temporally delineated workday and employment contracts 'labourers' were created as was 'labour', which became a temporally finite act undertaken by an individual agent in exchange for cash payment. I have shown similar processes at work in creating labourers in Kuala Lumpur and peasants in Bengal. These practices produced colonial subjects whose substantial identification, and presumably loyalty and self-interest, were not to local customary practices regulating labour and work but to the terms of the contract and the guarantee of wage payment, and thus by extension to the colonial state and the market economy (Cooper, 1993). Timothy Mitchell describes the colonizing of Egypt through the cultivation of the mental worlds of Egyptian subjects. These mental worlds constituted 'society', an abstraction that placed individual lives in a broader context that was run through with colonial concepts of order. Individual subjects were taught to see themselves as productive and efficient, and that productivity and efficiency were to be demonstrated in colonially established roles and concepts, such as that of paid, contracted freely given labour (Mitchell, 1991). Chapter three showed how colonial law on tenure effectively formed peasants in Bengal, giving these groups rights autonomous of their feudal relations with landowners and independent of their status in local hierarchies and customs.

These colonial practices of subject creation were then not only about individual transformation. They were also about creating moral and conceptual orders that would order and regulate economic, social and political patterns. It is this entrenching of a particular order that is the real and abiding basis of colonial domination. In the colony this order was often an abstract concept of modernity, to the extent that this also plays out in Iraq, the order is a concept of liberal democracy and a free market.

Building a Moral and Conceptual Order

Broadly, the CPA's Orders and Regulations did three things. First, they sought to delegitimise, and sometimes demonise, the previous hegemony and its moral and conceptual orders. Second, they sought to impose a new hegemonic order. Third, they called upon an Iraqi public. This broader public represented the body served by the CPA. Invoking an Iraqi public was not to simply invoke a general population; the term denoted an organised and networked body that conveyed certain information and allowed for the development of public policy.

The first Order of the CPA was the "De-Ba'athification of Iraqi Society" issued in May 2003 (CPA, 2003b). That Order prevented former senior Ba'ath party members from joining the civil sector and removed some thirty thousand senior and junior Ba'ath party members currently working in the public sector (Dobbins et al., 2009). Order Number 2, also issued in May 2003, dissolved the Iraqi army and a number of government bodies and public institutions associated with the previous regime (CPA, 2003c). Larry Diamond, a former senior advisor to Bremer, describes these moves as a part of a process of transforming a "political culture of fear, distrust, brutal dominance and blind submission" (Diamond, 2005: 9).

The de-Ba'athification Orders (there are two follow-up Orders and two memoranda outlining the process for inquiring into possible affiliation with the party: CPA 2003d; CPA 2003e; CPA 2003f; CPA 2003g) have been described as problematic and somewhat ill-judged because it removed at a stroke expert and useful individuals from public life. It also punished individuals who may have joined the party to further careers and not because they were ideologically committed (Chandler, 2004), though the CPA did through various moves try to take this into account. The iterative metonymy connecting Saddam and Ba'ath moreover passes over the movement's historical role as a secular, nationalist and modernist party (Milton-Edwards, 2006). The de-Ba'athification process is important for other reasons: it describes an Iraqi people, a public, and is the first step in narrating an order onto the social chaos of Iraqi space and in outlining the moral order of the occupation.

An Iraqi public comes into being in relation to the Orders. This public is invoked in the preamble of Orders to do with de-Ba'athification:

> Recognizing that the Iraqi people have suffered large scale human rights abuses and depravations over many years at the hands of the Ba'ath Party,
> Noting the grave concern of Iraqi society regarding the threat posed by the continuation of Ba'ath Party networks and personnel in the administration of Iraq, and the intimidation of the people of Iraq by Ba'ath Party officials. (CPA, 2003b)

The public, "the Iraqi people", here is a body organised and made coherent by a common experience of having been persecuted. The preamble contains a narrative about the Iraqi people and gives them a commonality and purpose. The process of de-Ba'athification abstracts a generalised public from a chaotic sectarian and ethnic space and is an important step in reconciling that chaos. The general national-scale public is inscribed against local scale ethnic and sectarian affiliation, taken to be a divisive state of affairs to which Iraq would revert without a sense of national-scale society. In an interview on PBS, Bremer would say in 2007:

> It was pretty clear from the start that you had both sectarian tensions between the Shi'a and the Sunnis and potentially ethnic tensions between the Arabs and the Kurds, because that's the complexity that is Iraq. (PBS, 2007)

A public is a recognisable network of people greater than the sum of its individual parts; the public that is invoked is the larger concept within which individuals are to be understood and to understand themselves (Warner, 2002). The identification of a public, of a means of narrating a togetherness and coherence amidst chaotic space, is an act of power, of a wilful determination that here stands a people connected by this shared moral concern. It is a way of arraying a population so that they may transmit information about themselves.

This would quickly however read more like an act of desperation, an act of an administrator struggling to quell the complex social relations of Iraqi social space. Iraqi group affiliations ran far beyond 'everyone against the Ba'athists'. Local, national and transnational political affiliations intruded onto this dyadic representation with numerous aims that were not readily or easily contained by later attempts at simplification through categorisation. From summer 2003 killings rose and the insurgency, or perhaps the multiple insurgencies, grew in force, skill and violence. In Baghdad by autumn

2003 the CPA was increasingly confined to the Green Zone, a ten-square-kilometre area in the heart of Baghdad surrounded by walls and barbed wire with entry points manned by soldiers. Movement within and beyond the Green Zone required escorts and military conveys. By the end of 2003, requests for such conveys had reached such a level that a week's notice was required (Rathmell et al., 2005). For Iraqis to get in they had to be escorted and wait in long queues and checkpoints (Ward, 2005). The CPA had little presence outside Baghdad, only able to send its personnel to other provinces towards the end of its existence (Dobbins et al., 2009). It was increasingly apparent that a coherent Iraqi public did not necessarily exist outside the wilful imagination of the CPA.

Making Politics

Nevertheless, the CPA sought to get a grip on this public and to reassert it as the basis for public policy. The preferred way of doing this was through establishing a political infrastructure that would either bolster a sense of the Iraqi public as cohesive or actually occlude questions about national cohesion. The Future of Iraq project was dedicated to the development of a democratic culture that would develop both a democratic mindset and a sense of unity and commonality among Iraqis. It was not necessarily about overcoming the crisis of representation in the political vacuum of post-Saddam Hussein Iraq. The CPA's proposal for a governance structure in Iraq would seek to quell dissension in the public sphere by creating a decentralised and federalist governance structure that would train Iraqis to view themselves as local consumers of public services, and not necessarily as grassroots political actors, and not as ethnically or religiously different from each other. The CPA's governance structure, as we shall see, technicalised politics. The political infrastructure presumed demanding citizens as consumers, and made government and politics the identification and fulfilment of these needs therefore quarantining away problematic questions about representation.

At the core of the CPA's plan was the conveying of hard statistical data about the physical conditions of Iraqis throughout the country and about the physical land resources available. Geospatial information became crucial to development strategies by which is meant the provision of public services (which was the raison d'être of the new governance structure proposed by the CPA). The governance structure proposed by the CPA was similar to that of the previous Ba'athist regime with a few exceptions, one notable one being that money for projects was to be independently utilised by local political institutions. The focus is on development and on the availability of scientific data against which development strategies may be assessed. The institutions of governance themselves were designed as didactic models; they were to impart political subjectivity. All these appeared to critics, not least the Grand Ayatollah Sistani, as a sop designed to prevent political representation of the Iraqi public rather than enable it (Cole, 2005).

In April 2004, CPA Order Number 71 titled 'Local Governmental Powers' was issued. That Order set out the roles and responsibilities of local government, noting that the Iraqi form of government "shall be republican, federal, democratic, and pluralistic" (CPA, 2004a). The aim of establishing local government is clear: "by appropriately empowering government bodies at the governorate, municipal and local levels, the Order is designed to improve the delivery of public services to the Iraqi people and make the Iraqi government more responsive to their needs" (CPA, 2004a). Governorate councils (formerly Provincial Councils) were appointed by the CPA in consultation with local leaders or they may have been hangovers from the previous regime (the CPA was to later insist on a de-Ba'athification of these) and in some cases they may have been appointed by coalition military forces or the basic structure of these councils may have been drawn up by a private enterprise, the Research Triangle Institute, working on contract for USAid. Governorate councils would then appoint municipal councils who would elect mayors. There was thus a political system established which would have little direct citizen participation. Presumably thus it would also be non-self-sustaining and lacking legitimacy. The system proposed by the CPA was not rooted in local politics nor did it seek legitimacy from those it sought to serve.

The emphasis is on service delivery. These institutions of local governance in Iraq were not intended to be forums for political contestation and argument. By focusing on service delivery, the CPA passes over issues of representation. Local authorities are recognised as such within a broader federalist Iraq: a linear federalist structure imprints onto Iraqi space the unifying ethos of an overarching state. Local government focused on the delivery of public services passes over the problematic question of national representation. It does not necessarily pass over questions of inequality and social justice but contain these within questions about the equitable provision of public goods. USAid writes of its Local Governance Programme:

> Resolution of intergovernmental tensions often occurred at meetings where opposing points of view could be discussed as *technical rather than political issues*. Such meetings gradually helped to build trust between governmental rivals. These meetings have proven effective, increasing the ability of local government in Iraq to overcome political, religious, and tribal barriers. (USAid/RTI, 2007: 19; my emphases)

Associated with a concept of service delivery is an idea of the citizen as consumer. The construction of the structure of local government by the CPA seems to have at its core a notion of the Iraqi public composed of demanding consumers. Citizen involvement with local government focuses on the articulation of needs; there is no forum for asking questions about the legitimacy of the structures themselves. To partake in local governance structures in this way is to enact and perform an identity given by the overall structure of governance. In this case it appears that the model subject taken is the western consumer-citizen. This is the didactic function of institutions of governance. It creates pathways for what is deemed to be democratic participatory politics while effectively displacing political questions thus limiting citizens to the performance of themselves as subjects as demanding consumers of public services (Clarke et al., 2007).

It is in this way that national-scale society is effected in Iraq, ironically through a decentralisation of state power but a decentralisation that goes hand-in-glove with a political structure that seeks to restrict and contain the types of political claims that can be made. Politics becomes the efficient delivery of public services to a consumer citizen who is essentially the same in any quarter of Iraq. A political structure contains the local scale and its potential chaos within a broader national mode of doing politics. It is this cultivation of a way of doing politics that creates a broader mental order, a recognisable national-scale society of Iraqis.

The decentralisation of governance plan put in place by the CPA was notable in that it elided popular sovereignty in favour of a series of caucuses and the development of political subjectivity in favour of consumers. Individuals were appointed to governorate councils who in turn would appoint members of municipal councils who would then elect mayors. On 15 November 2003 Bremer announced a plan for the transfer of sovereignty. Governorate councils would elect a two-hundred-member proportionally represented interim parliament who would then elect a prime minister. The whole process was to be completed by 30 June 30. Grand Ayatollah Sistani objected to the plan, noting that it did not seek to create a body representative of the Iraqi people, but rather sought to filter the political identities of Iraqis through a series of caucuses. Sistani and other leading Shi'ite clerics were deeply distrustful of the municipal and governorate councils, many of who were appointed by the CPA (Cole, 2005).

The CPA's plan was an attempt at dealing with the chaotic Iraqi social space, of which they appeared to have a deep-seated mistrust, by establishing a political infrastructure that would bypass this social space. The abstract geography of a coherent and unitary Iraqi state would be maintained by displacing the question of national representation and political sovereignty. Sistani would call for protests in a *fatwa*, and the Iraqi street would become that contestatory public sphere so feared by the CPA. Negotiations would follow and a deal struck in early 2004 following UN intervention where popular elections would be held by 2005.

It may be that the CPA feared making the Iraqi political system adequately representative of the Iraqi street. It is difficult to say why that was the case with any certainty. We may recall that the creation of political subjects involved the development of a greater moral and conceptual order. The political system that was to be established should be reflective of this greater order. The architects of such orders are rarely united; different interests come into the picture, reading what it means to be democratic, or even political, in different ways. This is either because vested interests need to be protected or because there are immanent inconsistencies in the meaning of such concepts to different actors or interested parties.

Coalition, or perhaps more properly American, policy in Iraq may be understood as a contested social field (Steinmetz, 2008). This means that American policy was not conceived by a single isolated figure or office but was subject to the varied interests of a broad group of actors from the Pentagon, the State Department, the CPA, the White House, USAid and private companies. It is by now a matter of public record that the State Department and the Department of Defence disagreed about postwar planning in Iraq. The Defence Department allegedly obstructed State Department involvement in postwar planning to the extent of preventing the appointment as assistant to General Franks, Bremer's predecessor, the head of the State Department's Future of Iraq project. The Future of Iraq project began well before the war at the State Department and comprised of seventeen working groups developing contingency plans for a post-Saddam Hussein Iraq. The Defence Department appears to have disregarded that report in its entirety. Initial postwar planning was the responsibility of civilians in the Pentagon headed by Donald Rumsfeld. Their plans centred on installing Ahmad Chalabi, a member of the opposition-in-exile Iraqi National Congress, as Prime Minister, apparently in the belief that Chalabi would quell Islamic based politics and allow American neoconservative agendas—particularly the development of American military presence in Iraq and encircling Iran (Hersh, 2002; Landay and Strobel, 2003). The State of Department was more or less frozen out till mid-2003. The recommendations of the governance working group of the Future of Iraq programme were however shared with Bremer's CPA after the White House stepped in to insist on moving beyond the Chalabi option. The CPA itself was subject to the pettifoggery and sheer obstruction of Rumsfeld's civilian coterie at the Pentagon.

Whatever the reasons, the CPA sought to bestow a political system that favoured a technicalised version of politics centring on the identification and provision of public services. In this they relied on an abstract Iraqi public, removed from the immediacy and chaos of multiple and confusing political associations that were taken to be rife in Iraqi space. The elision of popular sovereignty however proved difficult. United Nations intervention following Sistani's *fatwa* led to popular elections being held in Iraq in 2005. Local authorities were also subject to the popular vote and not appointed by caucus.

Capitalism Underpins and Sustains Technicalised Politics

A radical free-market economy was established by the CPA through a series of Orders that would gradually remake Iraq into a free-market haven. Trade barriers were almost completely eliminated, a regressive flat tax rate was imposed, barriers to the foreign ownership of Iraqi companies and industries were removed in all sectors with the exception of oil and all profits and dividends could be transferred abroad tax free (CPA Order Nos. 37, 47 and 84 regarding tax; No. 54 regarding trade liberalization; and Nos. 39 and 46 regarding foreign investment). The Iraqi constitution of 2005 affirms this arrangement by encouraging the development of the private sector (article 25) and the development of investment in all sectors (article 26). Article 109 commits the Iraqi state and local governments to the development of "oil and gas wealth" by "using the most advanced techniques of the market principles and encourages investment". Article 25 calls further for the reforming of the economy in accordance with "modern principles". In 2009 the first auction of drilling rights took place.

The decentralisation of the state and of political power instigated by the CPA allowed for the decentralised exploitation of economic resources. Local authorities were responsible for the identification and exploitation of local resources and for providing public services. This structure aided a radical free market economy. A decentralised political structure, the limiting of state ownership of industry, the development of the private sector and the liberalization of foreign investment created a terrain which meant that local authorities would be actively competing for investment. This has been described as a typical aspect of contemporary neoliberalism (Brenner, 1999). Provincial Investment Commissions were established to market different regions. In 2006 a National Investment Law was passed which will ensure a ten-year tax- and fee-free period for foreign investors (Republic of Iraq National Investment Commission, 2013). The CPA's flat-rate tax of 15% for companies remains in force, with the exception of those working in the petroleum sector (who are taxed at 35%) (Deloitte, 2013).

One difference in post-CPA Iraq is that local authorities, since 2005, have been elected. This means a constitution that is explicitly pluralist insofar as it offers a consociational form of politics, marked chiefly by proportional representation of ethnic minorities. This system was presaged by the CPA in its appointed Interim Governing Council (McGarry & O'Leary, 2007). It also means that the structure of economic exploitation put in place by the CPA is open to contest. The constitution places an ethnic register onto Iraqi politics perhaps overlooking crosscutting networks that connect Iraqis in favour of a more "atavistic" reading of political affiliation (McGarry & O'Leary, 2007: 672; Said, 2006). By ceding rights to ethnic groups and guaranteeing their protection, political contest and political recognition becomes ethnic-centred. The constitution explicitly protects the rights of ethnic minorities and religious minorities as well as stating that no law in contravention of Islamic principles may be passed (article 2). All this contains the political within a particular frame; and it means that those aspects of the political system that feed into and succour market economics is not directly the subject of contest; indeed the constitution itself guarantees the development of the private sector and the reforming of the economy.

While the pluralist constitution may contain and restrict questions of the political, claims made on ethnic principles can spill over and address questions of economic principle. More directly, unions have restricted attempts to restrict their voice and they remained—and may continue to remain—a significant voice against the ongoing marketisation of the Iraqi economy. Capitalism is not simply imposed onto pliant space but is a contested process (Herring, 2008).

The CPA created a political structure that remains in post-CPA Iraq. A number of CPA Orders remain in effect. The structure produced by the CPA was marked by a decentralisation of the economic power of the state and ostensibly also a decentralisation of political power. The terrain within which decentralisation takes place is important. The CPA's Orders placed a capitalist pattern onto economic space in Iraq. This pattern provided a frame for economic activity and also for political and social activity, but this does not mean that social activity is simply overwhelmed by these frames.

At the core of capitalist economics is an abstraction of the immediacy of space. Capitalism is marked by the free flow of finance and goods—but not necessarily people—across space. Localities would compete to facilitate this free flow. This process abstracts the vagaries of local spaces. Capital accumulation occurs by dispossession, by making local voices and local moral economies unheard within a dominant political imagination and structure (Harvey, 2003). The CPA sought to decentralise state power. It gave emphasis to local politics but sought to restrict that politics to the articulation of material needs. The ethnic frame is secondary to a broader technicalised politics. The rigidity of this structure was weakened in post-CPA Iraq when elections of local representatives were allowed. Another core component of the capitalist frame imposed is the idea of the citizen as consumer (Clarke et al., 2007). The consumer citizen is at the root of the CPA's political—and economic—structure. This is a citizen that outlines a series of material needs to be met by local government, and it is a citizen that is satisfied with the creation of the conditions deemed necessary for the accumulation of personal wealth.

At the core of the decentralisation of political power is then a general and abstracted Iraqi citizen, recognisably a part of a generalised Iraqi public. In the CPA's Orders, it matters little where that citizen is in Iraq; the vagaries of the local do not enter into the picture. There is instead an abstracted public whose individual citizens shared concern for the provision of public services—above all other considerations—connects them into an organised whole and provides a state effect. This is a moral order, it is a means of recognising a broader mental world within which individuals exist connected to each other by a shared set of practices and attitudes. This connection creates an integral Iraqi space, one where local issues are passed over. And it is of course an aspiration, a representation, that requires considerable work in delegitimising or quarantining claims made on the basis of the local. One argument is that this structure prevents the dissolution of Iraq into many different ethnically ordered mini-states. It is also however to suppose that ethnic connection trumps other connection in Iraqi social space. This aspirational representation of Iraqi people and space and of the possibility of a moral order trumping the vagaries of local space is a useful means of furthering neoliberal accumulation by dispossessing others of rights to use and view space in different ways.

THE LIMITS OF MAPPING

The geodetic survey of Iraq undertaken by the 175th Company is at face value a sophisticated terrain analysis undertaken with the intention to support with an adequate technical archive a series of civil and military activities. The 175th Company's geodetic survey can also be read as a *production* of space, territory, geography and place. Maps produced by the geodetic survey actively construct a particular type of knowledge about Iraq and are important in producing particular types of social change (Crampton & Krygier, 2006).

The geodetic survey is based on a complex process of triangulation. The desired end product is an ordered and structured archive of spatial knowledge completely covering Iraqi space, indeed sitting in stead of the immediacy of Iraqi space. The integrity of Iraqi space is presumed prior to the geodetic survey; it is also however actively produced through the referential CORS system. Triangulation locates specific points in relation to other points. Iraqi space becomes an intertwined mutually referenced web. The onus is on the maintenance and improvement of the accuracy of the relation points in a triangulation network with the ensuing goal being the development of a "complete spatial reference system" (Yenter et al., 2005). The accuracy of triangulation is such that it holds the potential of a perfect depiction of a given space. Its coordinates may aspire to a complete and accurate congruence to surface space. Matthew Edney writes of triangulation,

> The net result of the greater accuracy of triangulation, of its greater congruence with the land, of its greater degree of control, . . . is that triangulation is held to offer the potential perfection of the map's relationship with the territory mapped. Triangulation defines an exact equivalence between the geographic archive and the world. Triangulation makes it possible to conceive of a map constructed at a scale of 1:1. Not only would this be the same size as the territory it represents, it would *be* the territory. The "technological fix" offered by triangulation has served to intensify the Enlightenment's "cartographic illusion" of the "mimetic map." (Edney, 1997: 21)

Edney goes on to note that the emergence of triangulation as a technology of mapping in the eighteenth century was a key component of time-space compression central to Marxist analyses of capitalism. The identification of a generalised and integral 'Iraq' is precisely based on the removal of the immediacy of Iraqi space from the register and its replacement with a series of quantifiable abstractions that when taken together constitute 'Iraq'. This abstraction of space, the elision of the immediacy of place and the complex social relations that constitute it, creates a level of analysis and a semantic register that studies and bestows meaning onto an abstraction (Harvey, 1990). The abstraction of Iraqi space, an abstraction common to most modern societies and certainly not unique to Iraq, contributes to its commodification and to the sense that technicalised politics, capitalist modes of production, and indeed in Iraq, military activities, can function and produce on an abstracted plane where the production of real commodities, or the killing of real peoples, is at best a secondary consequence of the way that capital and the military operate. Governance, capitalism and the military are increasingly able to function in an abstracted space bereft of immediacy.

While the geodetic survey is easily attached in both the popular and academic imagination to scientific certitude, aspects of the triangulation process call this to question. Triangulation involves multiple calculations and their gradual reduction to single, plottable values (Edney, 1997; Wood, 1992). The mathematics of triangulation are complex and need not trouble us here. What is important is that a complex series of reductions from multiple datasets is required for triangulation and for the IGRS for the location of the CORS. In an article written for the professional magazine *American Surveyor*, members of the 175th Company write,

> Because their purpose is to be used as reference stations for precise applications, CORS themselves must have positions that are virtually free of error. NGS [the US National Geodetic Survey] calculates the positions and velocities of the Iraqi CORS by processing data from each new station with data from a set of "hub" stations that are part of the existing global CORS network. . . . NGS processes the positions of new CORS with their custom-developed software PAGES. This program uses the method of double differences to remove clock errors in GPS satellites and the hub stations. Once synchronized time is established, the precise locations of the satellites along their arcs of orbit may be calculated epoch by epoch. The positions of the Iraqi stations are then determined through triangulation to the solved locations of the satellites. . . . Measurements from a minimum of four satellites are necessary at each epoch of triangulation to solve the four unknowns of X, Y, Z position and time. (Yenter et al., 2005)

There are a series of consequential calculations required in order to accurately position the CORS hubs, the foundation of the geodetic survey. The process is similar to other applications of GPS technology and involves initial synchronisation of GPS satellites. A minimum of datasets from four satellites across their epochal movements need to be tracked, processed and reduced before values corresponding to "X, Y, Z position and time" may be reached. The reduction involved is not the only gremlin, the authors of the report note that the technology to measure the movement of tectonic plates is imperfect, it cannot take into account "deformable plate boundaries, such as the boundary between the Eurasian Plate and the Arabian Plate upon which Iraq lies." The earth, the subject of all these satellite measurements and reductions, moves. It is not still and cannot be represented as such by measuring satellites.

The standard solution is a series of mathematical estimations about the "velocity" of tectonic movements, which are, the authors say, normally accurate up to "a few millimetres", so long as no earthquakes or other changes in normal velocity occur. However the tectonic plates under Iraq are subject to movements that cannot be estimated by the existing program (it is not a question of technology but the location of the technology, the United States, where there is no need for measuring deformable plate boundaries). At the end of the series of abstracted mathematical measurements of the earth's surface, where the surface is to an extent treated as placid, the vagaries of the land itself arises.

> Predicted velocities for CORS in Iraq developed from any plate-tectonic model are expected therefore to be relatively inaccurate, requiring revisions of coordinates every few years until an accurate velocity can be calculated from the accumulated record of data. . . . Whether a surveyor chooses to ignore or include the contribution of plate tectonics to site coordinates depends on the duration and accuracy requirements of the application. (Yenter et al., 2005)

In a preceding section, I have taken note of the latent promise of a perfect mapping of Iraq, one that could correspond on a 1:1 basis, to the denoted space of Iraq. This representation of Iraq, and its realisation through a networked web of triangulation, has the potential to sit in stead of the space of Iraq. Rather than a study of the complex social and political geographies of fragmented Iraq, there is in its place a scientific abstraction known as Iraq, duly surveyed, appropriated and a useful instrumental tool to be paraded in different types of actuarial representation. The argument is not then about the relative influence of the 175th Company's plotting of 'Iraq', it is rather about how symbolic representations of what passes for 'Iraq' are founded upon a technical register of surveying and scientifically knowing space. Thus it is because of the primacy accorded to a technical register of knowledge, and the consequent archive of knowledge that it generates, that the geography of Iraq is malleable. It is because of this technical or scientific resolution of the nature of Iraqi space, and its borders, that Iraq as a symbol may be placed in different contexts and instrumentally employed for symbolic and indeed political, social and economic ends. It is also worthwhile repeating the ruse of scientific knowledge. Its claim to accuracy and to an unimpeach-able depiction of the nature of Iraqi space can be questioned from within its own knowledge register. I have noted that the accuracy of triangulation is inherently doubtful simply because of the large number of calculations required and the need to reduce these to workable single or small values in order to pinpoint CORS stations. I have also noted that the abstraction of scientific knowledge ironically leaves the earth as a blank slate. The faulty tectonic plates under 'Iraq' mean that the accuracy of surveys are strictly limited. The option that the IGRS gives is to ignore the shifting of physical land, to ignore the immediacy of the earth if you will.

Such immediacy is, however, more difficult to straightforwardly ignore in other mappings of Iraqi space. These are mappings that begin from a differ-ent experiential relation with Iraqi space. If the 175th Company's survey and mapping of Iraq is intended to create a networked space of interrelated and triangulated points, a self-referential system that aggregates into a viable space of development called Iraq, then other mappings and encounters with Iraqi space demonstrate some of the difficulties of so caging the multiple scales of Iraq. The 175th Company's mapping is one that assumes and cre-ates a sense of Iraqi space as knowable, and largely indeed known, as a necessary basis for thinking development. The 175th Company's map is one particular move in a many-tiered and many-sited process of imagining an integral space of Iraq enveloped by a state.

CONCLUSION

Geographical and political representations of Iraqi space cultivate a par-ticular sense of stateness, of a state that names and envelops its domain. In other words, what is being represented by cartographical and actuarial practices is a state who lays claim to a space that it suffuses. The flattening and elision of contrary elements and political claims that is a fundamental part of actuarial and cartographic representations allow for the ruse of a state entirely sovereign over the entirety of a given space. Maps and numbers then become tools for activities such as reconstruction or nation-building rather than specific cultural practices designed to imbue onto Iraqi space a particular stateness. This then places a national scale as the privileged site of the political, overseeing and regulating the local and acting as a mediator of global flows. The suffusing of Iraq with the authority of a particular state-ness also serves to delegitimise other types of political claims. Insurgents are seen as de facto unlawful because of the representation of a particular legitimate sovereignty over Iraq.

Space can only be regarded as an empty vessel to be filled by movement and activity of the preconceived state or state-like agent if the state is reified above 'its domain'. It is more useful to see a series of practices of stateness that work, in Iraq, to make a state and make that state viable.

The imprinting upon space of what may be called cosmologies of state creates patterns of behaviour and ways of relating to institutions of governance that enact a form of political community which, cyclically, invokes the state and legitimises its managerial role over society. I have noted that crucial to this is the actuarial politics derived from processes of making spaces knowable. Such actuarial practices work to create a population, divorced from society as a whole and its colourful multiplicities, whose common bond is primarily the ongoing pursuit of patterns of development which together invoke the state. At stake then is a mode of representation, and the institutions of governance that do the representation, that recognises a people, and makes a people recognisable to themselves, in terms of their relative positionality before the state and its ethoi of development. Such ethoi (the plural of ethos) shift over time in response to changing local and international contexts, shifting the relative positionality of different groups of people and creating and uncreating ties that bind.

The political and economic model designed by the CPA is then not simply imposed wholesale onto a pliant space. It is a process and a struggle; it requires force and a mode of representation that would delegitimise or diminish in importance types of economic and political claims and behaviour that are contrary. The dominance of the CPA model of the economy and politics is perhaps largely a result of the creation of a greater moral and conceptual order realised in a political structure that connects Iraqis as citizen-consumers of public services.

NOTES

1. Geodetic surveys are systems of representation concerned with positioning in a temporally variable field. Such surveys measure the Earth's gravity field as well as tidal variation and polar motion in a three-dimensional time-varying space. They allow thus for time-specific positioning.
2. Definitions at CPA's website, http://www.iraqcoalition.org/regulations/#Orders. Accessed 13 August 2010.

6 "The State Needs to Protect Itself"
Acts of Citizenship by Asylum Seekers in Hungary

(with Zsuzsanna Arendas)

This chapter studies how asylum seekers and asylum policy itself is governed in Hungary. Asylum policy in Hungary transposes very closely European Union directives that aim to make asylum an administrative matter. In its implementation, however, the coherence of asylum policy is threatened. Asylum policy is implemented and conceived in a relational field, involving discussion and contest between different parties. The key relation in Hungary is between the immigration bureaucracy, the Office of Immigration and Nationality (OIN) and the judiciary. Asylum policy is not necessarily coherent, its aims and intentions are challenged and distorted by other actors who have, or who claim, a legitimate right to be involved in questions of asylum. This can lead to the questioning of the extent to which asylum should be considered an administrative and depoliticised issue to be contained within the field of 'policy' and not, for instance, an issue of politics and human rights. This questioning amounts to a challenge to the boundaries of 'the political' and the privilege of the state, and here its immigration bureaucracy, to mark the limits of politics and who may be counted as political. It is in this questioning that I perceive "acts of citizenship" (Isin & Saward, 2013), which are challenges that seek to question the bordering of the political to a national-scale society with the state at its head.

The argument in this chapter is derived from interviews made with members of the Hungarian judiciary and the immigration bureaucracy. The overall aim of the chapter then is to question the enclosing of the problem of asylum, which is a problem of responsibility and its limits, within the field of 'policy'. This enclosure serves to exclude or marginalise important questions about how asylum, a claim to protection, is always an assertion of deep-seated connections between the state, rights, responsibility, community and the individual. Asylum claims are claims of those who have no inherent right to protection and this has come about because of the territorialisation of politics and of rights, where both centre on a state. In what follows, I study how the Hungarian state, in the guise of the immigration bureaucracy, strives to narrow the question of asylum to a problem of managing others who are outside the normal political community and so subject to a bureaucratic relationship with the state, rather than a political one based on rights and obligations. But the judiciary, the other principle partner in the relational field of asylum, emphasises a human rights reading that seems to "make strange" again the connections between the individual, community, rights and responsibility and the state and the ethical and moral limitations of these. In what follows, I examine the governance of asylum policy in Hungary where in recent times, and at the behest of the European Union, it has taken the form of a citizenship regime. Asylum policy is a way of affirming national-scale societies.

This chapter begins with a further account of what is at stake: I begin by accounting for the connections between the state and responsibility and rights (or the state and ethics as shorthand) and how this is related to issues of asylum and protection. I move then to describe Hungarian asylum policy and its wider context, European Union directives on common asylum approaches. The section following examines a court case where a Tibetan asylum seeker's appeal of the immigration bureaucracy's decision to reject his claim for refugee status seems to lead to a questioning of the connections between state and ethics and the depoliticisation of asylum. The last section before a conclusion focuses on an interview with a member of the immigration bureaucracy.

ASYLUM, TERRITORY AND RESPONSIBILITY

Questions of asylum are questions about responsibility and its limits (Warner, 1999). In a territorial order, asylum is at best a contingent right, no one has a right of protection unless various conditions are met (Guild, 2006). How, why and what conditions are stipulated and how they are assessed point to an arrangement of political life that takes 'a state' as its foundation (Dillon, 1999).

Protection is finite, it generally stops at state borders (or in aggregates of states such as the European Union) and the responsibility to protect is distributed among different state parties by relevant international legislation. This arrangement has arisen over time and centres on the privileging of a national community headed by a state as the basis for thinking social or political subjectivity (Favell, 2003) and responsibility. Rights are (unevenly) distributed and enclosed within national boundaries (Soguk, 1999; Nyers 2006; Prem Kumar & Grundy-Warr, 2007; Chatterjee, 2004).

The relationship of asylum seekers to the state is sometimes understood dichotomously, where the state stands for political subjectivity and asylum seekers represent an abjection outside of politics. This depiction is true up to a point, rights tend to be citizens' rights, but it can lead to a depiction of a timeless relationship of asylum seekers to the state. In this representation the historical process of constituting the state, rights, its distribution and limits have limited bearing on the relationship to asylum seekers. 'The state' is taken as a distinct and integral basis of the political, and can appear more settled than it is. One consequence is that the connections of issues to do with asylum to the making of territory becomes difficult to discern.

When a state is the basis for thinking politics, and is the guarantor of rights, it constitutes a universality of its own. That is, it encompasses political being and political personhood. This is not to say that it does so successfully, many states fail, nor that it successfully restricts appeal to other sources of political authority. Religious, legal, ethnic and economic transnational fields provide alternative networks of subjectivity and, often, rights. Dissension within the ranks of 'a state' provide pathways to new and broader forms of political subjectivity and rights, as I will explore here. All of these constitute possible points of intervention and disruption into 'a state' aspiring to a closed domain of subjectivity and rights with itself at the core.

How and to whom rights are distributed, by what logic, extends and changes over time. While the state is the repository of rights it does not distribute them evenly, nor does it often have the power to do so. Different variables restrict the capacity of different types of subjects to access and enact rights (Isin & Saward, 2012). Among these are economic arrangements such as private property or liberal notions of individual rights taking precedence over community responsibility (Chatterjee, 2004).

The right to protection is an aspect of a broader set of rights to political personhood, to citizenship, but how these have been distributed even to those who ostensibly have rights points to the biases (class, ethnic, religious) underpinning any civic arrangement. Even amongst those who are guaranteed rights because they are recognised as citizens, there remain official and unofficial economic regimes, bureaucracies and security arrangements that can prevent many people from accessing and enacting those rights (or even having knowledge of them). Further, a liberal perspective asserts that people who have no rights can make claims to equality. Political practice becomes the claim to equality of access by subjects who have been blighted by having been unable to access rights due them. This arrangement strengthens the underpinning limits of political community and responsibility; it does not address the limitations on responsibility but rather appears to strengthen the spatialisation of justice and responsibility by extending equality.

This chapter makes the case that the question of responsibility and its limits arises in relation to territorialising projects that enclose political subjectivity and rights within a state. I will try to locate this argument in relation to two arguments about political community and citizenship.

The first stems from the idea that the state encloses rights and therefore political subjectivity. Rights are distributed unequally and while this is admitted, the (liberal?) way out is the idea that equality can be striven for and achieved. Striving for equality is however a limited politics, it can leave questions about how things have been arranged, for what purpose and for whose benefit aside. What is at stake then is not simply the fact that rights are unevenly distributed but the attempted foreclosure of political struggle, and questions of ethics and morality. Not only are political rights limited, but the boundaries of the political are strengthened against challenge by the promise of eventual equality.

I think this has a perhaps unexpected impact on the understanding of asylum and the treatment of asylum seekers. A politics that privileges the quest for equality may centre on the provision of social welfare. This type of politics, the provision of services to a public, can narrow the meaning of politics and the political, with claims for services dominating and questions of why things have been arranged and for what purpose being clouded (Newman & Clarke, 2009). In Hungary, a primary reason for restricting the right to refugee is cost, as I will show below. Politics becomes the competition for goods by the subjects of a state by people seeking equality. Asylum seekers do not directly encounter "a state" but a regime of resource distribution that has the aim of furthering equality among recognised political subjects. The result in parts of Europe has been that cost-benefit assessments take primacy in assessing asylum seekers (Sales, 2002) or related security regimes directed at those that have no right to partake in a community of equals (Bigo, 2002). The key issue becomes the cost to state and society of extending its community of equals, rather than the atrocity that asylum seekers flee from. Questions about responsibility that are at the heart of asylum claims lose their force as state interests take precedence. Historically determinate arrangements of the political, of citizenship and its purpose influence the way asylum claims are understood and responded to.

The second kind of argument comes from the idea that the state constitutes a universality that allows for the sustained practice of exclusion. While not all citizens are equally able to access and enact rights, they all have the right to do so. That they have not can be explained in one way or another, everyone can (eventually) become equal. This contains and forecloses political subjectivity. Those outside of the normal political system do not readily figure as political subjects. For asylum seekers in Hungary, and broadly in the European Union, this means that they encounter not a state or a society but a specialised bureaucratic system of procedures, sequences, vocabularies and forms that fragment and disregard their political subjectivity. This bureaucracy may be seen as a means of containing and excluding political subjectivity and can give primacy to cost-benefit assessments, as I argue here. The depoliticisation of asylum, aided by both the externalisation of asylum seekers and an effective depoliticisation of politics itself (where resource distribution takes priority over contests about justice and the way things have been arranged), is conducive to the bureaucratisation or technicalisation of asylum.

Asylum and asylum claims are not distinct from the political. The way they are understood and managed stem from how politics and the political are arranged. While the details of this change over space and time, a commonality may persist. As I have argued with reference to CPA Iraq, the territorialisation of politics leads to a government of a population, which means effectively the extraction of a governable and regulable 'public' and 'society' from the inchoate population (Newman & Clarke, 2007; Mitchell, 1991). The site and focus of government is made legible, the limits of community and responsibility are mooted, and an orientation point for understanding and making legible claims to asylum from 'outsiders' is formed.

THE HUNGARIAN AND EUROPEAN CONTEXT

Asylum policy in Hungary is the result of how two different institutions, the Office of Immigration and Nationality and the judiciary, interpret and implement asylum law. These institutions have different ideas on how to interpret asylum (the OIN emphasises questions of order and state interest, the judiciary a language of rights). Asylum policy is then not always coherent, and it is often contested. The law moves across different institutions: the aspiration of state bodies to depoliticise asylum seekers and place them under administrative rule is contested. Politics, and questions of justice and citizenship rights, enter as the would-be technical and administrative asylum law encounters institutions and agents that interpret or contest this technicalisation.

Rather than a political or human rights issue, the Hungarian state aims to make asylum an administrative and bureaucratic issue. But in the relational field where asylum policy is worked out and contested, the aims of the immigration bureaucracy are distorted by challenges from other institutions, chiefly the judiciary. And so attempts to question administrative rule and lay claim to the political, what I call here 'acts of citizenship', are neither isolated nor unusual. They are also not necessarily revolutionary or extraordinary. Acts of citizenship of asylum seekers in Hungary are embedded in and a normal part of the structure of rule. Acts of citizenship may occur because the structure of governing asylum seekers is contested and not always coherent.

Articulations between groups, when a sense of commonality about how to conceive of asylum claims and what to do about them are worked out, are the building blocks for asserting a hegemonic dominance over the field of asylum policy. Further, each group also brings to the dialogic field other different networks that lead to the transnationalisation of the issue of asylum governance in Hungary, along with a normative stance on the question of asylum. For example, the judiciary locates asylum within a transnational "judicial continuum" (Guild, 2007) of treaties and international legal precedents, while the OIN frames asylum as a problem of nation-building and state-making and makes reference to the scope and intent of EU asylum directives.

The trajectory of asylum policy is debated within this fluid field. At this juncture in Hungary, because of a range of reasons explored here, the state-centred OIN-led depiction of asylum policy and asylum seekers is hegemonic. Hegemony is not flat or dominant; the persistence of hegemonic power depends on its success in controlling institutions and counter-hegemonic practices formed by alternative constellations of institutions and actors.

There are points when claims to belonging and protection exceed the categories of control that the OIN has developed. There are certain points when the hegemonic veneer of the OIN over asylum policy slips, and consequently claims are made that cannot be contained by the categories that the OIN puts forward. The OIN's categories are modes of identifying and managing asylum seekers that depend on a restrictive interpretation of law. These administrative categories are attempts to render law static; law is inherently mobile in that it is subject to interpretation and contest as different subject positions arise to make claims that question how categories are devised and implemented. The law in question here is the 2007 Hungarian Asylum Law (Act LXXX of 2007), which is a faithful transposition of EU directives onto national contexts. One response of the immigration bureaucracy to the contests over the way it has interpreted the law is to restrict the possibility of interpreting the law. This is done partly in a new draft law where some of the loopholes of the 2007 Asylum Law are addressed, leaving a restrictive scope of interpretation for the judiciary and taking jurisdiction away from courts seen as recalcitrant. This study covers the period before the new law came into force in 2012.

The European Union is a project of territorial integration premised on the management of migration. This means that the space of mobility that is at the core of the EU depends on the policing of the right of mobility of third-country nationals. The Schengen Agreement, which came into force in 1995, created a borderless zone in the European Union where sanctioned goods and people had freedom of mobility. Schengen does not apply to asylum seekers or refugees. Refugees and asylum seekers who have been granted status under the terms of the Geneva Convention do not have the right to mobility within the European Union in the same way that migrants from third countries with appropriate visas and/or family connections do. Asylum seekers are restricted by the Dublin Regulations, which determine the EU member state in which they must make their claims. Guild (2006) writes:

> Among the most telling aspects of the treatment of asylum seekers in these two conventions [Schengen and Dublin] is that they are the objects of state acts. They have no effective rights, nor is either instrument designed to give voice to their protection. They are the passive bodies on whom is visited the will of the Member States. (Guild, 2006: 636)

European territorial integration is organised upon the bodies of asylum seekers and refugees. The juridicial, political and ethical limits of European citizenship may be seen in the way refugees and asylum seekers are managed. The EU asylum regime is a way of containing more expansive notions of social belonging and participation that may be present in Europe especially through the prism of human rights. Asylum seekers are reduced to virtual speechlessness. They are refused entry into the social and political life of the Union. This restriction of the asylum seeker to the borders of the European Union is the first step enabling her technicalisation. Priority is given to technical and administrative procedures for controlling movement. Reception, or detention, at holding centres is the norm for asylum seekers throughout the process of their assessment in many member states. Asylum is, as I will show in the Hungarian case, a means by which an administrative state asserts its capacities.

When it comes to assessing asylum, an EU priority is the restriction of the right to free movement to EU citizens and third-country nationals with appropriate visas. The EU treaties allow member states to collectively reject the appeal of an asylum seeker if her application has been rejected in one member state; this is the first stage of asylum assessment under EU common directives. The treaties further allow member states to restrict application for asylum to the first country of entry, regardless if that person has cultural, familial or employment ties or prospects in another member state. If the asylum seeker is given refugee status, her mobility continues to be restricted by national borders, effectively restricting her social incorporation into Europe (Guild, 2006: 636–7). Asylum claims may be the subject of an administrative decision without considering the case itself or may be unfounded on the basis of the Dublin Regulations.

The most important element in the EU directives on asylum is the clarification of a zone of mobility by making an exception of asylum seekers. This may be part of a process of creating a common cultural identity among Europeans, extending the idea of Europe *as* the EU (Hansen, 2002), furthering perhaps the securitisation of asylum seekers as 'others'. The clarification of such a zone of mobility requires common standards and norms in assessing asylum seekers. The imperative placed on shared responsibility requires shared norms and practices. Such norms and practices have territorial integration and mobility for citizens as their organising principles; this means that member states may seek ever more technical procedures of assessing— or refusing to assess—asylum claimants because such claims, if successful, requires an exception to be made to a norm (Guild, 2006).

The EU's perpetuation of common practices is not intended to restrict the role of the state when it comes to managing migration flows; indeed, the core of EU common directives on irregular migration and asylum is the protection of the right of states to control their borders. The EU's asylum regime technicalises asylum; by making it thus an administrative and bureaucratic matter, the EU restricts the political and social participation of asylum seekers.

Hungary is not a major country of migration. In 2007 there were 166,693 foreign citizens legally registered. This amounts to 1.6% of the population. Some two-thirds of this migrant population is made up of ethnic Hungarians from neighbouring countries, while approximately 12% are from China and Vietnam and 12% from the EU-15 (Futo, 2009). In 2009 there were

4,672 registered applicants for asylum. There has been a gradual rise since 2005, when there were 1,609 applications. The numbers remain low in comparison to other EU countries. A very large proportion of asylum applicants enter the country irregularly; in 2009 4,476 of asylum seekers did so. Very few asylum applications are accepted; in 2009 172 were granted refugee status with a further sixty-two receiving temporary protection status (OIN, 2010).

Asylum is part of alien-policing[1] policy. The Office of Immigration and Nationality is a "bureaucratic conglomerate" (Tóth 2007: 18) dealing with the issue of alien policing, asylum and naturalization issues. Hungary does not have a migration policy as such nor does it have an office dealing with integration and other social issues that migrants may encounter. The OIN is an office of the Ministry of Justice and Law Enforcement. Asylum issues tend to be mixed with issues of irregular or illegal immigration. Asylum policy tends then to be cast as an issue of internal security and order (Kovats, Nyiri & Toth, 2003).

The importance of asylum and migration issues to the European Union seems to mean that states justify illiberal policies in the name of Europe (Guiraudon, 2000). In Hungary pressures from Vienna and Berlin may play a significant role in tightening border controls (Byrne et al., 2004). Asylum seekers and refugees are subject to hostile portrayals in the media (Vicsek and Marcell, 2008) and to a general xenophobia (Novak, 2007). These portrayals seem to stem from a concern about the threat posed to social cohesion (Novak, 2007) and to an already stretched economic market (Hars & Sik, 2008) by migrants, particularly irregular migrants.

Giraurdon argues that the Europeanisation of immigration has not weakened state control but has rather outlined a field where ministries and government departments may approach their goals autonomously of other pressures within the state. This administrative turn may be attributed to the rescaling of governance and the dislocation of territorial orders (Squire, 2009) given impetus by the European Union.

There are two pieces of regulation that apply to asylum seekers in Hungary. One is Act II of 2007, which applies to all third-country nationals. Its provisions for the detention of aliens directly applies to asylum seekers. The second is the 2007 Asylum Act (Act LXXX of 2007). Hungary transposed into national law Council Directive 2004/83/EC of 29 April 2004 on minimum standards for the qualification and status of third-country nationals or stateless persons as refugees or as persons who otherwise need international protection and the content of the protection granted ("Qualification Directive"). The 2007 Asylum Act fundamentally changed national asylum policy, and divided the formerly uniform asylum procedure into two distinct phases: the preliminary assessment procedure and the in-merit procedure.

The preliminary assessment procedure occurs in a closed reception centre where the asylum seeker's claim is assessed against the Dublin Regulations. The asylum seeker may then be moved to a second reception centre where the claim for asylum is assessed and the "in-merit procedure" begun. All assessment is carried out by the Office of Immigration and Nationality. Asylum seekers are throughout their time in Hungary normally placed in a closed world of reception centres with limited access for outsiders, though the asylum seeker may request a private domicile to be his or her place of residence during the in-merit procedure. If a positive decision is made after the in-merit procedure, the asylum seeker is normally placed in a third reception camp as part of an integration procedure.

At the preliminary assessment stage there are two possible outcomes. One is a refusal of the right to apply for asylum based on the Dublin Regulation and a return to the country of first entry to the European Union. There is a right of nonlitigious appeal to the Budapest Metropolitan Court. The asylum seeker or his or her representative is not present in this appeal, which is to be handled by the Court within eight days. The second outcome is to pass through and move to the next stage, the in-merit procedure.

There are four possible outcomes once the asylum seeker moves to the in-merit procedure. The first is that the claim may be rejected on the basis of noncompliance with the procedure or the law and the asylum seeker is given an order to leave or is removed from the country within thirty days of the decision being made. The second is that the asylum claim may be rejected but there may be imposed a nonrefoulement rule preventing the return of the asylum seeker to their country of origin because of a general condition of insecurity in that country. This "tolerated status"—sometimes also described as "temporary protection"—requires renewal every year based on conditions in the home country. Third, subsidiary protection in the form of a temporary protection visa may be given for a period of up to five years. Refugee status is the fourth option. Both subsidiary status and refugee status are normally dependent on the individual experiencing persecution, or having a fear of such persecution, specifically directed at her because of her membership of a social group or nationality subject to persecution within that state or because of her race, religion or political activity. Refugee status and subsidiary status holders share similar rights and have access to a similar range of benefits.

Rejection of the asylum claim may occur for any of the following reasons: if the asylum seeker's country of origin may be deemed safe or if she transited in a "safe third country"; if the asylum seeker's identification materials are forgeries or false or if she destroys identification papers *and* wilfully obstructs attempts to clarify her identity; if she supplies data on her persecution that is incoherent and contradictory to the extent that assessment of persecution experienced, or threat thereof, is impossible; if the asylum seeker provides false or misleading data; or finally if the claim to asylum may be shown to be undertaken solely for the purpose of obstructing a previous removal order. In order to achieve a positive outcome, the asylum seeker must demonstrate persecution, which is liberally defined in the 2007 Asylum Act, or fear thereof from a state party, or nonstate party aligned with the state or by private actors whose persecution of her the state is unable or unwilling to act against. People eligible for protection are those who comply with the conditions of the 1951 Geneva Convention on the Status of Refugees. People eligible for temporary protection are those forced to flee armed conflict, including ethnic clashes and civil war, or gross human rights violations. The temporary protection category does not require that the applicant demonstrate individualized persecution. Refugees and those with subsidiary protection are entitled to the same rights as Hungarian citizens with the following exceptions: they are only allowed to vote in local elections, they may not hold office or a job intended for Hungarian citizens, and they do not have the right of mobility that EU citizens have.

Under the terms of the 2007 law, the asylum seeker is allowed to appeal in court against a rejection of refugee or subsidiary protection status. Appeal must be made to the Budapest Metropolitan Court within fifteen days of the OIN's final decision; no further appeal may be made. It is at the appeal stage that the OIN's and judiciary's differing interpretations of the intent and purposes of the 2007 asylum law becomes most apparent. Following the passing of the 2012 law, the Budapest Metropolitan Court is no longer the sole court for assessing asylum claims. This amounts, our interviewees among the judiciary tell us, to the dissipation of expertise and dissension by the state. Appeals to the OIN's decisions will be undertaken in provincial courts with little to no experience or expertise in asylum cases.

CEVANG TSERING NAMGYAL[2]

This section illustrates how claims made by asylum seekers to courts of appeal can exceed the bureaucratic categories of the OIN. In the following example, a claim is made that the OIN failed to consider to its fullest and proper degree the protection obligation towards an asylum seeker, preferring to confine that individual to a temporary protection regime based on a technicality.

In 2008 a Tibetan asylum seeker, Cevang Tsering Namgyal, made an appeal to the Budapest Metropolitan Court after he had had his application for refugee status turned down twice by the OIN. Cevang had been granted tolerated status—temporary protection—to be renewed yearly. Temporary protection is given to individuals who have not proven individualized persecution or a reasonable fear thereof but in whose country of origin conditions of general insecurity prevail. In Cevang's appeal he—or rather his lawyer—sought to show that Cevang did have good reason to fear individual persecution and therefore was eligible for refugee status. Cevang sought thus to question how his experience of flight and persecution had been categorized by the OIN. The court would argue in favour of Cevang's appeal, but they would do so from a different, and more radical, basis.

In her statement, the presiding judge would say that the OIN's attempts to draw administrative categories from the 2007 Asylum Act was itself erroneous. The court did not pay much attention to Cevang's claim that he had been politically active and seemed to accept the OIN's argument that this claim may be doubted because it was made only at the appeal and was not presented to the OIN while Cevang's case was being assessed there. The court rather questioned the basis on which the OIN distinguished between the categories of tolerated status (or temporary protection) and subsidiary protection. Cevang's case, as we will show below, was seen by the court as exceeding both the categories and the logic of categorization.

The management of Cevang's case by the OIN was a straightforward means of restricting social and political participation and agency along the lines suggested by EU directives on asylum policy. But the implementation of these directives, as we have noted, must deal with the contests between institutions that is a part of the field in which asylum policy is conceived and implemented. From these contests (in this case, the one between the immigration bureaucracy and the judiciary) there arises a potential opening for acts of citizenship. These centre on recognising that the EU directives about how to manage asylum seekers foreground their bureaucratic management, over and above human rights issues. The judiciary, with its human rights stance towards asylum seekers, is sometimes able to highlight the ethical and moral compromises made by the EU directives. This is what happened in Cevang's case.

Cevang was a Chinese citizen of Tibetan origin who arrived in Hungary in August 2005. In September 2005 Cevang claimed refugee status, rejected by the OIN in November 2005. Cevang was however granted a nonrefoulement status, therefore temporary protection status, because of the general prejudice against Tibetans shown by the Chinese government that may constitute a generalised threat of human rights violations.

In March 2008, on the basis of the 2007 Asylum Law, the OIN officially reviewed Cevang's temporary protection status. The OIN found that Cevang had nothing new to say. In June 2008 the nonrefoulement order was maintained as the situation in Tibet had not improved, but a higher category of protection was precluded. In June 2009, as his protection status was up for review again Cevang appealed the OIN's decision at the Metropolitan Court.

In his statement at the September 2005 hearing before the OIN, Cevang stated that he had left Tibet after he was caught praying to a picture of the Dalai Lama by two Chinese individuals. These two individuals hit him and shot his dog. His attackers ascertained where he was living and left. He slept elsewhere that night and left Tibet the next day via Nepal. Cevang had not been politically active nor had he taken part in demonstrations against the Chinese authority in Tibet. Based on the above information the OIN reasoned that Cevang did not experience individualized persecution. Neither could he lay claim to having a reasonable fear of future persecution as he was not politically active. However, the OIN's country information service indicated that individuals leaving through Nepal were, upon return, subject to jail and a fine.

When deciding to uphold their earlier decision in June 2008, the OIN stated that the Tibetan situation did not specifically affect Cevang. The condition of general insecurity in Tibet affected all residents. In this reasoning the OIN admitted the possibility of the claimant being subject to torture and inhumane or degrading punishment upon return as he would likely be taken for a political supporter of the Dalai Lama. But the OIN insisted that a higher level of protection was not called for as the persecution he experienced was of a general nature and not individualized.

On appeal at the Metropolitan Court in June 2009, Cevang added new information: he had participated in a demonstration outside the Chinese embassy in Budapest (it is unclear when exactly). Embassy officials had taken his photograph and he would now be accused of political activity against the Chinese state were he to return to Tibet. Cevang also stated that it was likely that the two Chinese individuals who interrupted him in his prayers were policemen as the prayers were conducted at a site known to be frequented by religious—not political—followers of the Dalai Lama. Cevang stated that he did not give this information to the OIN in earlier hearings because he was not asked a direct question about it. On this basis, Cevang's lawyer argued that he qualified for refugee status. The OIN lawyer reacted by remarking that Cevang had full opportunity to present any relevant information about political activity in his hearing in June 2008.

In her judgement, the presiding judge argued that the OIN's distinction between the category of temporary and subsidiary protection was largely correct (one requires individualized persecution, the other does not) but the OIN derived erroneous conclusions from the distinction. The judge argued that both categories, subsidiary and temporary protection, are based on the sense that an individual would experience degrading or inhumane treatment or punishment were he to be returned to his country of origin. The OIN sought to qualify this by saying that subsidiary protection status requires the threat or existence of individualized persecution at a higher level than that experienced by the rest of society. Judge Dudas in her statement argued that the relative level or intensity of persecution, actual or probable, cannot be the basis for distinguishing between the two categories because at whatever level it may be experienced the threat or reality of torture or cruel and degrading punishment constitutes serious prejudice and is therefore, in the terms of the 2007 Asylum Law, a basis for protection. The court noted that there was reliable information that Tibetan returnees were subject to persecution. The OIN's claim that such persecution was more or less on par with a general level of insecurity experienced by the Tibetan population, and thus not constituting individualized persecution, was rejected by the court. The point is not whether the level of persecution threatened is greater or lesser than a general feeling of insecurity; the point is that individual persecution can reasonably be expected by a Tibetan national were he to return to Tibet after leaving illegally. On this basis the court granted subsidiary status to the applicant and ordered a new refugee procedure to be undertaken on the basis of Cevang's participation in a demonstration outside the Chinese embassy in Budapest. In June 2009, the OIN released a statement to the press stating that Cevang had been granted refugee status.

The OIN insisted through three refugee procedures that Cevang was eligible only for temporary protection because he did not face a threat of persecution greater than the general persecution faced by the Tibetan people as a whole. There was nothing special about Cevang, and nothing more could be done for him. The court's 2009 judgement rejected the terms of the OIN's argument and decisions. What was important was that Cevang, as an individual, had a reasonable fear of persecution, that it may be less or more than that experienced or feared by the Tibetan population as a whole was not relevant.

The OIN had sought to diminish the importance of individual persecution, choosing to reduce Cevang's admittedly well-founded fear of persecution to an experience relative to the general insecurity of individuals in Tibet. The court's ruling reasserted the importance of the individual's experience over and above any interests of the state when it comes to refugee assessment—a fundamental principle of refugee assessment which the OIN had sought to diminish.

In its decision, the court cut through the OIN's quibbling about the importance of differentiating between persecution at an individualised and generalised level. To the court, Cevang deserved protection regardless of whether the persecution he had experienced or might experience was greater than that faced by Tibetan people in general. In doing so, the court placed the importance of an individual's human rights at the foreground. The OIN waters this down, not least by implying that a different standard of measuring atrocity should apply across different countries. Against the OIN's relativist definition of protection and obligation, the judiciary in this case applies a universal individual-centred notion of human rights. The OIN's differentiation between measures of persecution speaks to state-centred notions of rights and responsibility. One consequence of this is the difficulty of referring to universal human rights standards and the possibility of quibbling about what in different countries is a normal state of affairs. Also underpinning the OIN's reasoning is then a sense that individuals outside their countries have only a limited claim for protection from another state. The attempt to differentiate between normal and unusual levels of persecution could occur because the Hungarian state, in the guise of the OIN, could claim that it had no obligation to protect people who were not its citizens. Rather than the actual case of the individual at stake, state interests gain precedence. But refugee assessment was not easily a means by which the administrative capacity of the state could be strengthened.

To what extent is the OIN's procedure determined by state interests? The next section, where we summarise our interviews with OIN officials and the judiciary, seeks to clarify this. The Europeanisation of asylum gives further leverage to the state. Whereas some aspects of the new territorial dimension of the EU may disrupt the trinity of state–nation–society, EU directives on asylum asserts that they are fundamentally connected. EU asylum directives to date centre on the strengthening of the external border and the social and political exclusion of asylum seekers. Both of these aims take the state as its primary actor. Rhetoric and practice both see individual member states as frontline agents protecting the integrity of the EU and as managers and protectors of a European society from a risky externalised other (Haddad, 2007). National society is taken as an extension of a broader European society and the protection of its purity from an external other assumed to possess disruptive properties is part of the Europeanisation of that society and is one way in which member states quickly become integrated into the norms of the EU.

Cevang's case was successful in questioning the validity of the OIN's decision. More than that however, the presiding judge questioned the basis for the OIN's decision. The OIN had hoped to be able to block off questions about how Cevang's human rights may be devastatingly impinged upon if he were to return to China. Doing so successfully would have allowed the OIN to keep Cevang under a temporary protection regime thus preventing his—albeit still limited—entry into Hungarian and EU political community as a refugee. The court's insistence that the danger of persecution faced by Cevang was pertinent to the asylum case meant that the OIN's categories designed to govern asylum seekers bureaucratically were ruptured.

"The State Needs to Protect Itself": Governing Migration Policy

The Office of Immigration and Nationality was established in 2000 as a specialist office of the Ministry of Justice and Law Enforcement with responsibility for the management of asylum matters. The OIN does not manage a preformed migration policy, as Hungary does not have one. There is no parliamentary or ministerial body dealing with issues of immigration. Immigration policy is formed in the process of translating asylum law into procedural practice. Except where it is intertwined with issues of nationality, asylum is not framed as a social issue in Hungary: it comes under the aegis of the Ministry of Justice and Law Enforcement and is framed as a security and policing issue. This contributes to the conflation of issues of irregular migration and asylum.

Migration in Hungary, other than the migration of ethnic Hungarians from neighbouring countries, has not been the subject of political discussion. Migration policy is not formed through debate and with the representation of appropriate social groups, including minority groups (migration policy is not formed at all). This state of affairs places issues of immigration and asylum as procedural and administrative matters centring on the application of bureaucratic procedures derived from relevant law. Asylum becomes an issue of administrative governance.

In 2009 the OIN's control over issues of migration increased with the closing down of the immigration department within the Ministry of Justice and Law Enforcement. This was a consultative and advisory body intended to guide the implementation of asylum and immigration policy and was chiefly responsible for drafting the 2007 Asylum Act. With the demise of this body, the OIN is established as the single state entity where asylum and immigration issues are dealt with. It is directly answerable via its Director-General to the Minister.

The OIN thus takes precedence in the initial implementation of asylum law. It is only at the point of appeal, if a case goes to appeal, that the OIN's approach to asylum law may be questioned. At that point, asylum seekers are able to position themselves and to lodge claims in ways that may rupture the OIN's administrative categories. The institutional location of the OIN leads to an initial rendition of asylum procedure that places state interests as the organising principle. The 2007 Asylum Act becomes an instructional sheet through which the sovereignty of the state and the borders of national and European political community are organised. The OIN's location within the Ministry of Justice and Law Enforcement leads to an emphasis on the security threat posed or potentially posed by asylum seekers. Because the OIN is the only state authority with any scope of authority over migration and asylum, the issue of asylum becomes framed as an issue of the administrative state; asylum is, initially at least, governed in a space where regulations and state interest take precedence over political claims and human rights.

The trajectory of asylum policy becomes adversarial at the point of appeal. The law is not easily reduced to regulation. The relative capacity of administrative governance depends largely on the extent to which it is able to implement a particular reading of the law. Law, however, as the literature on the anthropology of the law teaches us, is difficult to contain (Merry, 1992). Rights are open predicates and are not adhered to particular subject positions (Ranciere, 2004); individuals who may be marginalised by an administrative framework may be able to challenge their marginalisation by contesting how law has been read and implemented. A reading of law which emphasises the precedence of technical and bureaucratic procedures over questions of justice and the boundaries of political community may be challenged when the OIN's decisions are appealed at court by asylum seekers. The following paragraphs summarise our interviews with members of the Budapest Metropolitan Court and the OIN. These centre on the conflict between the law and state interests.

In our interview with a member of the OIN's asylum assessment department, the law is described as volatile, thus making the ordering and regularizing work of the OIN difficult. Noting that the OIN's multi-stage screening process now makes the "juggling" between categories more difficult, the interviewee goes on to say that although this is the case the law "builds possibilities" to keep the legal process running because of the nature of its practice. It is because of this that "asylum applications have multiplied". These are expected to go down in time because the 2007 Asylum Law restricts the possibilities of appeal drastically: "The state must protect itself, and the society which it serves, from a liberalizing trend [of the law]" This protection is to be effected by the implementation of rules that would limit the processual nature of the law: "We need to work out a process that would allow the screening of applicants and, second, the filtering out of those who do not meet the conditions [of asylum] as this is the aim [of the law]."

In our conversation with Dr Sz, an official involved in asylum adjudication at the OIN, migration is described in a historical frame. In the pre- and immediate post-1989 world, migration was generally that of ethnic Hungarians and people from neighbouring countries. From the mid-1990s onwards the situation changed to focus on arrivals from "Africa". The first wave of migration is described thus:

Before 1989, migration was principally students from countries who know the Hungarian way of life/system [berendezkedest] and were from neighbouring countries. There were not so many. It is not possible to say if there were significant numbers but many who studied here later chose this country to be their home and were completely integrated into society.

In the account of the first wave, migrants are rendered unproblematic before society. This narrative is contrasted with the "second wave" of migration at the end of the 1990s, principally from Africa. This is a wave that is disorderly and unorganised, it does not have the teleological neatness of student migration and the moral stability of individuals who know the Hungarian way of life and integrate easily:

The second wave was at the end of the 1990s when in Africa travel become more free. There were many opportunities. In the first place they chose to go to former colonizers: France, Italy, Belgium, Germany. . . . This was not a planned thing, everyone chose that country about which he had heard something or possibly had relations, friends or acquaintances.

This is a narrative that emphasises and opportunistic and chaotic migration. The story takes a turn for the worse:

Then an interesting process occurred: the law changed. And in western Europe a stricter legal regime was put in place and from this an entirely new problem emerged: migration shifted to a new direction. Now this wave of migration is more and more oriented towards eastern Europe.

The OIN was established as a means of managing this disorder:

> Before the change in the system [i.e. before 1989] the police dealt with migration issues, from about 1998 the process of migration increased in intensity, so that, OK, we have a police procedure but an independent institution dealing with migration became necessary. In the year 2000 the OIN was established. It then became straightforward to direct or understand when, where and how [migrants] came to be before the office. . . .

Dr Sz's narration creates a space for the OIN because of the perceived disorder of this "second wave" of migration. This rendition is backed up by the gradual constitution of the OIN as the sole state body with any authority over issues of migration and asylum. Unlike the image of migrants in pre-1989 Hungary slipping easily and unnoticeably into Hungarian life, here we have numbers of migrants who arrive with no fixed purpose to Hungary, both legally and not, and one that could not easily integrate into society. Dr Sz goes on in his narrative to say that the disorder was heightened, until the coming into force of the 2007 Asylum Law in January 2008, by a legal landscape that was open to loopholes, tricks and ongoing and multiple appeals to remain.

> The law contributes to this disorder. Dr Sz casts the OIN as an office of the Hungarian state that must work against the permissive and liberalizing trend of the law as well as its inherent disputative and contestatory nature. Law and lawyers are treated with suspicion and the OIN is framed as stabilizers of a disordering tendency in the law:
> . . . there are no statistics about this, but there exists certain legal helpers who are able to direct a request [for asylum] in a particular way. It is difficult to confirm, but it seems that everyone has a right to a representative that can [mould his request accordingly]. . . .

This process constitutes a structure and practice of governing asylum seekers as well as asylum policy itself. Its intent is to manage the play of asylum law so that a well-honed and coherent policy may always apply. The management of asylum policy requires the cooperation of the courts, through which a coherent structure of governance of asylum seekers may be institutionalized: "the Courts are overburdened, or they are unreflexive [*nincsenek tisztaban*] with their decisions." In Hungarian the intent is to say that the courts do not make systematic, consistent and well-founded decisions; rather, they react to individual circumstances. Earlier Dr Sz is dismissive of the individualizing tendency of the law. Despite rigorous OIN screening processes, the law "creates opportunities" for individuals to insist on continuous hearings. It seems the OIN would prefer (and the 2007 Asylum Law establishes this) a general and stable approach to screening asylum seekers, one based on rigorous rules and limitations placed on interpretation and appeals.

To do this effectively however a cooperative relational field with the courts needs to be established:

> It is a joint or common task of the state . . . to bring together the [various parties], but not only on the matter of how to receive [or interpret] the law, but also in the process of executing or implementing that law . . . those who work with the rules of the law [i.e. how to interpret it] need to express their opinion. Until this is the case, it will often happen that the OIN makes a decision and the court decides exactly to the contrary of the original decision.

The OIN asserts the need for a functioning relational field that would constitute the mode through which both asylum policy and asylum seekers are governed. The 2007 Asylum Law is intended to restrict the scope of interpretation, effectively minimizing the role of those who interpret the law. Dr Sz asserts the need for the interpretative and the executive arms of the state to come together. The central organising principle would be state interests and the maintenance of order, over and above questions of individual justice. Our interviews indicate the priority accorded by the OIN to a technicalising and administrative regimen for governing asylum seekers. The OIN's attempt to strengthen rules is a means of solidifying different protection categories, perhaps, as our informant has it, as a means of reasserting the prior right of the state to control and limit migration flows. Dr Sz reveals a frustration that categories are not fixed; the court themselves spend too much time, he says, in interpreting them.

At the time of the interviews, the Budapest Metropolitan Court's (*Fővárosi Bíróság*) status as the only court where appeals to decisions made by the OIN are heard was subject to change (this change has been in place since 2012). The OIN is seeking to decentralise the process, allowing provincial courts to hear appeals. The judges at the Metropolitan Court are strongly against this, arguing that it is an attempt to end the court's critical stance towards the OIN.[3]

The critical stance towards the OIN is based on a perception among judges we interviewed that the logic of OIN asylum law implementation is removed from the imperative to protect couched in international refugee law. This logic makes an assessment of state interest primary. The OIN bureaucrats embody an illusion of state control, of sovereignty over a polity. Serving this illusion, state bureaucrats effect policies that aim to institutionalize the right or capacity of the state to determine who is and who is not a migrant and asylum seeker (Bigo, 2002). At the core of this issue though is not that the state's ideological interests are served by defining who may enter and who may not (though this certainly happens). At the core of the issue is that the organising principle or logic behind decisions about asylum becomes not international norms of protection but simply the maintenance of the state. If the technicalisation of asylum assessment (the limiting of interpretation and the emphasis on rules) is halfway successful then it becomes cloistered from broader political, legal and moral questions about right conduct towards individuals and groups claiming protection. It is in this sense that the state overdetermines the asylum seeker by making him or her unimportant—a depoliticised figure rent of disruptive claims and either expelled or allowed in with little ado. Dr Dora Virag Dudas, a judge at the court, spoke in an interview in November 2009 of her perception that the OIN's tendency to limit protection to a ban on return rested on banal financial reasons.

> You see more and more that . . . recently we have started to repeal and change the OIN's decisions. Because they do not follow the 2007 Asylum Law, but rather attempt to continue a restrictive interpretation of the law. And this is because there is no money. There is this category of "additional protection"—*oltalmazott* [temporary protection status]. And there is a third category—the ban on return. The *oltalmazott* status is similar to that of refugee status, benefits are given [i.e. social welfare]. [This means] that it is very expensive. The ban on return on the other hand is just a tolerated and temporary condition. Minimal accommodation and meals are offered and there is no integration [procedure]. It is given for one year and is subject to yearly examination.

The judge's concern about the banal foundations of the OIN's assessment procedure does not appear to be unfounded. The new asylum law explicitly states that the cost of asylum procedure justifies a streamlined asylum assessment procedure (Hungarian Helsinki Committee, 2010).

Judges at the court are critical of what is seen as the OIN's tendency to mould and interpret the terms of the 2007 Asylum Law to fit what is perceived to be state interest in limiting the numbers of individuals accepted as refugees. Dr Dudas is strongly critical of the terms of the 2007 Asylum law but insists that once the law is passed it should be followed:

> The subsidiary protection status is for five years. According to the terms of this status all those who are refugees from situations of war and civil disturbance are eligible. Large numbers of people have come to Hungary from Afghanistan, Iraq, Somalia because they know that here we have this rule, it is possible to get a good residence permit here. This strong status that we have here is a legislative error. Elsewhere in Europe it is not like this, that's why they flow here [to Hungary]. Now

that there is this legislative error, the authority [i.e. the OIN or the state] seeks to eliminate this error by stating that now in Afghanistan, Iraq, Somalia there is no civil war. And so they do not give subsidiary protection, simply a ban on return [nonrefoulement]. This you simply cannot do under current legislation. Thus we [the court] change decisions and we ourselves grant the subsidiary protection status or order that a new procedure be started.

The judge's depiction of the OIN's reticence in according subsidiary protection is played out in Cevang's case noted above. The issue is how categories of protection are distinguished through procedures that seek to override or ignore the actual experience of persecution in favour of state interests.

Judges at the court describe the relational field within which both asylum policy and asylum seekers are governed. The OIN is portrayed as an authority willing to transgress the borders of the law for its own purposes. While the OIN presents itself as a means of regularizing the law, limiting its contestatory and interpretative nature, judges at the Court similarly describe a regularizing process where the law, no matter how inadequate or ill-formed, remains the frame within which asylum policy should operate:

The 2007 Asylum Law has not been good. It has many mistakes . . . primarily the provisions for subsidiary protection. . . . But they [the OIN] do not remedy this by [reviewing] the law and modifying its points, rather they exempt the authority from a review of its legality, [this means] that there is allowed an official arbitrariness, the law is derogated.

The judge charges the state with seeking to exempt itself from the provisions of its law. The sovereign's exceptional right to stand above the law is here not taken for granted; it is subject to contest by different institutions of the state—here the court.

Our interviews show the way in which EU citizenship regimes increase state capacity particularly by giving state agencies the responsibility of distinguishing those who do not belong to EU space and excluding them. On the other hand, judges at the Metropolitan Court insist on treating asylum as a human rights issue. There is a legal contest mounted against attempts at making asylum seekers technicalised and instrumentalised components of the EU citizenship regime. The courts in Hungary are part of a transnational legal continuum, their oversight of the immigration bureaucracy based on case law of the court (Mink, 2007). This reminder of another Europe, based on law and human rights, makes the relational field of asylum policy adversarial, and in the contest between the immigration bureaucracy and the courts, acts of citizenship may be undertaken. There is also contestation over which 'Europe' can or should be invoked, the Europe of the EU, or perhaps the Europe associated more generally with human rights. Such broad contrasts are played out in specific contexts and cases, where contestation creates openings for challenging acts of citizenship.

CONCLUSIONS

EU asylum directives implemented in Hungary are a way of imposing specific terms of rule onto asylum seekers; they are designed to control the social and political mobility and participation of asylum seekers. The EU directives intend that the state—through its immigration bureaucracy—remain the authoritative actor in the field of asylum. Terms of rule however are contested, not straightforwardly imposed. We have described an adversarial field of asylum policy in which other actors contest the aims of the Hungarian state. In this contest claims to political and social belonging may be made, and citizenship may be enacted, by appeal to a legal and human rights discourse that questions the EU's insistence on the technicalised and bureaucratic governance of asylum. The chapter shows that asylum policy is made, implemented and defended in a complex relational field of governance. Terms of rule and citizenship regimes are studied on the ground and in the contests around their implementation on asylum seekers. Acts of citizenship are, on our reading, not always spectacular; they may be an integral part of the structure of governance.

The specific contribution that this chapter makes to the existing literature on citizenship is to show empirically the functioning of a citizenship regime. Ranciere has argued that citizenship is not a label affixed to some bodies and not others; how and to whom it applies changes over time particularly following contests over legal interpretation (as we also show here). Citizenship regimes are fluid and subject to change; there is an economy of power—a relational field of governance—with different institutions contesting political and social status and belonging.

Acts of (European) citizenship are not only those which question or seek to transcend existing citizenship regimes, through protest or spectacular change. This view can assume that citizenship regimes are more unitary and coherent than they actually are. Change and disruption occur inherently because citizenship regimes are fluid and contested. Accordingly, acts of citizenship should be approached relationally; they ought to be analysed in the context of the meaning of the institutions, discourses and ideologies from whose interrelation disruption and the possibility of citizenship acts can be made.

Acts of citizenship by asylum seekers in Hungary question the boundaries of EU citizenship by appealing to a human rights tradition and legal system that read the limits of citizenship differently. In some ways, such acts posit a wider tradition of European ideas about social and political belonging and participation against the EU's attempts to impose a restrictive citizenship regime. The extent to which categories may be exceeded by asylum seekers is the extent to which the boundaries of EU citizenship may be ruptured and rethought. The temporal frame is important. The structure of asylum assessment in Hungary may mean that any act of citizenship that successfully exceeds bureaucratic categories and the logic of categorization is fleeting. The chances are that such excesses will be folded back into the OIN's categories or that the OIN will take steps to prevent such excess coming to the fore again. This is again a normal part of the structure of governance. A dialectic exists between sites of power and sites of resistance. Resistance is met by further acts of power that seek to close off ruptures. The new asylum law, particularly with its attempt at shifting appeals from the Budapest Metropolitan Court to untrained provincial courts, is a clear example of the state seeking to dampen down opportunities for rupture and the possibilities of further excess.

NOTES

1. *Idegenrendészet*
2. Based on court proceedings and statement by Judge Dora Virag Dudas. *Fovarosi Birosag 17.K.33.301/2008/15.*
3. Fieldnotes, interview with Dr Dorottya Virag Dudas.

7 Spaces of Hope
Rethinking the Purposes of Citizenship

Administrative rule, or more specifically that form of government founded on and furthering depoliticisation and technicalisation, has then become an increasingly prominent form of rule. It has become especially prominent as the go-to mode of government in response to 'crises'. There is a very explicit and visible manifestation of administrative rule—when technocrats and experts are turned to—but there is also a much less visible, more banal but more insidious and deeply embedded in society form of administrative rule which has been the primary focus of this book. This is administrative rule as a power of depoliticisation where specific groups are cast as being unfit, unready or underserving of politics. These are groups that have been disqualified from the political and are to be administered. This is ruling the margins, both in the sense of defining the marginal to be excluded and the strategies of government exercised on those there confined.

My study has focused on the social practices of depoliticisation where groups of people are denied political agency (or have this restricted) and where issues that would seem to be political and moral become subject to regulation and technicalisation. I chose to engage in a fine-grained history, allied with ethnography, to study these practices. I did so in order to study the gap and tension between the aspirations and reality of administrative rule. Often studies of administration presume that its aims of depoliticisation and technicalisation have been met and the focus of study becomes an abstracted plane of policy whose terms are settled and entirely defined by an administration. I have largely accepted the argument that administrative rule tends to dominate, but I have sought—with the histories and ethnography—to show that this domination is tangential and even at times fragile. Administrative rule appears as complete when it can abstract away from the social and cultural relations that actually constitute rule (this abstraction is served by representational strategies ranging from statistics that create a picture of a land and people tamed, or of paintings and photography that establish the other to be ruled as weak). The histories and ethnography that I have pursued had one overriding aim: to "make strange" (Li, 2007a) accounts of administrative rule. I have tried, in other words, to unpack the constitutive features of administrative rule and to show that as a complex and thick social process: rule, and 'power' generally, cannot be reduced to a series of fine lines connecting localities, nations and states to a people. Such fine lines abstract the hidden geographies of rule (Prem Kumar & Grundy-Warr, 2007; Allen, 2003): the relational process by which power plays out and is encountered, relayed, received and responded to. More than that, my focus on power as made up of a series of cultural and social relations questions a scalar account of power. Rather than tracing a line between global, national and local, I am interested in the intensive and constitutive relationships that are not easily centred on a single scale which constitute the movement of and encounter with power (Allen, 2003).

My focus has been then rather on the *translation* of power (Newman & Clarke, 2009). How is an aspiration to rule translated into policies and regulations? If power is not seen as a concrete or abstract entity but itself made up of a series of social relations then it is important to note that this translation process is not directed by an unseen hand, or at least not successfully directed. Translating an aspiration to rule seems, at least from my evidence but also from the work of Janet Newman and John Clarke (2009) as well as Tania Li (2007a), to be a messy and contradictory business with side effects and unintended consequences.

I needed a site or two to examine this messy process, and I have chosen what may be difficult ones. It is not easy or straightforward to connect colonial histories of state-making (or rule-making) to contemporary political problems. I have argued that because administrative rule was prevalent in colonies it is important to study the social constitution of administrative power in colonial sites. The major reasons preventing us from doing so—the idea that colonial state-making is an essentially different animal from the making of the modern Euro-American state not least because natives could not 'resist'—is invalid. Another barrier to comparison stems from a too-close equation of the history of politics, polities and societies with a history of state and nation-building. The first objection is invalid because history shows that rule-making in colonies was beset by struggle. It is also invalid because it depends, it seems to me, on an insistence that there were at least two if not more parallel struggles (one colonial, one European), each focusing on a specific point—a state of some sort—to the extent that the rationalities and practices of state-making become secondary to the study of states. I focus on rule as a social process focusing on the social and cultural relations that constitute practices, rationalities and techniques of rule.

What does it mean then to think of power and administration in these ways? What does a focus on rule as a social process actually mean for anyone interested in analysing policy and rule? I want to emphasise two ideas, perhaps critical interventions, that I have made in this book and try to highlight their consequences for studying contemporary power and, hopefully, moving beyond power.

The first critical intervention is the idea that if we study rule as a social process we focus on intensive social relationships (Allen, 2003). The main consequence of this idea is that we should give an account of the marginal alongside the dominant (Williams, 1978). If we pay attention that is to the multiple foundations of power—most of which are probably social relations of one sort or another—the focus becomes then a breaking down of, first, the constitutive parts of rule—territory and authority for example—and then, second, understanding the social processes that seek to conceive and maintain a piece of space as 'territory' or a form of rule as 'authority' (Sassen, 2008).

I have tried to show in the book how territory is made and how authority over that territory is clarified. I have emphasised that these are social processes; while rule is often achieved, it is based on fragile social foundations and relations. Many of these relations are abstracted away, that is they are made out to be unimportant, but they do contain the seeds and bases of change. It is from the basis of social relations, and the attitudes that they embody towards territory and authority, temporarily and with varying degrees of success made out to be domesticated, that social change can be accounted for. By focusing on rule as deeply social, this book makes the case that accounts of territory and authority on which administrative rule is based are made up of a series of social relations.

The second critical intervention idea that I want to emphasise is that a focus on the social processes and constitutions of rule should turn then to rights (Sassen, 2008) and how they are thought in relation to constellations of territory and authority. I am interested in thinking through how the abstractions of administrative rule remove or denigrate a sense of purpose to politics. Efforts to reconcile or simplify issues of ethics and morality within a specific constellation of authority, territory and rights lends a specific sense of purpose to citizenship.

My critique is not only about the borders of our commonsensical notions of political belonging (McNevin, 2009). As I have argued, when we see citizenship as social practice and not a static status bestowed from above, the focus shifts to giving an account of the contests surrounding authority—the authority to bestow rights and to represent those with rights—and territory, the space where rights are to be played out. These contests can in theory question how rights are directed (to what sort of institution are they directed) and from what conception of community (how strong is territory as the arbiter of the limits of moral community?). Useful, and indeed integral, as these types of intervention are (there are a number of excellent critical scholars of citizenship working on these types of question), I think these do not question enough the idea that rights are directed to a state and are intended to give succour to a particular community. I think that if we begin by questioning the reconciliation of rights within a specific constellation of territory and authority then we are able to give an account of rights as something not centred on individual selves (or aggregations of like individuals in a community) but on others.

This last point is of course a normative ethical position, but it follows from empirical and historical critique. The key issue is the form and context that gives meaning to citizenship. Expanding citizenship is important, it allows for others to enter into the political norm and allows for the extension of rights, and security and dignity. But 'expanding' citizenship does not in itself question two basic properties of citizenship, that it centres on appeals to a to a state and that it is primarily aimed towards succour and representation of individuals or groups of like individuals. The insights offered by the enacting citizenship debate (Isin & Saward, 2013) point to citizenship as a series of social contests. My histories and ethnography in this book show what it means to think of power and politics as social process: the main point is that any hegemonic account of the purposes and arrangements of the political must hold in abeyance the messy social relationships through which they are constituted. They must also hold in abeyance the idea that rights are to be enacted by individuals or groups for themselves and with reference to a specific nexus of authority and territory.

Politics rests on the capacity to make a connection between authority, territory and rights. This connection centres on a relationship with the individual subject. Modern government is derived by delicately balancing a notion of popular sovereignty—government of the people legitimated by the people—and the agency of the individual citizen, which can disrupt the cohesion and purposiveness of a community of sovereign subjects. At the centre of this relationship is the state and a modern narrative of progress and security (Brown, 2001). These narratives contain and restrict what we understand by ethics, morality and order; they construct a commonsensical structure of what constitutes political action that places and repeats the state at its centre.

The histories that I have pursued in this text disrupt the clean narrative of order and progress. They show the multiple contests, debates and inefficiencies surrounding such narratives. Wendy Brown (2001) urges us to think politics out of history; what may the content and principles of politics be based on outside of this dominating and domineering history?

The narratives of progress and security that connect politics to the state (to specific constellations of the relationship between territory, authority and rights) suggest that we are abandoned to the state and its law (Agamben, 1998) and that we are in a state of competition for a greater share of the benefits of progress and materiality (this competition can be ameliorated by the state and its welfare programs, or it can be heightened by a laissez-faire state, or it can be ameliorated also by civil society). As a consequence political personhood is defined by the articulation of claims to the state and by making claims centred on self-interest.

If the orders that structure this reading of politics start to crumble, or can be shown to be not objective accounts but rather willed readings of linear purpose into history that do away with the memory of alternatives, and of the social relations that make alternatives always a possibility, then we may begin by thinking politics outside of the state. What this amounts to then is the possibility of thinking citizenship as ethical, moral and political practice not centred on the state and not centred on the pursuit of individual or group interest. Can we think citizenship as the condition of existing with and for others whose likeness or difference is not the basis for thinking the extent of political and social solidarity?

This is akin to the actions of a number of groups in different societies that struggle with and for irregular migrants, but it is not to be limited to the expansion of a prefigured political community centred on the state (it is not about making others more equal to a predefined us). Citizenship outside of the state may perhaps be most interestingly conceived as an attempt to recapture our moral compasses. That may mean figuring out political, ethical and moral practice without the teleology of the state and its narratives. It may mean thinking through the limits of justice with others, and it may mean that the horizons of the political are not foreclosed by territory.

To my mind, the centring of politics away from the states leads to an anxious politics: it is centred not on looking for limits to community and belonging but on ensuring that any limits are constantly questioned. An ethics and politics not centred on the self, a citizenship centred on others, is perhaps most marked then on the taking up of responsibility by citizens to figure out their moral compasses. This involves thinking with and for others and an ethics not merely of coexistence but of protecting and succouring others without thinking the foreclosing thinking of territorial or other limits to political and moral community.

Engaging with the "messy actualities" (Li, 2007b: 279) of politics is part of political practice. Politics and government are not to be considered as abstract and efficient policy-driven machines. The histories and ethnography that I have engaged in show the difficulties involved in this abstraction; abstraction does happen but only to the extent that social relations that structure and limit power are read out. What we understand as rule is doubly social. It is made up of a series of different relations and positions that need to be reconciled in order for government to take place, and as it takes place it does so through intensive social relations. The maintenance of clear lines of authority and sovereignty between a state, a place-as-territory and a population is tenuous; the social processes that constitute government can be appealed to even if they appear defeated or dormant.

From this basis it appears important to consider and move beyond the narratives of progress and security that contain politics within a state and that cede moral and ethical action and responsibility to that state. Moving away then from the individualisations of modern politics we may begin to consider politics and ethics as for and with others. The broader contribution then that I have hoped to achieve in this book is to ground the abstractions of administrative government in a messy social reality, and in so doing to then open up the linear narrative of history and progress that bind us to the state. The most important consequence of this binding is the foreclosing of responsibility along territorial lines. If administrative power can be shown to be made up of social relations then we can think beyond such limitations to ethics and consider a politics beyond the pursuit of self-interest and towards others without recourse to considering their membership of political or moral community.

References

Abu-Lughod, Janet (1965). "Tale of Two Cities: The Origins of Modern Cairo". *Comparative Studies in Society and History* 7(4): 429–457.

Act LXXX of 2007 on Asylum (2007 Asylum Act).

Agamben, Giorgio (1998). *Homo Sacer: Sovereign Power and Bare Life.* Stanford, Stanford University Press.

Allen, John (2003). *Lost Geographies of Power.* Oxford: Wiley-Blackwell.

Allen, John (2011). "Topological Twists: Power's shifting geographies". *Dialogues in Human Geography* 1(3): 283–298.

Appadurai, Arjun (1993). "Number in the Colonial Imagination". In C. A. Breckenridge and P. van der Veer (Eds.), *Orientalism and the Post-Colonial Predicament.* Philadelphia: University of Pennsylvania Press.

Appadurai, Arjun (1996). "The Production of Locality, in Arjun Appadurai". *Modernity at Large: Cultural Dimensions of Globalization.* Minneapolis: University of Minnesota Press.

Asad, Talal (1994). "Ethnographic representation, statistics and modern power". *Social Research* 61: 55–88.

Baden-Powell, B. H. (1892). *The Land Systems of British India, Volume One.* Oxford: Clarendon Press.

Bhabha, Homi (1990). *The Location of Culture.* London: Routledge.

Bigo, Didier (2002). "Security and Immigration: Toward a Critique of the Governmentality of Unease". *Alternatives: Global Local Political* 27(1): 63–92.

Bird, Isabella (1883). *The Golden Chersonese and the Way Thither.* New York: G. P. Putnam's Sons.

Bose, Sugata (1986). *Agrarian Bengal: Economy, Social Structure and Politics, 1919–1947.* New York: Cambridge University Press.

Brenner, Neil (1999). "Globalization as Reterritorialization: The re-scaling of urban governance in the European Union". *Urban Studies* 36(3): 431–451.

Brenner, Neil, and Nik Theodore (2002). "Cities and the Geographies of 'Actually Existing Neoliberalism'". *Antipode* 34(3): 349–379.

Brown, Wendy (2001). *Politics out of History.* Princeton: Princeton University Press.

Butcher, W. G. (1979). "Toward the History of Malayan Society: Kuala Lumpur District 1885–1912". *Journal of Southeast Asian Studies* 10(1): 104–118.

Byrne, Rosemary, Noll, Gregor and Vedsted-Hansen, Jens (2004). "Understanding Refugee Law in an Enlarged European Union". *European Journal of International Law* 15(2): 355–379.

Castells, Manuel (1978). *City, Class and Power.* London; New York, MacMillan; St. Martin's Press.

Chakrabarty, Dipesh (2000). *Provincializing Europe.* Princeton, Princeton University Press.

Chandler, David (2004). "The Problems of 'Nation-Building': Imposing Bureaucratic 'Rule from Above'". *Review of International Affairs* 17(3): 577–597.

Chatterjee, Partha (1986). *The Colonial State and Peasant Resistance in Bengal 1920–1947*. *Past & Present* 110: 169–204.

Chatterjee, Partha (1993). *The Nation and Its Fragments: Colonial and Postcolonial Histories*. Princeton: Princeton University Press.

Chatterjee, Partha (2004). *The Politics of the Governed: Reflections on Popular Politics in Most of the World*. New York: Columbia University Press.

Chaudhary, Zahid R (2012). *Afterimage of Empire: Photography in Nineteenth Century India*. Minneapolis: University of Minnesota Press.

Chin Yoon Fong (1972). "The Chinese Protectorate of Selangor 1896–1906". *Malaysia in History* 15(1): 30–43.

Clandestino (2008). "Undocumented Migrants in Hungary: Counting the Uncountable".

Clarke, John, and Janet Newman (1997). *The Managerial State*. London: Sage.

Clarke, John, et al. (2007). *Creating Citizen Consumers: Changing Publics and Changing Public Services*. London: Sage.

Coalition Provisional Authority (2003a, 16 May). *Regulation No. 1*. "The Coalition Provisional Authority". *http://www.iraqcoalition.org/regulations/20030516_CPAREG_1_The_Coalition_Provisional_Authority_.pdf*. Accessed 13 August 2010.

Coalition Provisional Authority (2003b, 16 May). *Order No. 1*. "The De-Baathification of Iraqi Society. *http://www.iraqcoalition.org/regulations/20030516_CPAORD_1_De-Ba_athification_of_Iraqi_Society_.pdf*. Accessed 13 August 2010.

Coalition Provisional Authority (2003c, 23 May). *Order No. 2*. "Dissolution of Entities". *http://www.iraqcoalition.org/regulations/20030823_CPAORD_2_Dissolution_of_Entities_with_Annex_A.pdf*. Accessed 13 August 2010.

Coalition Provisional Authority (2003d, 25 May). *Order No. 4*. "Management of Propery and Assets of the Iraqi Baath Party". *http://www.iraqcoalition.org/regulations/20030525_CPAORD_4_Management_of_Property_and_Assets_of_the_Iraqi_Ba_ath_Party.pdf*. Accessed 13 August 2010.

Coalition Provisional Authority (2003e, 25 May). *Order No. 5*. "Establishment of the Iraqi De-Baathfication Council". *http://www.iraqcoalition.org/regulations/CPAORD5.pdf*. Accessed 13 August 2010.

Coalition Provisional Authority (2003f, 3 June). *Memo No. 1*. "Implementation of De-Baathification Order No. 1". *http://www.iraqcoalition.org/regulations/20030603_CPAMEMO_1_Implementation_of_De-Ba_athification.pdf*. Accessed 13 August 2010.

Coalition Provisional Authority (2003g, 4 November). *Memo No. 7*. "Delegation of Authority Under De-Baathification Order No. 1". *http://www.iraqcoalition.org/regulations/20031104_CPAMEMO_7_Delegation_of_Authority.pdf*. Accessed 1 July 2014.

Coalition Provisional Authority (2004a, 26 April). *Order No. 71*. "Local Governmental Powers. *http://www.iraqcoalition.org/regulations/20040406_CPAORD_71_Local_Governmental_Powers_.pdf*. Accessed 1 July 2014.

Cole, Juan R.I. (2005). *The Ayatollahs and Democracy in Iraq*. Leiden: Amsterdam University Press.

Comaroff, J.L. (2001). "Colonialism, Culture, and the Law: A Foreword". *Law & Social Inquiry* 26: 305–314.

Cooper, Frederick (1993). "Colonizing Time: Work Rhythms and Labour Conflict in Colonial Mombassa." In Nicholas B. Dirks (Ed.), *Colonialism and Culture*. Ann Arbor: University of Michigan.

Cooper, Frederick (2005). *Colonialism in Question: Theory, Knowledge, History*. Berkeley: University of California Press.

Costello, Cathryn (2006). "Administrative Governance and the Europeanisation of Asylum and Immigration Policy". In Herwig Hoffman and Alexander Turk (Eds.), *EU Administrative Governance*. Cheltenham: Edward Elgar.

Crampton, Jeremy W., and John Krygier (2006). "An Introduction to Critical Cartography". *ACME: An International E-Journal for Critical Geographies* 4(1), 11–33.

Das, Abhay Charan (1881). *The Indian Ryot, Land Tax, Permanent Settlement and the Famine*. Howrah: Howrah Press.

Daston, Lorraine (2000). "The Coming into Being of Scientific Objects". In Daston (Ed.), *Biographies of Scientific Objects*. Chicago: University of Chicago Press.

Deloitte (2013). Middle East Tax Handbook. *http://www.deloitte.com/view/en_XE/xe/services/tax/9cf018bd0021f310VgnVCM1000003256f70aRCRD.htm#.* Accessed 1 July 2014.

Diamond, Larry (2005). "Lessons From Iraq". *Journal of Democracy* 16(1): 9–23.

Dillon, Michael (1999). "The Scandal of the Refugee: Some Reflections on the 'Inter' of International Relations and Continental Thought". In David Campbell and Michael J Shapiro (Eds.), *Moral Spaces: Rethinking Ethics and World Politics*. Minneapolis: University of Minnesota Press.

Dirks, Nicholas (1997). "The Policing of Tradition: Anthropology and Colonialism in Southern India". *Comparative Studies in Society and History* 39(1): 182–212.

Dirks, Nicholas (2001). *Castes of Mind: Colonialism and the Making of Modern India*. Princeton: Princeton University Press.

Dobbins, James, et al. (2009). *Occupying Iraq: A History of the Coalitional Provisional Authority*. Santa Monica: RAND Corporation.

Eastern Daily Mail and Straits Advertiser. 22 January 1907. "Kuala Lumpur Notes".

Edney, Matthew H. (1997). *Mapping an Empire: The Geographical Construction of British India, 1765–1843*. Chicago: University of Chicago Press.

Elwood, Sarah (2006). "Critical Issues in Participatory GIS: Deconstructions, Reconstruction and New Research Directions". *Transactions in GIS* 10(5): 693–708.

Falconer, John (1984). "Ethnographical Photography in India 1850–1900". *Photographic Collector* 5(1):16–46.

Farina, Cynthia (1998). "Interpretation and the Balance of Power in the Administrative State". *Columbia Law Review* 89(3): 452–528

Favell, Adrian (2003). "Integration Nations: The Nation State and Research on Immigrants in Europe." *Comparative Social Research* 22(1): 13–42.

Federated Malay States (1921). *Laws of the Federated Malay States 1877–1920*. London, Aylesbury: Printed by Hazell, Watson & Viney, ld.

Feldman, Allen (2005). "The Actuarial Gaze: From, 9/11 to Abu Ghraib." *Cultural Studies* 19(2): 203–226.

Ferguson, James (1990). *The Anti-Politics Machine: 'Development', Depoliticization and Bureaucratic Power in Lesotho*. Cambridge: Cambridge University Press.

Finucane, M. and Ameer Ali (1913). *A Commentary on the Bengal Tenancy Act (Act VIII of 1885)*. Calcutta: The Cranenburgh Law Publishing Press.

Foucault, Michel (1978/1990). *The History of Sexuality* (Vol. 1). (Robert Hurley, Trans.). New York: Vintage.

Foucault, Michel (2003). *"Society Must be Defended": Lectures at the College de France, 1974–1975*. Mauro Bertani and Alessandro Fontana (Eds.) (David Macey, Trans.). New York: Picador.

Futo, Peter (2009). "Undocumented Migrants in Hungary: Counting the Uncountable". The Clandestino Research Project, 6th Framework Program, European Commission. *http://www.eliamep.gr/en/wp-content/uploads/2009/07/research_brief_hungary.pdf.* Accessed 30 November 2010.

Future of Iraq Project (2003). *Local Government Working Group*. United States Department of State. Archived at *http://web.archive.org/web/20060405034753/www.thememoryhole.org/state/future_of_iraq/.* Accessed 13 August 2010.

Geddes, Mike (2000). "Tackling Social Exclusion in the European Union? The Limits to the New Orthodoxy of Local Partnership". *International Journal of Urban and Regional Research* 24(4): 782–800.

Grabbe, Heather (2002). "Europeanisation Goes East: Power and Uncertainty in the EU Accession Process". In K. Featherstone and C. Radaelli (Eds.), *The Politics of Europeanisation*, Oxford: Oxford University Press.

Gramsci, Antonio (1971). *Selections from the Prison Notebooks of Antonio Gramsci.* Quentin Hoare and Geoffrey Nowell Smith (Eds. and Trans.). London: Lawrence and Wishart.

Gregory, Derek (2004). *The Colonial Present.* Oxford: Blackwell's.

Guha, Ranajit (1996). *A Rule of Property for Bengal: An essay on the idea of Permanent Settlement.* Durham. NC: Duke University Press.

Guild, Elspeth (2006). "The Europeanisation of Europe's Asylum Policy". *International Journal of Refugee Law* 18(3–4): 630–651.

Guild, Elspeth (2007). "The Foreigner in the Security Continuum: Judicial Resistance in the United Kingdom". In Prem Kumar Rajaram and Carl Grundy-Warr (Eds.), *Borderscapes: Hidden Geographies and Politics at Territory's Edge.* Minneapolis: University of Minnesota.

Guiraudon, Virginie (2000). "European Integration and Migration Policy: Vertical Policy Making as Venue Shopping". *Journal of Common Market Studies* 38(2): 251–271.

Gullick, John M. (1955). *"Kuala Lumpur, 1880–1895".* Kuala Lumpur: Malayan Branch of the Royal Asiatic Society.

Gullick, John M. (2004). *A History of Selangor, 1766–1939.* Kuala Lumpur: Malaysian Branch of the Royal Asiatic Society (MBRAS).

Haddad, Emma (2007). "Danger Happens at the Border". In Prem Kumar Rajaram and Carl Grundy-Warr (Eds.), *Borderscapes: Hidden Geographies and Politics at Territory's Edge.* Minneapolis: University of Minnesota Press.

Halchin, Elaine L. (2005). *The Coalition Provisional Authority (CPA): Origin, Characteristics, and Institutional Authorities.* Washington, DC: Congressional Research Service.

Hall, Stuart (1996). "Gramsci's Relevance for the Study of Race and Ethnicity". In David Morley and Kuan-Hsing Chin (Eds.), *Stuart Hall: Critical Dialogues in Cultural Studies.* London and New York: Routledge.

Hansen, Peo (2002). "European Integration, European Identity and the Colonial Connection". *European Journal of Social Theory* 5(4): 483–498.

Hars, A. and Sik, E. (2008). "Hungary – Towards Balanced Tightening of Regulations on Irregular Employment". In M. Kupiszewski and H. Mattila (Eds.), *Addressing the Irregular Employment of Immigrants in the European Union: Between Sanctions and Rights.* Budapest: International Organization for Migration.

Harvey, David (1990). *The Condition Of Postmodernity: An Enquiry into the Origins of Cultural Change.* Cambridge: Blackwell.

Harvey, David (2003). *The New Imperialism.* Oxford: Oxford University Press

Hayes, Patricia (1996). "'Cocky' Hahn and the 'Black Venus': The Making of a Native Commissioner in Southwest Africa, 1915–46". *Gender & History* 8(3): 364–392.

Herring, Eric (2008). *Neoliberalism versus Peacebuilding in Iraq.* Governance Research Centre, University of Bristol, Working Paper No. 02–07.

Hersh, Seymour (2002). "The Debate Within". New Yorker. March 11.

Hersh, Seymour M. (2003). "Annals of National Security: The Debate within the Objective Is Clear—Topple Saddam. But How?" *The New Yorker* 11 March.

Hirschman, Charles (1987). "The Meaning and Measurement of Ethnicity in Malaysia: An Analysis of Census Classifications." *The Journal of Asian Studies* 46(3): 555–582

Hoffman, Herwig, and Alexander Turk (2006). *EU Administrative Governance*. Cheltenham: Edward Elgar.

Hornaday, William T. (1885). *Two Years in the Jungle: Experiences of a Hunter and Naturalist in India, Ceylon, the Malay Peninsula and Borneo*. New York: Charles Scribner's Sons.

Hume, Ethel Doulas (1907). *The Globular Jottings of Griselda*. Edinburgh and London: William Blackwood and Sons.

Hungarian Helsinki Committee (2010). "Vélemény migrációs törvénytervezetről". ["Opinion on the Draft Migration Law"]. *http://helsinki.hu/Friss_anyagok/htmls/732*. Accessed 30 November 2010.

Innes, Emily (1885). *The Chersonese with the Gilding Off*. London: Richard Bentley and Sons.

Isin, Egin (2005). "Citizenship after Orientalism: Ottoman Citizenship". In F. Keyman and A. Icduygu (Eds.), *Challenges to Citizenship in a Globalizing World: European Questions and Turkish Experiences*. London: Routledge, 2005.

Isin, Engin, and Mike Saward (2013). "Introduction". In Engin and Saward (Eds.), *Enacting European Citizenship*. Oxford: Oxford University Press.

Jackson, James C (1963). "Kuala Lumpur in the 1880s: the Contribution of Bloomfield Douglas". *Journal of Southeast Asian History* 4(2): 117–127.

Johnstone, Michael (1981). "The Evolution of Squatter Settlements in Peninsular Malaysian Cities". *Journal of Southeast Asian Studies* 12(2): 364–380.

Kalpagam, U. (2004). "Colonial Governmentality and the Public Sphere in India". *Journal of Historical Sociology* 14(4): 418–440.

Kovats, Andras, Pal Nyir, and Judit Toth (2003) "Hungary". In Jan Niessen et al. (Eds.), *EU and US Approaches to Immigration*. Brussels: Migration Policy Group.

Kraus, Werner (2005). "Raden Saleh's Interpretation of the Arrest of Diponegoro: An Example of Indonesian "Proto-Nationalist" Modernism". *Archipel* 69: 259–294.

Kratoska, Paul H. (1982). "Rice Cultivation and the Ethnic Division of Labour in British Malaya". *Comparative Studies in Society and History* 24(2): 280–314.

Kratoska, Paul H. (1983). "'Ends That We Cannot Foresee': Malay Reservations in British Malaya". *Journal of Southeast Asian Studies* 14(1): 149–168.

Landau, Paul S (2002). "Empires of the Visual: Photography and Colonial Administration in Africa". In Paul S. Landau and Deborah Kaspin (Eds.), *Images and Empires: Visuality in Colonial and Postcolonial Africa*. Berkeley: University of California Press.

Landay, Jonathan S., and Warren P. Strobel (2003). "Pentagon Civilians' Lack of Planning Contributed to Chaos in Iraq". *Knight Ridder* 12 July.

Leach, Edmund (1961). *Rethinking Anthropology*. London: The Athlone Press.

Legg, Stephen (2007a). "Beyond the European Province: Foucault and Postcolonialism". In Jeremy Crampton and Stuart Elden (Eds.), *Space, Knowledge and Power: Foucault and Geography*. London: Ashgate.

Legg, Stephen (2007b). *Spaces of Colonialism: Delhi's Urban Governmentalities*. Oxford: Blackwell.

Levine, Philippa (2008). "States of Undress: Nakedness and the Colonial Imagination". *Victorian Studies* 50(2): 189–219.

Li, Tania (1999). "Compromising Power: Development, Culture and Rule in Indonesia". *Cultural Anthropology* 14(3): 295–322.

Li, Tania (2007a). *The Will to Improve: Governmentality, Development and the Practice of Politics*. Durham: Duke University Press.

Li, Tania (2007b). "Practices of Assemblage and Community Forestry Management". *Economy and Society* 36(2): 263–293.

Ludden, David (1993). "Orientalist Empiricism: Transformations of Colonial Knowledge'. In Carol A. Breckenridge and Peter van derVeer (Eds.), *Orientalism and the Postcolonial Predicament*. Pittsburgh: University of Pennsylvania Press.

158   References

National Archives Malaysia: SSF 4505/1891. "Bapoo Mandor & Others".

Mackenzie, John (1995). *Orientalism: History, Theory and the Arts*. Manchester: Manchester University Press.

Malay Mail (1907, 14 May). "Editorial".

Malay Mail (1907, 14 March). "Editorial".

Malay Mail (1907, 25 April). "Editorial".

Malay Mail (1907, 3 January). "Editorial".

Malay Mail (1912, 4 January). "Health of Kuala Lumpur. Report by Dr Gerrard".

Malay Mail (1908, 6 August).

Malay Mail (1907, 16 August). "Editorial".

Malay Mail (1912, 22 February).

Malay Mail (1912, 22 February). "Letters to the Editor".

Malay Mail (1912, 28 February).

Mamdani, Mahmood (1996). *Citizen and Subject: Contemporary Africa and the Legacy of Late Colonialism*. Princeton: Princeton University Press.

Mamdani, Mahmood (1999). "Historicising Power and Responses to Power: Indirect Rule and its Reform". *Social Research* 66(3): 859–886.

Markham, Clements (1878). *A Memoir on the Indian Surveys*. London: W H Allen & Co.

Marx, Karl (1857). *The Eighteenth Brumaire of Louis Napoleon*. Saul K Padover and Progress Publishers, Moscow (translators). Marx/Engels Internet Archive. *https://www.marxists.org/archive/marx/works/1852/18th-brumaire/*. Accessed 1 July 2014.

Maxwell, Anne (1999). *Colonial Photography and Exhibitions: Representations of the 'Native' and the Making of European Identities*. London: Leicester University Press.

Mbembe, Achile (2001). *On the Postcolony*. Berkeley: University of California Press.

McClintock, Anne (1995). *Imperial Leather: Race, Gender and Sexuality in the Colonial Context*. New York: Routledge.

McGarry, John, and Brendan O'Leary (2007). "Iraq's Constitution of 2005: Liberal consociation as political prescription." *International Journal of Constitution Law* 5(4): 670–698.

McLane, John R. (1993). *Land and Local Kingship in Eighteenth-Century Bengal*. Cambridge: 1993.

McNevin, Anne (2007). "Irregular Migrants, Neoliberal Geographies and Spatial Frontiers of 'The Political'". *Review of International Studies* 33(4): 655–674.

McNevin, Anne (2009). "Doing What Citizens Do: Migrant Struggles at the Edges of Political Belonging". *Local-Global: Identity, Security, Community* 6(2009): 67–77.

Merry, Sally Engle (1992)."Anthropology, Law, and Transnational Processes". *Annual Review of Anthropology* 21: 357–379.

Milton-Edwards, Beverley (2006). "Faith in Democracy: Islamization of the Polity after Saddam Hussein". *Democratization* 13(3): 472–489.

Mink, Julia (2007). "Detention of Asylum Seekers in Hungary". Budapest: Hungarian Helsinki Committee. *http://helsinki.hu/dokumentum/Detention_of_ Asylum-Seekers_in_Hungary.pdf*. Accessed 15 August 2011.

Mitchell, Timothy (1991). *Colonising Egypt*. Berkeley: University of California Press.

Mitchell, Timothy (2002). *Rule of Experts: Egypt, Techno-Politics, Modernity*. Berkeley: University of California.

Mookerjee, Radharomon (1919). *Occupancy Land Rights*. Calcutta: Calcutta University Press.

National Archives Malaysia: NAM 1957/0162594. "Memorandum on the Action Taken by Government in Connection with the Chinese Reform Movement."

National Archives Malaysia: MD 691/85 Sel Sec. "Report of the Filthy State of the Brothels".

National Archives Malaysia: SSF 4435/1911. "Notes Complaints against Protector of Chinese and Memorandum from Protector of Chinese".

Newman, Janet, and John Clarke (2009). *Publics, Politics, Power: Remaking the Public in Public Services.* London: Sage.

Novak, Anita (2007). "Racism in Hungary". *ENAR Shadow Report. http://cms. horus.be/files/99935/MediaArchive/national/Hungary%20-%20SR%202007. pdf.* Accessed 30 November 2010.

Nyers, Peter (2003). "Abject Cosmopolitanism: The Politics of Protection in the Anti-Deportation Movement". *Third World Quarterly* 24(6): 1069–1093.

Nyers, Peter (2006). *Rethinking Refugees Beyond States of Emergency.* New York: Routledge.

O'Looney, John (2000). *Beyond Maps: GIS and Decision Making in Local Government.* Redlands, CA: Environmental Systems Research Institute.

Office of Immigration and Nationality (OIN) (2010). *Statistics 2005–2009. http:// www.bmbah.hu/statisztikak.php.* Accessed 30 November 2010.

O'Malley, Pat, Lorna Weir and Clifford Shearing (1997). "Governmentality, Criticism, Politics". *Economy & Society* 26(4): 501–517.

Ong, Aihwa (2000). "Graduated Sovereignty in Southeast Asia". *Theory, Culture & Society* 17(4): 55–75

Ong, Aihwa (2006). *Neoliberalism as Exception: Mutations in Citizenship and Sovereignty.* Durham, NC: Duke University Press.

Phillips, H. A. D. (1886). *Our Administration in India: Being a Complete Account of the Revenue and Collectorate Administration in All Departments With Special Reference to the Work of a District Officer in Bengal.* London: W Thacker & Co.

Prem Kumar Rajaram and Grundy-Warr, Carl (2007). "Introduction". In Prem Kumar and Grundy-Warr (Eds.), *Borderscapes: Hidden Geographies and Politics at Territory's Edge.* Minneapolis: University of Minnesota Press.

Price, Liz (2002). "Some 19th Century Visitors to Caves in Peninsular Malaysia". *Acta Carsologica* 31(2): 233–247.

Provisional Authority. Santa Monica, CA: RAND Corporation.

Public Broadcasting Service (PBS) (2007). *Gangs of Iraq: Transcript of an Interview Conducted on Frontline with L. Paul Bremer 9 January. http://www.pbs.org/wgbh/ pages/frontline/gangsofiraq/interviews/bremer.html.* Accessed 13 August 2010.

Rai, Vipinichandra (1886). *The Rent Law of Bengal: being the Bengal Tenancy Act, VIII of 1885.* Calcutta: H C Gangooly & Co.

Rampini, R. F. and M. Finucane (1889). *The Bengal Tenancy Act Being Act VIII of 1885.* Calcutta: Thacker, Spink & Co.

Ranciere, Jacques (2004). "Who Is the Subject of the Rights of Man?" *South Atlantic Quarterly* 103(2–3): 297–310.

Rathborne, Ambrose (1898). *Camping and Tramping in Malaya: Fifteen Years Pioneering in the Native States of Malaya.* London: Swann Sonnenschein and Co., Ltd.

Rathmell, Andrew, et al. (2005). *Developing Iraq's Security Sector: The Coalition Provisional Authority's Experience.* Santa Monica: RAND Corporation.

Ray, Rajat and Ratna Ray (1975). "Zamindars and Jotedars: A Study of Rural Politics in Bengal". *Modern Asian Studies* 9(1): 81–102.

Regulation VI of 1895. A regulation to amend and consolidate the law relating to labour in the state of Selangor. [Labour Code, 1895]. *The Laws of Selangor, 1877–1895. Orders in council and regulations together with rules made thereunder having the force of law.* Compiled by J H M Robson (magistrate, Selangor), revised by A T D Berrington, (Chief Magistrate, Selangor). Kuala Lumpur: Selangor Government Printing Office, 1896.

Republic of Iraq National Investment Commission (2013). *Investment Guide to Iraq*. Baghdad: National Investment Commission.

Risley, H. H. (1891). "The Study of Ethnology in India". *The Journal of the Anthropological Institute of Great Britain and Ireland* 20: 235–263.

Robb, Peter (1997). *Ancient Rights and Future Comfort: Bihar, the Bengal Tenancy Act of 1885, and British Rule in India*. London: Curzon Press.

Rose, Nikolas (1999). *Powers of Freedom: Reframing Political Thought*. Cambridge: Cambridge University Press.

Rose, Nikolas, and Peter Miller (1992). "Political Power beyond the State: Problematics of Government". *The British Journal of Sociology* 43(2): 173–205.

Said, Edward (1978). *Orientalism*. New York: Vintage Books.

Said, Yahia (2006, Mar. 2–8). "Federal Choices Needed". *Al-Ahram Weekly. http:// weekly.ahram.org.eg/2006/784/sc6.htm*. Accessed 13 August 2010.

Sales, R (2002). "The Deserving and the Undeserving? Refugees, Asylum Seekers and Welfare in Britain". *Critical Social Policy* 22(3): 456–478.

Sassen, Saskia (2008). *Territory, Authority, Rights: From Medieval to Global Assemblages*. Princeton: Princeton University Press.

Scott, David (1995). "Colonial Governmentality". *Social Text* 43: 191–220.

Scott, James W. (2002). "A Networked Space of Meaning? Spatial Politics as Geostrategies of European Integration". *Space and Polity* 6(2): 147–167.

Selangor Journal, The (1897). *Jottings Past and Present* (Vol. 5). Kuala Lumpur: Selangor Government Printing House.

Selangor Secretariat (1888). *Government of Selangor Notice June 1888*. Selangor Secretariat Files 2214/3

Sen, Satadru (1999). "Policing the Savage: Segregation, Labor and State Medicine in the Andamans". *The Journal of Asian Studies* 58(3): 753–773.

Sen, Satadru (2013). "Nietzsche in the Tropics: Colonialism and the Photographic Imagination". *History and Sociology of South Asia* 7(1): 19–38.

Shamsul, A. B. (2001). "A History of an Identity, an Identity of a History: The Idea and Practice of 'Malayness' in Malaysia Reconsidered". *Journal of Southeast Asian Studies* 32(3): 355–366

Sharp, Joanne (2009). *Geographies of Postcolonialism*. London: Sage.

Singapore Free Press and Mercantile Advertiser, The (1911, 19 December). "An Arrest in the Malay States".

Soguk, Nevzat (1999). *States and Strangers: Refugees and Displacements of Statecraft*. Minneapolis: University of Minnesota Press.

Spaan, Ernst, Ton Van Naerssen and Gerard Kohl (2002). "Reimagining Borders: Malay Identity and Indonesian Migrants in Malaysia". *Tijdschrift voor Economische en Sociale Geografie*. 93(2): 160–172.

Squire, Vicki (2009). *The Exclusionary Politics of Asylum*. Basingstoke: Palgrave-Macmillan.

Steinmetz, George (2007). *The Devil's Handwriting: Precoloniality and the German Colonial State in Qingdao, Samoa and Southwest Africa*. Chicago: Chicago University Press.

Steinmetz, George (2008). "The Colonial State as a Social Field: Ethnographic Capital and Native Policy in the German Overseas Empire before 1914". *American Sociological Review*. 73: 589–612.

Steinmetz, George (2009). *The Devil's Handwriting: Precoloniality and the German Colonial State in Qingdao, Samoa, and Southwest Africa*. Chicago: University of Chicago Press.

Stoler, Ann Laura (1994). "Sexual Affronts and Racial Frontiers: European Identities and the Cultural Politics of Exclusion in Southeast Asia". In Cooper, Frederick and Ann Laura Stoler (Eds.), *Tensions of Empire: Colonial Cultures in a Bourgeois World*. Berkeley: University of California Press.

Straits Times Weekly (1912, 24 February). "Rioting at Kuala Lumpur".

Straits Times Weekly (1892, 24 February). "A Destructive Fire".

Straits Times Weekly (1904, 13 October). "FMS Notes".

Survey Office, Bengal (1894). *Annual Report on the Survey Operations in Bengal 1892–93*. Calcutta: Government Printing Press.

Surveyor-General, Bengal (1911). *Annual Report on the Survey Operations in Bengal 1909–10*. Calcutta: Government Printing Press.

Surveyor General of India (1881). *General Report on the Operations of the Survey of India Department, 1879-80*. Calcutta: Office of the superintendent of government printing.

Surveyor General of India (1882). *General Report on the Operations of the Survey of India Department, 1880–81* Calcutta: Office of the Superintendent of Government Printing.

Surveyor General of India (1888). *General Report on the Operations of the Survey of India Department, 1886–87*. Calcutta: Office of the superintendent of government printing.

Surveyor General of India (1889). *General Report on the Operations of the Survey of India Department, 1887–88*. Calcutta: Office of the superintendent of government printing.

Surveyor General of India (1890). *General Report on the Operations of the Survey of India Department, 1888–89*. Calcutta: Office of the superintendent of government printing.

Surveyor General of India (1891). *General Report on the Operations of the Survey of India Department, 1889–90*. Calcutta: Office of the superintendent of government printing.

Surveyor General of India (1892). *General Report on the Operations of the Survey of India Department, 1889–90*. Calcutta: Office of the superintendent of government printing.

Surveyor General of India (1893). *General Report on the Operations of the Survey of India Department, 1891–92*. Calcutta: Office of the superintendent of government printing.

Taussig, Michael (1984). "Culture of Terror—Space of Death. Roger Casement's Putumayo Report and the Explanation of Torture". *Comparative Studies in Society and History* 26(3): 467–497.

Thompson, E. P. (1991). *Customs in Common*. New York: The New Press.

Tóth, J. (2007). *Migration Movements in Hungary. http://www.migrationeducation.org/fileadmin/uploads/Hungarymigration_2007.pdf*. Accessed 20 October 2011.

Turner, Bryan S. (2000) "Outline of a Theory of Orientalism". In B. S. Turner (Ed.), *Orientalism: Early Sources*. New York: Routledge.

USAid (2008). *Iraq Local Governance Program (LGP) 2007 Annual Report.*

USAid/Research Triangle Institute (2008). *Local Governance Programme Annual Report, 2007*. Research Triangle Institute. *http://pdf.usaid.gov/pdf_docs/PDACM058.pdf*. Accessed 13 August 2010.

Vicsek, Lilla, and Marcell, Márkus (2008). "Representation of Refugees, Asylum-Seekers and Refugee Affairs In Hungarian Dailies". Journal of Identity and Migration Studies 2(2): 87–107.

Wallerstein, Immanuel (1974). "The Rise and Future Demise of the World Capitalist System: Concepts for Comparative Analysis". *Comparative Studies in Society and History* 16(4): 387–415.

Ward, Celeste J. (2005). *The Coalition Provisional Authority's Experience with Governance in Iraq: Lessons Identified*. Washington, DC: United States Institute of Peace.

Warner, Michael (2002). "Publics and Counterpublics". *Public Culture* 14(1): 49–90.

Warren, James Francis (2003). *Rickshaw Coolie: A People's History of Singapore*. Singapore: Singapore University Press.

Weber, Max (1968). *Economy and Society*. New York: Bedminister Press, 1968.

Williams, Raymond (1978). *Marxism and Literature*. Oxford: Oxford University Press.

Williams, Raymond (1982). *The Sociology of Culture*. New York: Shocken Books.

Wimmer, Andreas and Nina Glick-Schiller (2002). "Methodological Nationalism and Beyond: nation-state building, migration and the social sciences". *Global Networks* 2(4): 301–334.

Wood, Denis (1992). *The Power of Maps*. New York: Guildford Press.

Yen Ching Hwang (1987). "Class Structure and Social Mobility in the Chinese Community in Singapore and Malaya 1800–1911". *Modern Asian Studies* 21(3): 417–445.

Yenter, Colonel Mark W., et al. (2005). "Development of the Iraqi Geospatial Reference System". *The American Surveyor* (November).

Index

For Product Safety Concerns and Information please contact our EU
representative GPSR@taylorandfrancis.com
Taylor & Francis Verlag GmbH, Kaufingerstraße 24, 80331 München, Germany

www.ingramcontent.com/pod-product-compliance
Lightning Source LLC
Chambersburg PA
CBHW050523270326
41926CB00015B/3047